Early Retirement

The Decision and the Experience

Richard Barfield

James Morgan

This investigation was supported in part by grant number 277 from the Social and Rehabilitation Service and the Social Security Administration, United States Department of Health, Education, and Welfare, Washington, D.C.

Library of Congress Catalog Card Number: 70-626137

Printed by Braun-Brumfield, Inc.
Ann Arbor, Michigan

Manufactured in the United States of America

PREFACE

The study of decision making on early retirement was undertaken primarily as the result of a suggestion by Melvin A. Glasser[1] and several of his associates within the International Union—UAW.

During the fall of 1964, substantially liberalized early retirement benefits were negotiated by the UAW and various companies in the automobile and agricultural implement industries; these benefits covered almost one million workers. Mr. Glasser suggested that this development provided a large, relatively homogeneous group of workers who would be required to decide whether or not to retire early with a relatively high level of benefits. Furthermore, the UAW had sufficient data to identify persons in the age group immediately faced with this decision and was willing to encourage their cooperation in the study.

In response to Mr. Glasser's suggestion, the Survey Research Center developed a bipartite framework for the study, proposing that surveys be conducted both of older automobile workers and of a representative sample of the population as a whole. The latter sample would provide a broader framework in which to consider and evaluate results derived from the more homogeneous sample. Support for the research effort was obtained from the United States Department of Health, Education, and Welfare.

This monograph reports the findings from the first three years of the retirement decision study; a supplemental report, which will discuss the results of a planned reinterview with the automobile worker sample, will be forthcoming in 1970. James N. Morgan was principal investigator for the project; this report is the joint effort of Richard Barfield and Dr. Morgan. George Katona was extensively involved in planning the study, served as adviser during the study period, and also contributed to the writing of this monograph. The samples were drawn under the direction of Irene Hess, interviewing was carried out under the direction of John Scott, and coding under the direction of Joan Scheffler.

Tabulations and computations were performed on the IBM 1401 (and later on the IBM 360/40) computer located in the Institute for Social Research, and on the University of Michigan Computing Center's IBM 7090 (and later on the IBM 360/67). The computing operations were carried out under

---

[1]Mr. Glasser is Director, Social Security Department, International Union—UAW and Secretary-Treasurer, Michigan Health and Social Security Research Institute.

iii

the direction of John Sonquist and Duane Thomas. Alice Pruss, Janet Keller, and Karen Dickinson provided valuable technical assistance.

Virginia Eaton typed the tabular material which appears in this volume; Sue Hudson and Millie Dennis assisted in preparing tables and manuscript for printing.

The portion of the study involving UAW members (described in Chapters 6 through 10 and the related Appendices) reflects a joint effort by the Survey Research Center and the Michigan Health and Social Security Research Institute in selecting the samples, designing the questionnaires, and interpreting the replies. Appendices B and C were prepared by Howard Young and Eugene Loren, consultants to the Michigan Health and Social Security Research Institute; they also assisted in the preparation of Chapters 6 through 10.

Within the Survey Research Center, Judith H. Hybels assisted in the preparation of Chapters 2 through 4, Ismail Sirageldin contributed much to Chapter 5, Irene Hess authored Part II of Appendix C, and Jay Schmiedeskamp prepared Appendix D.

Finally, we are greatly indebted to William V. Haney for his contributions as the editor of this volume.

CONTENTS

LIST OF TABLES AND FIGURES

CHAPTER 6

CHAPTER 7

Chapter 1

INTRODUCTION, SUMMARY, AND CONCLUSIONS

I. Introduction to the Study

Early retirement[1] has become an increasingly important phenomenon in America. Slightly more than half the men who have retired recently have taken reduced social security benefits. Although retirement before a set conventional age was not especially uncommon in earlier years, such retirement was often associated with chronic unemployment, obsolescence of job skills, and/or earnings "that were characteristically low or that had dropped off substantially"[2] in the later years.

More specifically, Social Security Administration earnings records show that

—men who had elected to begin drawing social security benefits at age 62 were only half as likely as age-65-retirees to have had covered earnings of $4,800 in the year with largest earnings and that

—early retirees "were almost four times as likely to have earned less than $2,400 in their best year since 1950."[3]

The study also found, however, that "there seem to be more and more aged men who are well enough to work and who might get some kind of job if they were interested, but who prefer the leisure of retirement."[4] And, there have been substantial improvements in retirement-income-maintenance programs in recent years, improvements which have not been available to the great majority of previous early retirees. Increases in OASDHI benefits have

---

[1] "Early" is defined throughout this study as "before age 65."

[2] Lenore A. Epstein, "Early Retirement and Work-Life Experience," *Social Security Bulletin* (March 1966), p. 3.

[3] *Ibid.,* p. 7.

[4] Lenore A. Epstein and Janet H. Murray, *The Aged Population of the United States* (Washington: U. S. Government Printing Office, 1967), p. 105.

1

been significant, if not spectacular; perhaps more important has been the spread of private pension plans, many of which contain more or less comprehensive early retirement provisions. In particular, substantially liberalized early retirement benefits were negotiated during the fall of 1964 by the International Union—UAW and various companies in the automobile and agricultural implement industries; under the new agreement an auto worker could retire as early as age 60 with a monthly pension of up to $400.

With this development as a major impetus, and with the belief that "a study of . . . the circumstances that favor or oppose early retirement is greatly needed in order to predict future trends and to assess their impact on the economy and the well-being of millions of people,"[5] the Institute for Social Research and the Michigan Health and Social Security Research Institute began, in the fall of 1965, the study of decision-making on early retirement. The primary focus of the study has been on finding those factors which are important for the decision to retire voluntarily (that is, before one is compelled to retire by institutional arrangements or for health reasons); the factors investigated included attitudes toward employment (including positive or negative evaluation of income earned and of the kind of work done) as well as the evaluation of conditions expected under retirement (including satisfaction or dissatisfaction with expected retirement income and appreciation of or antipathy toward leisure). Supplementing this major part of the study was a survey of the situations and attitudes of the already-retired.

The study design provided for data collection from two sources: a representative sample of the national population and a random sample of older workers—those around 60 years of age—in the automobile industry. The later sample was seen as particularly relevant for a study of retirement decision-making, since the auto workers formed a fairly homogeneous group which was eligible, as stated earlier, for a relatively attractive early retirement benefit program and which was involved at the time of initial contact in making a decision on early retirement. Yet homogeneity—blue-collar workers in a mass production industry who are entitled to similar retirement provisions—has obvious disadvantages; ability to generalize from findings obtained with a special group would be limited unless it were possible to place those findings in their proper broad frame. Thus the representative sample, with all the heterogeneity of age, current income, occupation, and retirement provisions which this implies. Interviewing of the national sample was completed during 1966;[6] mail

---

[5]"Study of Decision Making on Early Retirement" (Unpublished study proposal of the Institute for Social Research, The University of Michigan, Ann Arbor, 1965).

[6]A smaller, supplemental national survey was also taken during August-September 1968.

contact was initiated with the auto workers during the same year, and personal interviews were conducted in the summer of 1967. (Reinterviewing of the auto worker sample was planned for the second half of 1969; a supplemental report of the results of this investigation was scheduled to be issued in 1970.)

II. Summary of Findings

As stated earlier, the study analyzed the effect on retirement planning of both situational and attitudinal variables, the expectation being that both types of factors would loom important in a decision to retire. *The major finding of the study (derived from both national and auto worker sample data) is this, however: that financial factors—primarily expected retirement income— are of principal importance in the retirement decision, with attitudinal variables having less influence, though usually operating in expected directions.* For both national and auto worker sample respondents, there was found a "threshold" level of retirement income which most people seem to consider necessary to insure a reasonably adequate post-retirement living standard. Currently this level is about $4,000 per year; it is likely, though, that $4,000 is not an absolute figure, but one which reflects a current consensus about the minimum income necessary to provide reasonably comfortable living after retirement. Thus, the "threshold" level may shift upward over time as living standards generally rise—and this upward movement should be all the faster if price level increases are not kept within reasonable bounds. Other economic aspects of retirement—number of dependents expected at retirement age, house equity at retirement age, and expected income from assets at retirement age—were also importantly related to retirement plans in both parts of the study.

Another situational variable, subjective evaluation of health, was found to be substantially correlated with planning early retirement in both parts of the study; persons seeing their health as relatively declining were more likely to express plans for early retirement. Generally, other situational variables demonstrated little correlation with retirement plans.

In the national sample analysis, persons who looked forward to enjoying recreational activities—hobbies, sports, travel, etc.—were substantially more likely to opt for retirement before age 65. Persons who expressed dissatisfaction with their job, either directly or by stating that they had thought of moving to a more promising or lucrative job, were more responsive to the idea of early retirement, as were those whose overall commitment to the "work ethic" seemed somewhat tenuous. For perhaps a variety of reasons age was found to be negatively correlated with plans for early retirement; finally, the perception of pressures toward retirement—from the employer, from the union, from colleagues—tended to induce a little accommodating behavior. But current income, occupation, education, whether the respondent supervised others as a regular part of his job, and the time required to travel to work all exhibited no systematic relationship with retirement plans.

In the auto worker sample analysis, an investigation of the factors underlying actual retirement behavior as well as retirement planning was possible, since about a third of the workers had retired between the time of initial mail contact (in 1966) and personal interviews (in 1967). As implied above, both having retired early and planning to retire early were found to depend most directly on available retirement income (from both social security, if the worker had reached age 62, and private pension benefits). Further, persons who had difficulty keeping up with the job, and who were unable to do anything about it, were rather more likely either to have retired or to be planning to retire early. Some differences were uncovered in the analysis, however. *Having retired early* was correlated fairly strongly with subjectively feeling that one's health had improved during recent years, while persons who saw their health as declining were most likely to express *plans to retire early*. (This finding is entirely consistent with other findings that health—or at least *feelings* about health—may improve after retirement.) For those auto workers who had retired when interviewed, no other factors—including satisfaction with job and with place of work, ease or difficulty in getting along with superiors, extent to which the work was repetitive, and ability to control the pace of the work—were found to be systematically related to having retired early. For those workers who were still working when interviewed, several other factors seemed to be associated with planning retirement before age 65: having talked about "the question of when to retire" with people outside the immediate family; thinking that most younger people feel that older workers should retire to provide job openings; preferring less work than one is now doing, or not preferring more work; planning to spend time on leisure activities after retirement; and finding the trip to work annoying were among those factors. From our analysis of the auto worker retirement decision we concluded that, in the main, the auto worker tended to make prompt use of the new early retirement provision if his available retirement income was of a size to enable reasonably comfortable living; he remained at work—perhaps only so long as was necessary to raise his prospective income—if this were not so.

While the major focus of the study was on the decision to retire or to remain at work, sufficient information was obtained from retired individuals, both in the national and in the auto worker samples, to enable some investigation of the factors associated with being generally satisfied with life after retirement. In both parts of the study about three-fourths of retired respondents reported being "satisfied" or "very satisfied" with their life since retirement. For national-sample respondents, satisfaction with retirement was substantially correlated with having an annual (retirement) income of $4,000 or more and with viewing one's present living standard as better than or the same as that enjoyed before retirement. Retirees who had retired as planned, rather than unexpectedly, were more likely to be enjoying retirement, as were those who had not had health problems serious enough to interfere with their pre-retirement work. Finally, relatively younger retirees, and those who had re-tired between ages 60 and 65, were somewhat more satisfied with retirement than others.

For auto worker respondents, several situational factors were important-ly associated with retirement satisfaction; these included owning one's home mortgage-free, having over $10,000 in assets, being married, and having a sub-stantial pension income. After the effects of the important situational vari-ables were accounted for, the following other factors were found to be posi-tively correlated with satisfaction:

—having retired as planned, rather than unexpectedly
—being in relatively good health
—having attended at least one retirement information meeting (spon-
    sored by the union and/or the company of employment)
—having retired earlier (in 1965-66) rather than later (1967-68)
—participating in leisure activities.

By far the most important reason for auto worker dissatisfaction with retire-ment seemed to be serious health problems, either for the respondent himself or for other family members.

III. Conclusions

The study of retirement decision-making implies that, even allowing for some wishful thinking, the proportion of people retiring early will increase. Evidence from the national sample part leads one to believe that, during the last 5 or 6 years, there has been some tendency for early retirement *planning* to become more common. It is likely, then, that more and more early retirees will be people who planned for early retirement and are financially prepared for it. The result is likely to be an increasing discrepancy among the retired between those who retired as they had planned to and those who retired un-expectedly, often without planning and hence in most cases with inadequate retirement incomes. The discrepancies probably will be accentuated by the growth of private pension plans covering only some workers and (in some cases) not even all the workers in any particular company or industry. One of the authors of this monograph has offered the following as a suggestion for alleviating this dichotomization of future retirees:

The implications of this for policy with respect to OASDHI are that perhaps the most important revision might be the introduction of a provision by which workers would make voluntary supplemental contributions to the system and thereby raise their retirement benefits. In this way workers in jobs without supplemental private pensions could provide similar supplemental benefits through the Social Security System efficiently. There would be some competition with private pension and annuity plans, but for the most part only with the individual, not the group, plans; and the proposed scheme would be a great deal more efficient than individual private schemes.

Earlier retirement could also be handled this way, by allowing additional worker contributions to build a fund similar to the supplemental early retirement benefits the auto workers now have. Indeed, it could be left flexible whether the worker would use his extra payments to provide earlier retirement, or to provide higher benefits upon regular retirement.[7]

The vigorous response of auto workers to the improved early retirement package (two-thirds either having retired or planning to retire early) would seem to imply that an increase in pension benefits will lead to a significant increase in early retirees. It is important to realize, though, that the increase in negotiated pension benefits provided by the 1964 agreement was indeed a substantial one;[8] and it seems quite likely that a gradual improvement in pension levels, either through the social security mechanism or via private pensions, will not have such a dramatic impact on the number of early retirees. Given the "threshold" phenomenon discussed before, it is probable that a continuation of the present pace of OASDHI improvements and private pension expansion will have a notable effect on early retirement only after we are well into the 1970's. A speeding up of the early retirement process (beyond that which is apparently occurring now) would seem to require either large increases, generally, in retirement-income-maintenance schemes or a selective distribution of available funds among particular groups of workers.

A finding which certainly bears repeating is that retirement can, apparently, be a genuinely satisfying time of life for many, if not most, people. The design of the study renders this judgment somewhat tentative for national-sample respondents, but a reading of the auto worker responses (see Chapter 10) leads one to believe that it certainly can be true for this type of mass-production-industry worker. And this is important to know, for some observers, noting the considerable increase in leisure time which future productivity increases likely will make possible, have questioned whether a choice to appropriate a large part of this increase to the retirement years would be wise. Juanita Kreps in particular has suggested the wisdom of "diverting more and more of our time to education, investments in education being the corollary

---

[7] Letter from James N. Morgan to Harrison A. Williams, in Special Committee on Aging, United States Senate, *Long-Range Program and Research Needs in Aging and Related Fields* (Washington: U. S. Government Printing Office, 1968), p. 262.

[8] See Appendix B for a discussion of this point.

of our high current growth, and the *sine qua non* of future, even higher, rates."[9] Certainly the argument is a persuasive one. But the expressions of joy in the freedom of retirement on the part of a large majority of auto workers are also persuasive and should perhaps be considered when we arrange our priorities. At the least further investigation into the satisfactions afforded by retirement would seem to be worthwhile before a decision on the allocation of leisure time is made.

IV. Organization of the Book

Chapters 2 through 4 present the results of our analysis of factors influencing the retirement decision for national-sample data. Chapter 2 is concerned with the plans of all economically active family heads age 35 to 59, Chapter 3 investigates the early retirement decision within several interesting subgroups (all older persons, older union members, and persons with some college training), and Chapter 4 touches on the late retirement decision. Chapter 5 details our findings on the situation and attitudes of those family heads who were retired when interviewed in 1966 (and 1968).

Chapters 6 through 10 discuss early retirement in the auto worker context. Chapter 6 presents an overview of the negotiated early retirement provision and sets forth the (univariate) relationships between various situational and attitudinal factors and having retired or planning to retire early. Chapter 7 details the results of multivariate analyses of actual early retirement, Chapter 8 reports on the analysis of auto worker retirement plans, and Chapter 9 presents the findings with respect to retirement satisfaction. Chapter 10 summarizes the auto worker findings and reproduces some actual responses to the question on retirement satisfaction.

Six appendices follow the main text. Appendix A explains the multivariate techniques used in the data analysis. Appendix B discusses auto worker retirement and employment conditions; Appendix C, the auto worker sample. Appendix D details sampling methodology for the national part of the study. Finally, Appendices E and F present percentage distributions of answers to all questions asked of national sample and auto worker sample respondents, respectively.

---

[9]Juanita M. Kreps, "Lifetime Tradeoffs Between Work and Play" (Paper delivered at the annual meeting of The Industrial Relations Research Association, 1968), p. 17.

Chapter 2

THE NATIONAL SAMPLE: FACTORS INFLUENCING THE EARLY RETIREMENT DECISION

A comparison of information gathered in surveys conducted in 1963, 1966 (the year in which the major study was conducted), and 1968 affords some evidence of an increasing desire to retire early. Table 2-1 shows, for selected relevant groups, the proportions in those three years planning to retire before they are 65 years of age.

Some differences in the questions asked of the respondents and in what preceded them may have had some effect on the responses. Yet it seems clear,

TABLE 2-1

PLANS TO RETIRE EARLY, BY AGE[a]

	Proportion who plan to retire before they are age 65		
Age	1963 survey	1966 surveys	1968 survey
35-44	25	43	34
45-54	23	33	35
55-64	21	22	26

---

[a]For family heads in the labor force, age 35 to 64 and with family income $3,000 or more; nationwide samples.

Note: In surveys conducted in 1963, in connection with a study of individual saving and participation in private pension plans, the following question was asked: "Now I have a few questions about retirement. When do you think you will retire from the work you do; I mean at what age?" In surveys conducted in 1966, in connection with the study of early retirement, the question asked was: "When do you think you will retire from the main work you are now doing—I mean at what age?" The 1966 question followed other questions about retirement and about what things would be like later on. In the 1968 survey, the question was: "At what age do you think you will retire from the main work you are doing now?"; the 1968 question was contained in the retirement section of a larger survey.

9

first, that younger people are rather more likely than older people to think of retiring early and, second, that recent developments have influenced retirement plans. Indeed, the differences between the 1963 survey and the later surveys suggest a trend toward more purposeful early retirement. To be sure, the apparent decline from 1966 to 1968 in the proportion planning early retirement among younger persons (age 35 to 44) casts some doubt on the validity of such a trend, but it should be noted that the overall proportion planning to retire before age 65 was essentially identical in both years (34 percent in 1966 and 33 percent in 1968). Thus, the approximately 10 percentage point increase in planned early retirement which was observed between 1963 and 1966 was maintained in the results from the most recent survey.

While in the past early retirement has been often associated with trouble—illness, obsolescence of job skills, unemployment—a new source of early retirement may have arisen among people at the other end of the scale: those who planned to retire early, saved for this purpose, and retired because they could afford it. While at present the majority of those who have retired early did not retire as planned (see Chapter 5, page 3), in the future a different relation between planning and early retirement likely will prevail.

The distributions of *when* people said they planned to retire are given in Table 2-2. As was mentioned above, in recent years about one-third of labor force members expressed plans to retire early, with a majority of the rest planning to retire between the ages of 65 and 69.

As the tendency toward planned early retirement would imply, Americans generally are optimistic about and look forward to retirement. A substantial majority believe that current retirees are generally satisfied with their financial situation; an overwhelming majority—about 90 percent—believe that they will be even better off when they themselves retire. Three-quarters of those currently in the labor force expect few, if any, financial problems after retirement; they see themselves as enjoying a comfortable standard of living then. Of those whose ideas about retirement have undergone some change during the last several years, about two-thirds report a change in a direction more favorable to early retirement. Forty percent now feel that if a person can be financially secure in retirement he has some moral obligation to retire early in order to make more jobs available for younger workers. Finally, about 60 percent of American family heads state that they look forward to retirement as a time in which to enjoy leisure-time activities and to be relieved from the burdens of work; only one-third expressed some skepticism about retirement.

The 1966 sample of family heads was asked not only about their expected retirement age and their outlook toward retirement, but also about situational and attitudinal factors which were expected to be relevant for the retirement decision. Of the 3,647 individuals interviewed in 1966 for the

TABLE 2-2

WHEN PEOPLE PLAN TO RETIRE

(Percentage distribution of heads of families)

Planned retirement age	Age 35-64 in labor force, with family income $3,000 or more			All those age 35-64 and in labor force	
	1963 survey	1966 surveys	1968 survey	1966 surveys	1968 survey
Under age 60	4	10	12	9	11
60-64	20	25	21	25	22
65-69	50	37	44	35	43
70 or older	3	3	⌐ 9	4	⌐ 9
Will work as long as possible	⌐ 23	⌐ 25	⌐	13	⌐
Don't know when will retire; not ascertained when will retire	⌐	⌐	14	14	15
Total	100	100	100	100	100
Number of cases	1,853	1,463	582	1,853	1,024

study, 2,764 were in the labor force and had not retired from any previous work. This economically active group included persons in their 20's and 30's as well as others in their 60's and 70's, and it seemed reasonable to exclude from the analysis both working family heads under age 35, since they likely had thought about retirement only vaguely, if at all, and those older respondents age 60 and over, since for them early retirement (retirement before age 65) is less and less possible with increasing age. For the multivariate analyses discussed in this chapter, then, the relevant sample became the 1,652 respondents in the labor force and between the ages of 35 and 59.

I. Regression Analysis of Retirement Plans

Regression analyses were undertaken of the 1,652-person group and of the following subgroups, which are discussed in subsequent chapters:

—those having some college training
—those in the 50 to 59 age range
—those in the 50 to 59 age range who are also members of labor unions

—those interviewed in the second part of the 1966 survey,[1] who were asked several questions not included in the first part.

The dependent variable in these regressions was dichotomous, with a value of one for respondents who planned to retire before age 65 and of zero otherwise; the various factors whose influence was investigated were the following:[2]

(1) expected retirement pension income, which includes government and private pensions, plus any annuities payable to the respondent;

(2) an index of other economic aspects of retirement, ranging from 0 to 4 and constructed as the sum of

    1 point for expecting to have no dependents other than the respondent's wife after age 59,

    1 point for expecting to earn $500 or more per year from post-retirement work,

    1 point for expecting to receive an income from retirement-age asset holdings (including anticipated equity in the respondent's home) of $1,000 or more, and

    1 point for expecting to have no mortgage payments to make after age 60;[3]

(3) an index of the respondent's health, ranging from 0 to 5 and constructed as the sum of

    2 points for feeling better now relative to "several years ago,"

    1 point for having missed few workdays because of illness during the last 5 years,

    1 point for not having a work-limiting disability, and

    1 point for having missed no work weeks because of illness in 1965;

(4) the respondent's having hobbies which he wants to pursue after retirement;

---

[1]The first wave of interviews was taken in the period January through March (2,419 interviews); the second—of a completely independent sample—in August through September (1,228 interviews).

[2]These predictors are listed in order of their importance in explaining the variance in retirement plans, for all 1,652 respondents; Table 2-3 displays the square of their beta coefficient and the direction of their effect on retirement plans.

[3]These factors are grouped together into an index because they may encourage early retirement *alternatively*; one is relevant for some persons, another for others. This sum, then, is more useful analytically than its parts. A search-technique analysis (see Appendix A) which indicates the alternative nature of these variables is diagrammed in Footnote 8 of this chapter.

TABLE 2-3

PREDICTORS BY THEIR IMPORTANCE IN EXPLAINING PLANS FOR EARLY RETIREMENT[a]

Predictor	Using unadjusted means	Using adjusted means	
	Importance taken singly (Correlation ratio squared)	Importance in regression (beta squares)	Direction of (net) effect on plans to retire before age 65
Expected retirement pension income	.043	.035	+ with increasing income
"Other economic variables" index	.039	.025	+ with more favorable position
Health index	.010	.012	− with better health
Whether hobbies	.015	.007	+ with hobbies to pursue
Ranking of "short hours" criterion	.004	.006	− with low ranking
Job satisfaction	.004	.005	− with increasing satisfaction
Age	.013	.005	− with increasing age
Current family income	.011	.004	No discernible direction
Sex	.001	.001	− for males
Race	.001	.001	+ for Negroes/Latin Americans
Whether self-employed	*	.002	No discernible direction

*Less than 0.0005.

[a]For 1,652 respondents in the labor force, age 35 to 59.

(5) low ranking of "short hours" as a criterion for occupational preference;

(6) the respondent's evaluation of his current work (that is, whether he sees it enjoyable or not);

(7) age;

(8) current family income;

(9) sex;

(10) race; and

(11) whether self-employed.

The most important single influence on early retirement plans of all persons age 35 to 59 in the labor force was the pension and annuity income expected after retirement.[4] Those who looked forward to a financially advantageous position in their sixties were, indeed, the persons more likely to express plans for early retirement. The "threshold" level here seemed to be about $4,000 per year; above this level the proportion planning to retire before age 65 rose systematically with rising (expected) income, becoming well over 55 percent after the $7,500 level. (Overall, the mean proportion of respondents planning to retire early was about 36 percent.) Below the threshold amount the proportion hovered around 30 percent, except for an anomalous few expecting less than $1,000 per year in pensions. Apparently this latter group included persons whose current income was also low (necessitating perhaps only a small income cut after retirement, even at this low retirement income level) and/or persons whose employment history had been unfavorable (implying little or no accumulation of private pension benefits and general discouragement with continued labor force participation). The relationship between pension income and retirement plans is indicated in Figure 2-1. As one might have expected, the anticipated pension income amount was rather strongly correlated with the current family income of the respondent and with his age (see Table 2-4).

Investigated in other multivariate analyses was the effect on retirement plans of a variable which measured the extent to which expected retirement

_____

[4]The pension and annuity income figure was calculated from respondent estimates of all government and private pension receipts expected at age 65, plus any annuity payments which he expected at that time. Amounts were assigned whenever the respondent was unable to provide an estimate. In the 1968 survey, the respondent was asked to give a global estimate of total expected retirement income. Here, though about half those asked were unable to furnish an amount, a similar strong association between expected income and retirement plans was evident: 22 percent of those who expected a retirement income of less than $3,000 planned early retirement, while 44 percent of those expecting $3,000 or more had such plans.

TABLE 2-4

ASSOCIATION BETWEEN CURRENT FAMILY INCOME, AGE, AND EXPECTED RETIREMENT PENSION INCOME[a]

(In percent)

	Expected pension and annuity income during retirement							
	Less than $1,000	$1,000 -1,999	$2,000 -2,999	$3,000 -3,999	$4,000 -4,999	$5,000 -7,499	$7,500 -9,999	$10,000 or more
Total family income								
Less than $3,000	49	25	3	1	1	*	-	-
$3,000-4,999	19	32	18	5	2	3	-	-
$5,000-7,499	8	19	29	26	19	13	8	2
$7,500-9,999	16	10	21	30	35	19	13	7
$10,000-14,999	5	9	17	27	31	37	42	27
$15,000 or more	3	5	12	11	12	28	37	64
Total	100	100	100	100	100	100	100	100
Age of family head								
35-44	19	28	39	43	44	47	52	59
45-49	16	20	20	23	23	23	23	24
50-54	30	23	21	20	18	19	20	13
55-59	35	29	20	14	15	11	5	4
Total	100	100	100	100	100	100	100	100

* Less than 0.5 percent.

[a] For 1,652 family heads in the labor force age 35 to 59.

FIGURE 2-1

PROPORTION PLANNING EARLY RETIREMENT, BY EXPECTED RETIREMENT PENSION INCOME

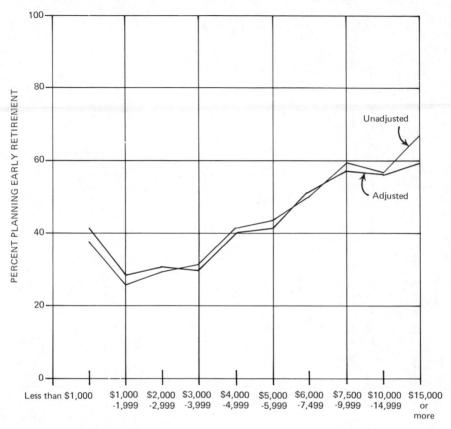

EXPECTED RETIREMENT PENSION INCOME

income differed from current family income. When this variable contributed little additional explanatory power it was excluded from further consideration. However, as will be noted subsequently, a similar variable proved quite important in determining the retirement plans of automobile workers.

The other economic aspects of retirement—defined above in the predicator list—vied with expected pension income in influencing the retirement decision. In fact, as is evident from Table 2-5, the proportion of respondents planning early retirement increased monotonically with the index. It is apparent that asset levels, post-retirement earnings, and mortgage payments and number of dependents expected around retirement age were indeed taken into account when considering retirement behavior. (The relation between early retirement and the four components of the index is revealed in Table 2-6.)

TABLE 2-5

PROPORTION[a] PLANNING EARLY RETIREMENT, BY "ECONOMIC VARIABLES" INDEX

(In percent)

Expected economic outlook	Number of cases	Unadjusted	Adjusted
Relatively unfavorable (index value of 0 to 1)	505	22.5	24.8
"Average" (index value of 2)	599	37.9	38.6
Relatively favorable (index value of 3 to 4)	548	45.8	43.0

[a]For 1,652 family heads in the labor force age 35 to 59.

It is obvious from the preceding discussion that economic considerations are of preeminent importance for the early retirement decision. This does not mean, however, that everything else is insignificant. As will be seen later in this chapter, several other variables were found to be importantly correlated with planning to retire before age 65.

Relatively poor health was found to encourage plans for early retirement; although its effect was somewhat erratic, those respondents whose health index scores were relatively low expressed such plans more frequently than did relatively more healthy individuals.

Evidence gathered on hobby plans for the post-retirement years suggests that those persons who have made provision for leisure-time pursuits are more likely to plan retirement before the conventional age. More than this, however, the data indicate that substantial numbers of people may not plan a large-scale disengagement from ordinary activities in their later years; almost two-thirds of those in the sample planned to continue their hobbies after retirement.

The results of a recent study of rural Kentuckians age 45 to 60 are worth noting here. Youmans reports that a large majority of persons contacted in the study were currently pursuing hobbies (respondents reported participation in an average of two hobbies—active and sedentary—per person) and that almost as many were planning to continue such hobbies in their old age. While the relation between planned hobbies and retirement age was not investigated in the Kentucky study, its results confirm the relative lack of planned disengagement evident from our data.[5]

[5]E. Grant Youmans, "Orientations to Old Age," *The Gerontologist,* Vol. 8, No. 3 (Autumn, 1968), pp. 154-155.

TABLE 2-6

PROPORTION[a] PLANNING EARLY RETIREMENT
BY COMPONENTS OF "ECONOMIC VARIABLES" INDEX

Component	Percent
Age at which respondent will have no dependents other than his wife	
Under age 51	36.9
51-54	43.1
55-59	39.0
60-64	32.2
65-69	30.6
70 or older	29.5
Expected earnings from post-retirement work	
Less than $500	30.7
$500-1,999	47.1
$2,000-4,999	53.3
$5,000 or more	54.3
Not ascertained	36.0
Expected post-retirement income from assets (including house equity)	
Less than $1,000	24.3
$1,000-1,999	41.0
$2,000-2,999	37.9
$3,000-3,999	43.7
$4,000-5,999	45.7
$6,000-9,999	41.3
$10,000 or more	40.8
Age at which head owns/will own home mortgage-free	
Under age 51	35.7
51-55	41.2
56-60	42.0
61-64	39.5
65-70	36.8
71 or older	20.3
Nonhomeowner	33.2

[a]For 1,652 family heads in the labor force age 35 to 59.

TABLE 2-7

PROPORTION[a] PLANNING EARLY RETIREMENT, BY HEALTH INDEX

(In percent)

Health	Number of cases	Unadjusted	Adjusted
Relatively poor (index value of 0 to 2)	577	40.7	41.7
Relatively good (index value of 3 to 5)	1,075	33.2	32.6

---

[a]For 1,652 family heads in the labor force age 35 to 59.

TABLE 2-8

PROPORTION[a] PLANNING EARLY RETIREMENT
BY PLANNED POST-RETIREMENT HOBBY ACTIVITIES

(In percent)

Category	Number of cases	Unadjusted	Adjusted
Respondent has hobbies which he plans to pursue after retirement	1,046	40.3	38.9
Respondent has no hobbies	606	28.1	30.5

---

[a]For 1,652 family heads in the labor force age 35 to 59.

Attitudes toward work in general and the respondent's job in particular affected retirement plans: those who ranked "working hours are short, lots of free time" last in a field of six occupational criteria[6] were rather more apt to plan work after age 65; and persons who expressed a dislike of their current work were more likely to plan early retirement.

For perhaps a variety of reasons age was found to be negatively correlated with plans for early retirement; whether the observed difference reflects a genuine inter-generational shift in attitudes about retirement, whether retirement simply seems less attractive as one ages, whether the fact that for younger people age 60 is far away and does not seem particularly "early" is sufficient to generate this negative correlation—our data really do not enable us

---

[6]The other criteria of occupational preference were "the work is important, gives a feeling of accomplishment;" "income is steady;" "there's no danger of being fired or unemployed;" "chances for advancement are good;" "income is high."

TABLE 2-9

PROPORTION[a] PLANNING EARLY RETIREMENT,
BY RANKING OF "SHORT HOURS" AS AN OCCUPATIONAL CRITERION

(In percent)

Rank of "short hours"	Number of cases	Unadjusted	Adjusted
Last of six items	792	32.6	31.9
Other than last	860	38.8	39.4

[a]For 1,652 family heads in the labor force age 35 to 59.

TABLE 2-10

PROPORTION[a] PLANNING EARLY RETIREMENT,
BY EVALUATION OF CURRENT WORK

(In percent)

Evaluation	Number of cases	Unadjusted	Adjusted
Enjoys work	389	33.4	31.7
Enjoys work somewhat	901	35.5	35.8
Pro-con	233	36.5	39.0
Dislikes work somewhat	42	50.0	48.1
Dislikes work	53	43.4	42.2

[a]For 1,652 family heads in the labor force age 35 to 59.

to say (though the 1963 to 1968 trend would tend to support a "nongenerational" hypothesis). Perhaps more compelling than these speculations is the suggestion that plans to retire early may be viewed as a reflection of the prevailing wide-spread optimism, which occasions the common belief that the two purposes of earning income, to cover consumption needs and to acquire enough for retirement, can both be fulfilled by working 30 to 40 years. This, coupled with the fact that surveys have repeatedly shown that such optimism is by far most pronounced among young people,[7] may explain the observed age-associated differences (Figure 2-2).

Four variables were correlated hardly at all with retirement plans. The proportion of respondents planning early retirement varied erratically rather

[7]See George Katona, *The Mass Consumption Society* (New York: McGraw-Hill Book Company, 1964), Chapter 12.

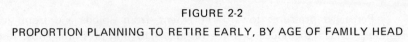

FIGURE 2-2

PROPORTION PLANNING TO RETIRE EARLY, BY AGE OF FAMILY HEAD

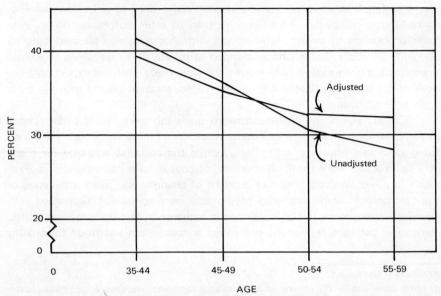

than systematically from income group to income group within the current family income predictor—and this was true both before and after the regression adjusted for its correlation with expected pension income. Similarly, the importance of sex, race, and whether the respondent was self-employed was quite small (although women and Negroes were slightly more likely to plan early retirement).

II. Further Multivariate Analysis of Retirement Plans

In addition to the regression analyses discussed above, other multivariate analyses were undertaken, using both regression and search techniques (the latter is described in Appendix A). These analyses investigated the effects on early retirement plans of numerous other variables, the more interesting of which are discussed here[8] and listed in Table 2-11.

---

[8]The predictor variables discussed here were used in the second of a two-stage search-technique analysis, the first stage of which adjusted for differences in expected retirement financial position. This analysis included respondents in the labor force, age 35 to 64 (that is, persons age 60 to 64, who were excluded from the previously discussed analyses, were retained here). These variables were included only in this analysis because (1) some of them are potentially circular, perhaps both causing and resulting from plans

Perceived pressures toward retirement—from unions and from younger workers—tended to induce positive responses to that pressure. Those respondents who felt that younger workers wanted older ones to retire to make jobs available were somewhat more likely to plan to retire before age 65; an even larger proportion of persons who agreed with this viewpoint planned early retirement. Similarly, those who responded affirmatively to questions of whether unions are encouraging early retirement were more likely to expect to leave work at an early age. (But thinking that employers want people to retire early made little difference.)

Various aspects of attitudes toward one's job were found to be related to early retirement plans. Respondents who desired more work than they were doing were less prone to retire early, while the converse was true for those who desired less work (both alternatives, of course, with corresponding adjustments in pay). Workers who had thought of changing to "more interesting or more promising" work, and who presumably were somewhat dissatisfied with their jobs, were more likely to plan early retirement. But there was very little correlation between retirement plans and a respondent's attitude toward his

---

(Footnote 8 Continued)

to retire early and/or (2) others, while correlated somewhat with retirement plans, nevertheless were able to explain very little of the total variance in such plans.

The first stage of the analysis produced the following figure:

FINANCIAL OUTLOOK AND RETIREMENT PLANS

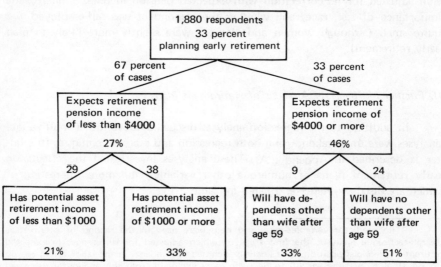

Residuals from the four end-groups were then pooled and used as the dependent variable in the second stage of the analysis.

TABLE 2-11 (Sheet 1 of 2)

PROPORTION[a] PLANNING EARLY RETIREMENT, BY VARIOUS PREDICTORS

(In percent)

Predictor	Number of cases	Unadjusted	Adjusted
Perceive union encouragement of early retirement			
Yes	565	44.1	40.5
No	438	32.4	32.2
Don't know	768	28.6	30.7
Perceive pressure toward early retirement from young people			
Yes	1,073	39.2	39.3
No	404	27.7	25.6
Don't know	206	28.2	30.2
Agree that older people should retire early			
Yes	698	46.1	46.8
Pro-con; depends	105	40.0	39.1
No	906	25.7	24.8
Would like to work more than now			
Yes	528	28.8	31.3
(Pro-con)	(13)	(53.8)	(54.1)
No	1,222	36.5	35.7
Would like to work less than now			
Yes	216	45.0	44.6
(Pro-con)	(16)	(25.0)	(18.3)
No	1,558	32.6	32.7
Have thought of changing jobs			
Yes	603	40.5	39.1
No	1,250	30.3	30.9

[a] For 1,880 family heads in the labor force age 35 to 64.

TABLE 2-11 (Sheet 2 of 2)

PROPORTION[a] PLANNING EARLY RETIREMENT, BY VARIOUS PREDICTORS

(In percent)

Predictor	Number of cases	Unadjusted	Adjusted
Industry of respondent's occupation			
Agriculture, forestry, fishing	154	31.2	35.6
Mining and extracting	18	33.3	27.9
Manufacturing	484	38.2	37.3
Construction	201	31.8	34.5
Transportation, communication, utilities	154	35.1	32.7
Retail, wholesale trade	245	29.8	29.6
Finance, insurance, real estate	73	30.1	29.4
Services	238	24.8	26.4
Government services	253	40.3	38.5
Amount of volunteer work respondent plans to do after retirement			
More than now	831	38.6	37.7
Same as now	363	33.1	33.0
Less than now	145	31.7	32.4
Don't know; not ascertained	519	27.4	28.4
Ranking of occupational criteria			
Achievement is ranked first	687	34.1	31.9
Steady income or job security is ranked first	794	34.0	36.1
High income is ranked first or second (if neither of above occurs)	203	31.0	30.6
Other rankings	196	31.6	31.5

---

[a] For 1,880 family heads in the labor force age 35 to 64.

coworkers (the question referred to the respondent's missing coworkers if he were to change jobs).

Several other variables whose importance had been anticipated were revealed to have little, if any, influence on the retirement decision. The relationship between retirement plans and occupation was quite erratic; education and socioeconomic status were of little relevance in explaining the variability in expected retirement age. Whether or not the respondent's wife worked made little difference, nor did whether he himself supervised others as a regular part of his work.

Three other variables were correlated to some extent with retirement expectations. Among industries, workers in government services (where retirement often may occur after a given length of service rather than at a given age) and in manufacturing (where negotiated private pensions—many with early retirement provisions—are prevalent) were somewhat more likely to plan early retirement. Respondents who had made plans to do more volunteer work ("for church, charity, or your children") were similarly disposed, as were those who ranked steady income or job security first among the six occupational criteria.

III. Search-technique Analysis of an Index of Involvement with Retirement

For several reasons it seemed unsatisfactory to base the entire analysis on the replies to a single question (when will you retire?). There are problems both of unreliability and of insufficient variance in the dependent variable. Some people may be uncertain as to when they will retire (14 percent did not give a codable reply), or their answers may merely reflect compulsory retirement ages. Further, the regression analyses of expressed retirement plans discussed earlier in the chapter explained a relatively small fraction of the variance of the dichotomous variable, about four percent with expected pension income alone and about eight percent with the entire set of predictors.

While it is necessary to be careful not to combine explanatory and dependent variables, we nevertheless have some other questions the answers to which can be thought of as representing "involvement with retirement" in terms of reported experience or behavior. Perhaps these could be combined in such a way as to form a new, better dependent variable. To test the possibility of building an index of involvement with retirement, we should look at their relationships with retirement plans and with each other.

Nearly half of those age 35 to 64 and not retired say they know someone who has retired early. Those who know an early retiree are also more likely (43 percent versus 23 percent) to have talked with someone outside the immediate family about retirement. Those who neither knew someone who had retired early, nor have talked about retirement with an outsider, are less likely to report hobbies they would like to pursue further when they retire. The proportions with such interest in more hobby activities are:

	Percent with interest in more hobby activity
Neither knew an early retiree nor talked about retirement	52
Knew an early retiree but did not talk about retirement	66
Talked about retirement but did not know an early retiree	70
Both knew an early retiree and talked about retirement	74

If we now build a simple index (see Table 2-12), giving one point each for knowing someone who has retired, having talked with others about retirement, and having hobbies he would like to do more of, index scores may vary from 0 to 3 and are highly correlated with plans to retire.

But if these components are thus positively correlated, we can properly combine them into a new dependent variable, adding one point for planning to retire before age 65 and one more point for planning to retire before age

TABLE 2-12

RELATION OF RETIREMENT PLANS TO INDEX OF INVOLVEMENT WITH RETIREMENT

(In percent)

Planned retirement age	0	1	2	3
Under age 60	2	7	12	17
60-64	17	21	29	32
65-69	34	37	35	36
70 or older, definite age given	25	22	12	9
Never; will work as long as can	22	13	12	6
Total	100	100	100	100

60. This results in another index of involvement with retirement (or, more properly, an index of involvement with and planning for retirement) which is reasonably well distributed:

Index value	Percent of sample
0	16
1	28
2	26
3	19
4	18
5	3
	100

One way to test the validity of a dependent variable is to ask whether we can do a better job of explaining it with our best explanatory variables. The mean value of the index at the various levels of expected retirement pension income are shown in Table 2-13.

Using the dichotomous variable, we can explain four percent of the variance (this is the correlation ratio, or if one thinks of using dummy variables

TABLE 2-13

RELATION OF EXPECTED PENSION RETIREMENT INCOME
TO INVOLVEMENT-WITH-RETIREMENT INDEX AND
EXPRESSED RETIREMENT PLANS

Expected pension retirement income	Average value of index of involvement with retirement	Percent who plan to retire early
Less than $1,000	1.35	38
$1,000-1,999	1.39	26
$2,000-2,999	1.60	30
$3,000-3,999	1.82	32
$4,000-4,999	2.08	42
$5,000-5,999	2.31	44
$6,000-7,499	2.52	50
$7,500-9,999	2.65	60
$10,000-14,999	3.03	57
$15,000 or more	3.30	67

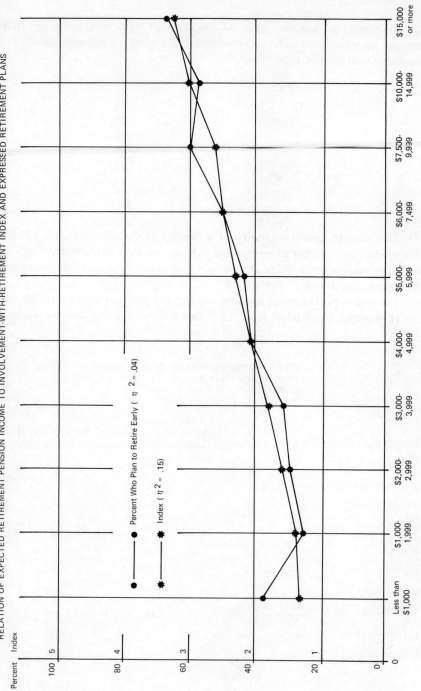

FIGURE 2-3

RELATION OF EXPECTED RETIREMENT PENSION INCOME TO INVOLVEMENT-WITH-RETIREMENT INDEX AND EXPRESSED RETIREMENT PLANS

for each expected retirement income class, it is the multiple correlation squared). Using the index, we can explain 15 percent of its variance, nearly four times as much. If we use this index as a dependent variable, then, we can also find better relations with other explanatory variables, including the additudinal ones. And we can ask what kinds of expectations and attitudes toward the job, and felt pressures from the union or from younger workers, seem to affect it.

When we use the index, converted by multiplying by 20 so that it ranges from 0 to 100, we find the same general patterns of explanatory factors as with the simple report of planning to retire early. Figure 2-4 shows the results of introducing, in a flexible search process, only four economic factors: expected income from pensions and social security, expected other retirement income (including imputations), age when there would be no remaining unpaid mortgage debt, and age when there would be no remaining dependents other than the wife. It is clear from the figure that the second (other retirement income) is important only when the first (pension and social security expected) is low, and that having dependents after age 54 becomes important when both kinds of expected income are low.

If we had forced more divisions, they would have been based largely on finer differences in expected pension and social security income; an exception would be the 622 cases with low expected pension income but substantial expected other income, where having a mortgage with payments extending beyond age 70 matters. It is common for such people to have big houses and long mortgages, the former giving them a higher expected non-money income when they retire, but the latter a larger set of obligations (mortgage payments).

But the five groups account for about 14 percent of the variance and provide a sufficient elimination of the effects of these economic forces so that an examination of the residuals (deviations from the five end-group averages repooled) will allow an examination of net relationships with other things.

Figure 2-5 shows the result of such an analysis. Here again, the asymmetry of forces becomes obvious. Expecting to do more volunteer work affects the involvement with retirement only for those who do not expect to earn money after retirement. Apparently work for money and work as a volunteer are substitute attractions. Health considerations appear to be important only for those who would like to work after retirement, but are vague about the amount of work they expect to do.

With some of the divisions of the diagram, there are factors which competed with the ones actually used in the division. These other factors universally come into the picture in a later division, but only for one of the two groups formed earlier; that is, they affected some people but not others.

FIGURE 2-4

INDEX OF INVOLVEMENT WITH RETIREMENT*

(For 1,652 family heads in the labor force, age 35 to 59)

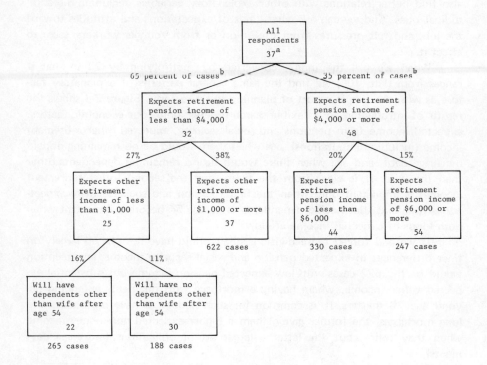

---

*Converted to range from 0 to 100.

[a]This figure is the average value of the index (times 20) for the subgroup defined in the box.

[b]This percentage relates the number of family heads who are in the subgroup specified in the lower box to the number of all heads included in the analysis.

For example, those who expect to retire from their present job but not completely from the labor force form a quite different group, more involved with that retirement now. But the next most important factors related to the whole sample of differences were felt pressure to retire from younger people, felt pressure from unions, and expecting to do more non-paid volunteer work after retirement. As we have seen, however, the volunteer work plans affected only those not planning to work for money after retirement. The felt pressures from younger people were important mostly for those expecting to do

FIGURE 2-5

INDEX OF INVOLVEMENT WITH RETIREMENT: ANALYSIS OF DIFFERENCES FROM END-GROUP

AVERAGES OF FIGURE 2-4

(For 1,652 household heads in the labor force, age 35 to 59)

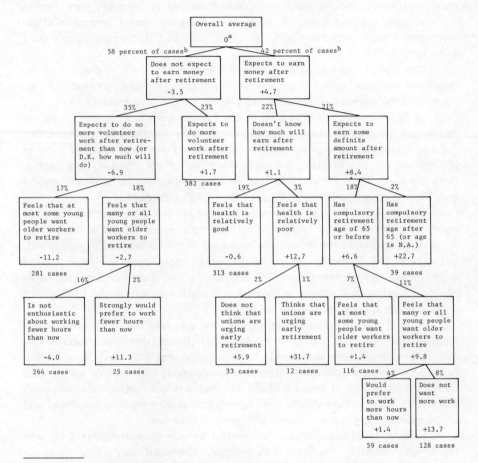

[a]This figure indicates the deviation from the overall mean involvement score associated with the subgroup defined in the box.

[b]This percentage relates the number of family heads who are in the subgroup specified in the lower box to the number of all heads included in the analysis.

neither paid nor unpaid work after retirement, although felt pressures also affect some with compulsory retirement ages who plan to work after retirement anyway (lower right in diagram). Felt pressure from unions affected for the most part those who reported themselves currently in relatively poor health.

Finally, wanting less work now (or at least not more) seemed to affect involvement with retirement only for those who feel that young people want oldsters to retire.

The eleven end-groups of Figure 2-5 account for over 10 percent of the *remaining* variance, about 9 percent of the *original* variance, so that the two figures combined account for some 23 percent of the *total* variance.

It is interesting to notice what the factors were that proved to be unrelated to involvement with retirement, not only for the whole sample, but for any major part of it. We noticed that having a mortgage which ran late in life almost came into play, but such situations affect relatively few people. Only 74 cases out of the 1,652 had mortgages that would continue beyond their 70th birthday, and only 207 past their 64th birthday.

Felt pressure from employers toward retirement was reported less commonly than pressure from unions or younger people, and it almost was powerful enough to divide the group who expected to do no work after retirement, but did not feel pressure from young people. In other words for those persons in the lower left part of Figure 2-5, the feeling that employers wanted older people to retire was almost as powerful a predictor as was the feeling that young people wanted oldsters to retire.

Among the background factors, age, sex, and race did not make any difference, not even for one of the subgroups. (Recall that the effects of the main economic factors had already been removed and with them the possibility of spurious correlations of retirement involvement with race or sex or age.) Being self-employed or being a union member did not matter either although there were small differences in the expected directions because employed and union members are more involved with early retirement.

Finally, two measures of enjoyment of the job were irrelevant. One, asking directly whether the work was drudgery, produced only a slightly larger interest in early retirement among those who disliked their job. The second measure, asking whether the respondent would miss the people he worked with if he should change jobs, also produced slightly larger interest in retirement among those who said they would not miss their fellow workers.

Even when we use the broader index of involvement with retirement rather than the narrower plans to retire early, we are left with a preponderance of economic and situational forces affecting retirement. And the reports that young people or unions or employers want older workers to retire may well be an effect of the desire to retire early rather than a cause. The only attitudinal variables that seem to work and may well be causal are the reports of wanting to work fewer hours now, or of not wanting more work now.

CHAPTER 2: APPENDIX

SUMMARY OF SEARCH-TECHNIQUE ANALYSIS OF THE INVOLVEMENT-WITH-RETIREMENT INDEX

I. First stage of the analysis

A. Rank of the predictors by their importance in explaining variance in the dependent variable (measured by this fraction: between sums of squares/total sums of squares)

Predictor	BSS/TSS
Expected pension income	.090
Other retirement income	.068
Age mortgage paid	.023
Age no dependents other than wife	.003

B. Variance explained: 13.6 percent

C. Mean values of the involvement index within the various predictors, for all respondents (grand mean x 20 = 37.6)

1. Expected pension income

Predictor categories	Number of cases	Mean value of index times 20
Less than $1,000	37	28.6
$1,000 - 1,999	292	26.6
$2,000 - 2,999	464	32.5
$3,000 - 3,999	464	36.7
$4,000 - 4,999	282	42.1
$5,000 - 5,999	131	47.3
$6,000 - 7,499	117	50.6
$7,500 - 9,999	84	53.1
$10,000 - 14,999	37	60.5
$15,000 or more	9	71.1

2. Other retirement income

Predictor categories	Number of cases	Mean value of index times 20
Less than $1,000	530	27.8
$1,000 - 1,999	437	39.5
$2,000 - 2,999	235	41.1
$3,000 - 3,999	142	46.5
$4,000 - 4,999	63	44.4
$5,000 - 5,999	77	47.0
$6,000 - 7,499	47	42.6
$7,500 - 9,999	45	42.2
$10,000 - 14,999	74	47.0
$15,000 or more	2	50.0

3. Age mortgage paid

Predictor categories	Number of cases	Mean value of index times 20
Younger than age 51	221	40.7
51 - 55	194	41.6
56 - 60	200	40.6
61 - 62	66	47.3
63 - 64	81	37.8
65 - 70	133	43.2
71 - 98	74	34.1
Does not own home	681	32.9

4. Age no dependents other than wife

Predictor categories	Number of cases	Mean value of index times 20
Younger than age 51	382	37.9
51 - 54	364	40.6
55 - 59	557	36.9
60 - 64	233	35.5
65 - 69	72	35.0
70 - 74	28	39.3
75 - 79	6	40.0
80 or older	10	24.0

II. Second stage of the analysis, with pooled residuals from end-groups of the first stage as the dependent variable

A. Rank of the predictors by their importance in explaining variance in the dependent variable (measured by this fraction: between sums of squares/total sum of squares), for all respondents

Predictor	BSS/TSS
Expected post-retirement earned income	.028
Whether feels that younger workers want older ones to retire	.023
Whether sees unions as urging retirement	.021
Whether plans to do more or less volunteer work after retirement	.018
Whether sees employers as urging retirement	.010
Whether would like more work than doing now	.009
Whether would like less work than doing now	.009
Compulsory retirement age	.008
Health index	.004
Race	.003
Whether would miss coworkers if left job	.003
Whether belongs to labor union	.002
Whether enjoys work	.001
Sex	.001
Whether self-employed	*
Age	*

*Less than 0.0005

B. Variance explained: 10.6 percent

C. Sum of grand mean value of the involvement index and mean value of residual (both multiplied by 20), within the various predictors, for all respondents

1. Expected post-retirement earned income

Predictor categories	Number of cases	Adjusted index value
None	952	34.2
$1 - 499	14	38.4
$500 - 999	29	50.7
$1,000 - 1,999	126	44.7
$2,000 - 2,999	51	42.0
$3,000 - 4,999	41	47.7
$5,000 - 7,499	42	48.4
$7,500 - 9,996	13	57.8
$9,997 or more	26	47.4
Not ascertained	358	38.7

2. Whether feels that young workers want older ones to retire

Predictor categories	Number of cases	Adjusted index value
Most do	950	40.8
Some do	89	35.3
Only a few do	6	26.8
None do	364	34.0
Don't know	179	32.9

3. Whether sees unions as urging early retirement

Predictor categories	Number of cases	Adjusted index value
Yes	521	42.9
Pro-con	29	29.5
No	378	37.5
Don't know	676	34.3

4. Whether plans to do more or less volunteer work after retirement

Predictor categories	Number of cases	Adjusted index value
More	748	41.3
Same	320	36.9
Less	124	36.6
Not ascertained, don't know	456	32.5

5. Whether sees employers as urging early retirement

Predictor categories	Number of cases	Adjusted index value
Yes	454	40.8
Pro-con	199	39.7
No	737	36.7
Don't know	224	35.0

6. Whether wants more work than doing now

Predictor categories	Number of cases	Adjusted index value
Yes, emphatically	413	33.7
Yes	66	39.9
Yes and no	13	43.9
No	28	43.5
No, emphatically	1,025	39.5

7. Whether wants less work than doing now

Predictor categories	Number of cases	Adjusted index value
Yes, emphatically	129	44.6
Yes	52	42.4
Yes and no	14	34.4
No	27	35.4
No, emphatically	1,352	37.2

8. Compulsory retirement age

Predictor categories	Number of cases	Adjusted index value
None	1,000	35.9
Before age 65	25	49.7
Age 65	428	38.3
After age 65	137	47.4

9. Health index

Predictor categories	Number of cases	Adjusted index value
Relatively poor health (0-2 on index)	577	39.8
Relatively good health (3-5 on index)	1,075	36.5

10. Race

Predictor categories	Number of cases	Adjusted index value
White	1,517	38.0
Negro, Latin American	135	32.9

11. Whether would miss co-workers

Predictor categories	Number of cases	Adjusted index value
Yes	867	38.7
Yes and No	90	39.8
No	598	36.7

12. Union membership

Predictor categories	Number of cases	Adjusted index value
No	876	36.8
Yes	453	40.1
Self-employed	300	37.2

13. Whether enjoys work

Predictor categories	Number of cases	Adjusted index value
Yes, emphatically	389	38.8
Yes	901	37.3
Yes and No	233	35.6
No	42	42.0
No, emphatically	53	40.8

14. Sex

Predictor categories	Number of cases	Adjusted index value
Male	1,479	37.8
Female	173	35.7

15. Whether self-employed

Predictor categories	Number of cases	Adjusted index value
Self-employed	306	36.7
Other-employed	1,346	37.8

16. Age

Predictor categories	Number of cases	Adjusted index value
35 - 44	662	37.3
45 - 49	357	39.1
50 - 54	340	36.6
55 - 59	293	37.7

Chapter 3

FACTORS INFLUENCING THE RETIREMENT
DECISION: SELECTED SUBGROUPS

The analysis of the whole sample of household heads 35 to 59 years of age in the labor force provided the best insight into retirement trends and plans and the various factors associated with expecting to retire early. For several reasons, however, it was desirable to investigate the retirement decision within various subgroups of respondents: those having some college training, those 50 to 59 years of age, and those 50 to 59 years of age who were also members of labor unions. Education beyond the high school years has become so common a part of American life that a larger and larger proportion of future retirees will have at least some college training. Further, it has been rather widely speculated that persons with more education would likely be more attached to their jobs and less satisfied with the idea of retirement than those with less education.

The nature of the auto worker part of this study suggested the inclusion of the older-respondent groups; as has been stated, all auto workers studied were around 60 years of age, and it seemed a natural extension of the analysis to study those persons in the national sample who were roughly equivalent in age, as well as those who also were union members. A fourth group was also analyzed separately: those persons who were interviewed in the second part of the 1966 survey. Here, several questions expected to be relevant for the retirement decision but not included in the earlier 1966 survey were asked; their importance in retirement planning is discussed below.

The same regression-type analysis which was used for the whole-sample investigation was utilized for the four subgroup analyses, and the same dependent and predictor variables were used in the regressions. The results of the college-trained and the older respondent analyses are summarized in Table 3-1, which indicates the relative importance (and the direction of effect) of the predictors for each group, and in Table 3-2, which details the relationship between the more important predictors and retirement plans.

The two financial factors—expected retirement pension income and the "other economic variables" index—remained relevant for the retirement decision in the three analyses; generally these continued as the most important

TABLE 3-1

PREDICTORS BY THEIR IMPORTANCE IN EXPLAINING PLANS FOR EARLY RETIREMENT

(For various subgroups indicated below)

| Predictor | Importance in regression (beta squared) and direction of (net) effect on plans to retire before age 65 (in parentheses) | | |
	College-trained group	Age 50 to 59 group	Older union member group
Expected retirement pension income	.034 (+)	.032 (+)	.022 (+)
"Other economic variables" index	.044 (+)	.025 (+)	.053 (+)
Health index	.028 (−)	.034 (−)	.052 (−)
Whether hobbies	.008 (+)	.012 (+)	.004 (+)
Low ranking of "short hours" criterion	.013 (−)	.016 (−)	.034 (−)
Whether enjoyed his work	.013 (−)	.008 (−)	.010 (−)
Age	.006 (−)	* (0)	.013 (+)
Current family income	.019 (+)	.007 (0)	.037 (+)
Sex (whether male)	.001 (−)	* (0)	.002 (+)
Race (whether Negro/Latin American)	.001 (+)	.002 (+)	.001 (+)
Whether self-employed	.003 (−)	.002 (+)	* (0)
Number of cases	430	633	176
Percent planning early retirement	38.4	29.5	34.7

*
Less than 0.0005

predictors (as measured by the squares of their beta coefficients). Table 3-2 reveals, however, that the association between expected pension income and retirement plans for both older-respondent groups is perhaps not as systematic as that for all respondents or for the college-trained group. It is true, certainly, that those older respondents who expect $4,000 or more in retirement income are more likely to plan retirement before age 65 than are those who expect to be less well-off; but the proportion planning early retirement does not increase smoothly with increasing expected income. The relationship between the other economic variables (consolidated into an index) and early retirement planning was, as is obvious, strong across the three groups.

The respondent's health remained important in all subgroups and, as seems reasonable, became more salient for the older respondents, particularly the older union members. Having hobbies one looked forward to spending

TABLE 3-2 (Sheet 1 of 2)

PROPORTION PLANNING EARLY RETIREMENT, BY VARIOUS PREDICTORS,
WITHIN THREE SELECTED SUBGROUPS OF RESPONDENTS

Predictor	Adjusted percent planning early retirement		
	College-trained group	Age 50 to 59 group	Older union member group
Expected retirement pension income			
Less than $2,000	30.8	27.0	26.5
$2,000-2,999	30.8	27.4	33.8
$3,000-3,999	28.0	22.1	34.2
$4,000-4,999	34.4	37.1	37.4
$5,000-5,999	44.9	25.7	32.9
$6,000-7,499	44.2	51.7	51.8
$7,500 or more	51.6	44.3	24.0
Other economic variables index[a]			
Relatively low value (index value of 0 to 1)	20.3	23.0	25.5
"Middle" value (index value of 2)	35.5	32.9	41.1
Relatively high value (index value of 3 to 4)	47.3	36.9	44.7
Health index			
Relatively poor health (index value of 0 to 2)	44.5	39.7	41.6
Relatively good health (index value of 3 to 5)	35.6	22.8	29.4
Whether has hobbies to spend time on after retirement			
Has hobbies	40.8	33.7	37.0
Has no hobbies	30.8	23.4	29.7
Ranking of "short hours" as a criterion of occupational preference			
Ranked last of six items	32.5	23.1	23.9
Ranked other than last	43.7	34.5	41.8

---

[a]Recall that the variables incorporated here were (1) dependents expected after age 59, (2) expected post-retirement earnings, (3) potential income from pro-jected retirement-age asset holdings, and (4) mortgage payments after age 60.

TABLE 3-2 (Sheet 2 of 2)

PROPORTION PLANNING EARLY RETIREMENT, BY VARIOUS PREDICTORS,
WITHIN THREE SELECTED SUBGROUPS OF RESPONDENTS

| | Adjusted percent planning early retirement | | |
Predictor	College-trained group	Age 50 to 59 group	Older union member group
Satisfaction with work			
Enjoys work	31.9	29.3	37.9
Enjoys, qualified	39.1	30.2	35.1
Pro-con response	46.8	34.8	35.2
Dislikes work	43.8	35.8	41.5
Age of family head			
35-44	39.1	b	b
45-49	40.3	b	b
50-54	41.0	30.1	29.5
55-59	29.3	28.9	40.2
Family income in 1965			
Less than $3,000	39.8	31.5	50.6
$3,000-4,999	48.6	24.7	33.3
$5,000-7,499	29.6	29.4	32.1
$7,500-9,999	40.6	34.7	42.7
$10,000-14,999	40.7	30.4	34.6
$15,000 or more	35.2	27.9	18.9

---

[b]These cells were empty for the two older-respondent groups.

time on was associated with planning to retire before age 65 across the board,
though its relative importance among the predictors was rather low for union
members. Ranking "short hours" last in the group of six criteria of occupational preference, which generally continued to be associated with planning a
longer stay on the job, was, on the other hand, of particularly high importance
for union members; probably this and having hobbies, both of which
may be construed as measuring a demand for leisure time, are in some sense
substitute factors.

For all groups, satisfaction with one's job was correlated with planning
to remain at work relatively longer, while dissatisfaction with the work was
associated, to a greater or lesser extent, with a tendency toward earlier retirement. In the group in which the full range of ages was represented, respondents older than age 54 were less likely to plan early retirement; but in the 50
to 59 year-old group there was little difference between the two age groups,

TABLE 3-3

PROPORTION[a] PLANNING EARLY RETIREMENT, BY CONTROL OVER THE PACE
OF WORK, TIME REQUIRED TO GET TO WORK, AND RELIGIOUS PREFERENCE

Predictor	Number of cases	Unadjusted percent	Adjusted perc
Work-pace control[b]			
Substantial control	353	37.1	37.1
Some control	49	46.9	44.4
Little or no control	145	40.0	40.9
Importance in regression:			
12th of 14 predictors			
Travel time[c]			
Less than 15 minutes	244	37.3	39.5
15 to 30 minutes	203	40.9	39.9
More than 30 minutes	96	39.6	37.5
Importance in regression:			
10th of 14 predictors			
Religious preference[d]			
Fundamentalist Protestant	168	33.3	35.4
Other Protestant	234	41.0	39.7
Roman Catholic	126	45.2	46.4
Non-Christian; not			
ascertained	42	28.6	24.4
Importance in regression:			
7th of 14 predictors			

---

[a]For 570 family heads in the labor force age 35 to 59.

[b]The question was: "Do you organize your own work or vary its pace, or is it all determined by a production line or a crew that has to keep together?"

[c]The question was: "How long does it take you to get from your home to where you work?"

[d]The question was: "Is your church preference Protestant, Catholic, or Jewish? (If Protestant) What denomination is that?"

and in the older union member group, the 55-or-older workers were *more* likely to plan early retirement (and this, recall, after the regression adjusted for differences in financial outlook, health, etc.). Family income in 1965, though its beta-square value in two of the three regressions was rather high, was related only erratically to early retirement plans in all three subgroups. Finally, neither sex nor race nor whether the respondent was self-employed were much important for the retirement plans of respondents in any subgroup.

As was indicated above, three additional questions were asked only of those persons interviewed in the Summer 1966 survey; these asked about

(1) amount of the respondent's control over the pace and organization of his work,

(2) time consumed in traveling to work, and

(3) religious preference.

The three variables, along with the eleven predictors used in the other analyses, were included in a regression which was restricted to the 570 Summer survey respondents age 35 to 59 in the labor force. The relationship between the three new predictors and early retirement planning is detailed in Table 3-3; as is evident from the table, only religious preference was at all important for the retirement decision.

To summarize the results of this chapter, then, the relatively strong association between planning for early retirement and expecting a favorable retirement financial position, so evident in the whole-sample analysis, was duplicated here. And, the substantial correlation between relatively poor health and early retirement plans was repeated. Finally, respondents with college training seemed at least as receptive to the idea of early retirement as the others and as strongly motivated by financial, health, and leisure-time considerations.

Chapter 4

THE LATE RETIREMENT DECISION

While the major focus of this study is on the decision to retire before it is compulsory or before one's personal circumstances force the cessation of work, it is interesting also to look at the decision to retire later than usual. About fifteen percent of economically active family heads age 35 to 59 expressed plans to retire after age 70 or to continue work as long as they were able, or said that they would "never" retire. Several questions are then suggested: Who are those who plan to retire late? Are they likely to form an increasing or a decreasing proportion of the population in the future? Are the factors which were influential in the early retirement decision also relevant here; that is, is the late retirement decision essentially the inverse of the early retirement decision, with persons who expect small retirement incomes, who enjoy good health, who like their work making up the bulk of those who want to postpone retirement? Accordingly, a separate regression analysis of the late retirement decision was undertaken, having a dichotomous dependent variable in which persons who planned to retire late (as defined above) received a value of one, and all others received zero. Predictors were the ones used in the previous, early retirement analyses; they are listed in Table 4-1 by their importance in the regression. (Predictor rank for the whole-group early retirement regression is also given to facilitate comparisons.)

The effects of the various factors were generally in directions consistent with those in the early retirement analyses, although the order of importance was, as is evident, substantially revised. Whether the respondent is self-employed was the single most important factor in late retirement plans, no doubt partly because late retirement is simply more feasible for the self-employed, who do not face compulsory retirement barriers. (In the whole-sample early retirement analysis self-employment was the least important of the eleven predictors. This striking difference in importance apparently results from the relative polarization of planned retirement age for the self-employed; such persons are quite likely to plan retirement either before age 65 or after age 69, with few falling into the intermediate age range.) Current and expected pension income were both importantly related to the late retirement decision, with those having and/or expecting relatively low incomes being generally more likely to plan to retire late. Respondents who claimed to enjoy their work

47

TABLE 4-1

PREDICTORS BY THEIR IMPORTANCE IN EXPLAINING PLANS FOR LATE RETIREMENT[a]

Predictor	Using unadjusted means Importance taken singly (correlation ratio squared)	Using adjusted means Importance in regression (beta squared)	Direction of (net) effect on plans to retire after age 70	Rank in "early retirement" regression
Whether self-employed	.044	.026	+	11
Expected retirement pension income	.048	.019	-	1
Current family income	.029	.015	-	8
Whether enjoyed his work	.008	.009	+	6
Age	.013	.006	+	7
Whether hobbies	.009	.004	-	4
Health index	.005	.002	0	3
"Other economic variables" index	.006	.001	0	2
Low ranking of "short hours" criterion	*	.001	+	5
Race (whether Negro/Latin American)	.001	*	0	10
Sex (whether male)	.002	*	0	9

*Less than 0.0005.

aFor 1,652 family heads in the labor force age 35 to 59.

TABLE 4-2 (Sheet 1 of 2)

PROPORTION[a] PLANNING LATE RETIREMENT, BY VARIOUS PREDICTORS

	Number of cases	Unadjusted percent	Adjusted percent
Predictor			
Employed status			
Self-employed	306	31.0	27.2
Other-employed	1,346	11.6	12.5
Current family income			
Less than $2,000	52	30.7	26.0
$2,000-2,999	57	19.3	17.3
$3,000-3,999	85	28.2	24.7
$4,000-4,999	123	25.2	22.6
$5,000-7,499	342	15.5	15.2
$7,500-9,999	344	11.3	13.1
$10,000-14,999	377	9.6	11.7
$15,000 or more	248	14.9	14.1
Expected pension income			
Less than $1,000	37	29.7	21.6
$1,000-1,999	292	20.5	15.8
$2,000-2,999	464	23.1	21.0
$3,000-3,999	282	14.9	16.5
$4,000-4,999	199	4.5	7.9
$5,000-5,999	131	6.9	10.2
$6,000-7,499	117	5.1	8.8
$7,500-9,999	84	4.8	10.7
$10,000 or more	46	6.5	9.3
Feelings about work			
Enjoy	389	20.3	20.4
Enjoy somewhat	901	14.8	14.8
Pro-con	233	10.3	10.4
Dislike somewhat	42	11.9	11.6
Dislike	53	11.3	10.0

---

[a] For 1,652 family heads in the labor force age 35 to 59.

TABLE 4-2 (Sheet 2 of 2)

PROPORTION[a] PLANNING LATE RETIREMENT, BY VARIOUS PREDICTORS

	Number of cases	Unadjusted percent	Adjusted percent
Predictor			
Age			
35-44	662	11.3	12.5
45-49	357	13.2	13.9
50-54	340	20.3	19.4
55-59	293	20.5	17.9
Whether hobbies			
Yes	1,046	12.6	13.5
No	606	19.6	18.1
Health index			
Relatively poor health (index value of 0 to 2)	577	15.3	14.7
Relatively good health (index value of 3 to 5)	1,075	15.1	15.4
Other economic variables index			
Relatively poor financial outlook (index value of 0 to 1)	505	18.4	15.2
"Middle" financial outlook (index value of 2)	599	15.0	14.6
Relatively good financial outlook (index value of 3 to 4)	548	12.4	15.7
Ranking of "short hours" as a criterion of occupational preference			
Ranked last of six items	792	15.7	16.1
Ranked other than last	860	14.8	14.4

---

[a]For 1,652 family heads in the labor force age 35 to 59.

were, as seems reasonable, more likely to plan a postponement of retirement. Age had an effect on late retirement planning analogous to that found for early retirement; older persons generally were more likely to express a preference for retirement after age 70. And, having hobbies to pursue after retirement was associated with a smaller proportion planning late retirement. [The effect of one of the variables included only in the Summer 1966 survey—amount of control over the pace of work—was also investigated in the late retirement regression; while this factor was relatively unimportant for the late retirement decision (as it was for the early retirement decision, also), there was some tendency for persons having substantial control over the pace of their work to plan retirement after age 70].

None of the other predictors was a significantly important influence on deciding to retire late, including the "other economic variables" index; apparently the financial factors which inhibit early retirement—dependents or a mortgage after age 60—become unimportant in inducing plans to retire late.

The person who plans to continue work until age 70 or later may, then, be characterized as follows: he likely is self-employed and over 50, earning less than $5,000 per year and expecting a retirement income of less than $4,000. He enjoys his work and has developed few outside interests which he could pursue in the event of retirement. While the pattern of factors which are associated with planned late retirement is somewhat analogous to that associated with planned early retirement, the relative difference in importance of such things as self-employment and economic factors other than expected retirement income implies that we are dealing here with something other than merely two sides of the same retirement coin. Planned late retirers *are* different, and, given their rather small expected retirement incomes, their decision to remain at work is probably socially advantageous.

It seems unlikely that the number of such persons will become proportionally greater in the future. Self-employed small businessmen, the source of a large part of this group, will probably not become relatively more numerous. As the general income level rises, and as social security and private pension improvements are forthcoming, there should be fewer persons with relatively low current and expected retirement incomes. Finally, if the trend toward a lowering of the average age of the labor force continues, and if the observed association between age and planned late retirement reflects real inter-generational differences in attitude, the incidence of late retirement would seem likely to decline.

It is possible that a genuine and pervasive improvement in the quality of jobs, and a related increase in job satisfaction, would tend to counteract these tendencies. And, there is some evidence that the results of recent technological change have been in this direction.[1] But, given the rather small number of persons who in fact express dissatisfaction with their work, even a significant increase in the quality of work and the work environment probably would not substantially increase the relative number of planned late retirers.

---

[1]Eva Mueller, *Technological Advance in an Expanding Economy: Its Impact on a Cross-Section of the Labor Force,* Chapter VI. Institute for Social Research, The University of Michigan (in press).

Chapter 5

THE RETIRED

I. Differences in Income Among the Retired

We know far too little about the current economic situation of retired people and the factors which make for the prevailing great differences in the well-being of the retired. Some data collected in the 1966 surveys will be presented here in order to indicate the importance of some crucial factors that influence the financial position of the retired and to provide a tentative basis for prediction.

The tabulations are based on data from 675 respondents and therefore on a fairly small number of cases. Yet they are derived from the same carefully drawn representative sample from which the data on retirement plans and expectations of those still in the labor force were obtained. As stated earlier, the total sample of the 1966 surveys consisted of over 3,600 families and single individuals. In about 18 percent of that sample the head of the family, or the single person living without close relatives in a selected dwelling unit, was found to be retired.[1]

Three criteria were selected for the purpose of comparing the economic position of different groups of retired: current age, age at retirement, and planned as against unexpected retirement. The three criteria are interrelated. Nevertheless, in studying the influence of the three variables, only the second and the third variable will be combined. This method of presenting the findings was chosen because of the probable predictive significance of data on the differences between currently younger and currently older retired people. Since the older retired people have much less formal education than the younger ones, and since many older retired people have neither social security nor private pensions, it is probable that in a decade or so the financial position of the average retired American will resemble the position of the younger ones among those who are now retired, rather than the average of all currently retired people.

---

[1] It should be noted that retired wives and retired people who live with their children are not counted separately because the analysis in this chapter relates to retired *heads of families.* A single retired person is counted as the household head. The analysis also excluded older females who have never worked and call themselves housewives or widows rather than retired, even if they live alone or are heads of units.

Table 5-1 presents the distribution of the retired people by their age, as well as the relation of age to the age at retirement. It appears that in 1966 only 27 percent of all retired (family heads and single persons considered together) were less than 65 years of age, while more than half were 70 years old or older. Naturally, all retired people in the two youngest age groups retired "early," i.e., before they were 65 years of age. Yet early retirement as defined was much more frequent; it comprised more than one-half of all retired.[2] Nevertheless, the majority of those who were over 70 years of age in 1966 retired "late," that is, at a time when they were 66 years old or older.

Following the question about their age at the time of retirement respondents were asked: "Had you planned to retire then, or did you have to?" Most respondents who did not answer that they retired as planned said that they retired unexpectedly (and frequently referred to health considerations). Some respondents explained that they had plans to retire but had to change them. These respondents are included among those who retired unexpectedly. Planned retirement is most common among people who retired at age 65; both early and late retirement are more frequently unexpected:

TABLE 5-1

DISTRIBUTION OF RETIRED PEOPLE BY
CURRENT AGE AND AGE AT RETIREMENT

(In percent)

| | | Retired | | |
Age in 1966	All	Early*	At 65	Late**
Under age 60	17	17	0	0
60-64	10	10	0	0
65-69	22	12	8	2
70-74	23	8	5	10
75 or older	28	6	5	17
Total	100	53	18	29

---

* Retired at age 64 or earlier.
**Retired at age 66 or later.

---

[2]In the 1968 survey, fewer than half (43 percent) the retired people had retired early; here, though, the number of cases was quite small (189).

Among those who retired

At age	As planned	Unexpectedly
64 or younger	39%	61%
65	70	30
66 or older	46	54

(The above distribution was essentially duplicated in the data obtained from the supplemental 1968 survey. Here, the "as planned" percentages were 39, 76, and 50; and the "unexpectedly" percentages were 61, 24, and 50.)

Income level is a crucial factor in assessing the economic status of the retired. The cash income of all respondents was determined in the 1966 surveys by a series of questions concerning the amount received from various income sources of the family head, as well as those of other family members. The resulting tabulation of total family income before taxes received in 1965 by retired people is given in Table 5-2.

The younger the retired family head (or single retired person), the higher is his income on the average. The median income of retired people who are age 70 or older is particularly low; in these age groups income of less than $2,000 is frequent and income of more than $7,500 infrequent (Table 5-2).[3]

TABLE 5-2

FAMILY INCOME BEFORE TAXES IN 1965
BY AGE OF THE RETIRED

Age in 1966	Median income	Proportion in age group (in percent) with income of:	
		Less than $2,000	$7,500 or more
Under age 60	$3,770	20	29
60–64	3,650	28	21
65–69	3,610	20	17
70–74	2,690	32	10
75 or older	2,350	44	10
All retired	3,140	33	16

[3]While a detailed break-down of income within age is not available from the 1968 survey, the tendency for younger retirees to have larger incomes was continued. Overall, 34 percent of 1968 retirees received less than $2,000 in annual income; nine percent received $7,500 or more.

How can these substantial income differences be explained? At least three hypotheses suggest themselves. Perhaps the most obvious is that earned income makes for the difference because the younger a person, the greater the probability that he will be able to work during retirement and earn some money. Or it may be that the before-retirement incomes of the younger retirees was larger and engendered larger retirement incomes via income-related government and/or private pension schemes. Alternatively, planning ahead for retirement may be associated with larger retirement incomes. Finally (and perhaps more likely), some combination of the above factors may account for the observed income differences.

Data from the 1966 surveys allow at least tentative conclusions about these hypotheses. All retired people were asked, "Did you work for money at any time during 1965?" Thirteen percent answered in the affirmative. Since, however, the proportion working was lower both among the younger and older retired people than among those 65 to 69 years old, it seems improbable that younger retirees as a group received enough in earned income to account for the age-associated retirement income differences.

While we did not obtain information on the pre-retirement income of the retired persons interviewed in 1966, other available information indicates that this is primarily responsible for the observed income differences. First, education, a factor known to be related to income level among those not retired, differs greatly among age groups. The distribution of educational attainment among the retired is related to their current age in Table 5-3. Close to 60 percent of the retired who in 1966 were 70 years or older had 8 grades of schooling or less; among those younger than 60, the proportion is 34 percent. Undoubtedly the older retired people had much lower incomes before retirement than the younger retired people, both because their retirement was at an earlier time, and because they had less education.[4]

Second, we asked survey respondents for a subjective evaluation of their standard of living in comparison with the one they had before they retired. In this respect practically no differences were found among younger and older retired people (Table 5-4). In each age group about one-third said that their current standard of living was lower than the one before retirement. The majority of retired prople said that their standard of living was the same. (Some respondents could not answer the question; all that may be said about the not-ascertained group is that they did not have a clear notion about a deterioration or an improvement in their standard of living.) It appears then that the substantial income differences between younger and older people did not make for major changes in their feelings about their standard of living. This finding reinforces the notion, derived from the relation between the age

---

[4]Educational differences were roughly similar in the 1968 data.

TABLE 5-3

DISTRIBUTION OF RETIRED PEOPLE BY AGE
AND EDUCATIONAL LEVEL IN 1966

(In percent)

Education of family head	Under age 60	60-64	65-69	70-74	75 or older	All retired
0-5 grades	10	13	18	23	23	19
6-8 grades	24	39	38	39	33	34
9-11 grades	20	11	14	12	14	14
12 grades plus other noncollege training	37	27	25	18	22	25
College, Bachelor's or advanced degree	9	10	4	5	6	6
Not ascertained	0	0	1	3	2	2
Total	100	100	100	100	100	100

TABLE 5-4

DISTRIBUTION OF RETIRED PEOPLE BY AGE
AND CHANGE IN THE STANDARD OF LIVING[a]

(In percent)

Present standard of living compared to preretirement standard	Under Age 60	60-64	65-69	70-74	75 or older	All retired
Better	5	7	4	6	5	5
Same	39	48	55	55	61	53
Lower	32	32	33	34	30	32
Not ascertained	24	13	8	5	4	10
Total	100	100	100	100	100	100

---

[a]The question asked was: "Considering income and expenses, is your standard of living about the same as before you retired, not quite as good, or what?"

of the retired and their education, that the income differences among the retired are greatly influenced by differences in their preretirement income.[5]

Third, the retired were asked to estimate the ratio of their retirement income in 1965 to their income in the year before they retired. The answers (Table 5-5) may not reflect the true income differences correctly because the recollection of preretirement income—often an income earned many years earlier—may be faulty or even biased in many cases. But they do reflect people's impressions about how retirement has affected their income. Older and younger retired people gave substantially the same answers; the impression about the extent of the reduction in income because of retirement varies little by age. Recalling that actual retirement income varies greatly by age, we again

TABLE 5-5

SUBJECTIVE EVALUATION OF DIFFERENCES BY AGE
BETWEEN RETIREMENT AND PRERETIREMENT INCOME[a]

(In percent)

Current ratio of income to preretirement income	Under Age 60	60-64	65-69	70-74	75 or older	All retired
Less than one-fourth	4	11	5	8	11	8
About one-fourth	15	23	27	32	27	26
Smaller, don't know how much	1	4	4	6	6	4
About one-half	27	25	29	24	26	26
About three-fourths	3	7	5	5	3	4
Nearly as large	11	13	17	11	14	14
Larger	5	7	3	4	4	4
Don't know, not ascertained	34	10	10	10	9	14
Total	100	100	100	100	100	100

[a]The question asked was: "How does your income last year compare with your income the year before you retired - is it closer to one-quarter as large, one-half as large, or almost as large as before you retired?"

[5]Within the less detailed age division available in the 1968 survey (younger than age 65/age 65 or older), there was also hardly any difference in the subjective living standard comparison. Here, however, about half each age group viewed their retirement living standard as lower than that enjoyed while working.

reach the conclusion that the income differences among the retired are influenced primarily by differences in preretirement income. (Education and the
current/preretirement income ratio are related in Table 5-6. No systematic relationship between the variables is discernible from the table, though persons
holding college degrees are somewhat more likely to report a ratio of 0.5 or
higher. To the extent, then, that education is a valid proxy for preretirement
income, there is little evidence that persons who received larger preretirement
incomes enjoy *relatively* larger current incomes than do others.)

It is true, certainly, that *planning* for retirement is also a relevant factor
in retirement income differences. The retired's median family income, for example, is related to their age at retirement and to planned versus unexpected
retirement. As is evident from Table 5-8, people who retired when they were
fairly young had much higher incomes during retirement than people who retired when they were older. Furthermore, those who retired when planned
had much higher incomes than those who did not.[6] In these respects, earned
income makes for a difference; those who retired as planned worked for
money after retirement far more often than did those who retired unexpectedly. We may summarize these findings as follows: the group of retired prople
with the highest incomes consists of those who retired at a relatively early age
as planned. Two groups with low income during retirement may be singled
out: those who are fairly old, and those who retired late and unexpectedly.
The same people often fall into both groups, but others fall only into one and
not the other group. Probably both considerations make for a difference.[7]

Further evidence for the importance of planning for retirement in the
observed income differences among the retired can be inferred from the relation between planning and the current income/preretirement income ratio discussed above. As is clear from Table 5-9, persons who retired as planned report higher such ratios than do those who were forced to retire unexpectedly.

Planning for retirement is, however, apparently not responsible for the
current-age-associated retirement income differences. Only about 32 percent of
the retirees who were less than 65 years of age at the time of interview reported having retired as planned, while 51 percent of those age 65 and older
had done so. We must conclude, again, that the higher retirement incomes of

---

[6]The same relationship (among income, age at retirement, and planning for retirement) was observed in the 1968 survey data. Here, for example, persons who retired as
planned before age 65 had a *mean* annual income of about $6,000, while those who re-
tired unexpectedly after age 64 reported a mean income of about $2,700.

[7]It is interesting to note that initial satisfaction with retirement seems to be overwhelmingly related to whether the family head retired as planned or unexpectedly. While
only 17 percent of the unexpected retirees responded positively to the question "How
did you feel about retirement (when you retired)?" almost 70 percent of those who retired as planned were pleased about leaving work (see Table 5-7).

TABLE 5-6

SUBJECTIVE EVALUATION OF DIFFERENCES BETWEEN RETIREMENT AND PRERETIREMENT INCOME, BY EDUCATIONAL ATTAINMENT

(In percent)

Current ratio of income to preretirement income	0-5 grades	6-8 grades	9-11 grades	12 grades (and any noncollege training)	College, no degree	College degree
Less than one-fourth	13	5	10	7	8	10
About one-fourth	31	28	25	27	8	7
Smaller, don't know how much	4	5	1	5	9	2
About one-half	22	31	24	19	29	38
About three-fourths	2	5	3	3	6	12
Nearly as large	11	12	19	17	11	10
Larger	6	4	4	6	6	2
Not ascertained	11	10	14	16	23	19
Total	100	100	100	100	100	100

TABLE 5-7

RELATION OF AGE AND PLANNING FOR RETIREMENT
TO INITIAL FEELINGS ABOUT RETIREMENT[a]

(In percent)

	Felt good	Felt neutral	Felt bad	Not ascertained	Total
Retired before age 56					
Expectedly	71	10	12	7	100
Unexpectedly	11	6	71	12	100
Retired between ages 56-64					
Expectedly	75	5	14	6	100
Unexpectedly	16	8	69	7	100
Retired at age 65					
Expectedly	68	9	21	2	100
Unexpectedly	24	6	64	6	100
Retired after age 65					
Expectedly	65	13	22	-	100
Unexpectedly	20	12	62	6	100
Not ascertained or don't know when retired or whether retirement was expected	22	5	15	58	100
All retired	38	8	41	13	100

[a]The question asked was: "How did you feel about retirement then [when you retired]?"

TABLE 5-8

MEDIAN FAMILY INCOME IN 1966 BY AGE AT RETIREMENT
AND PLANNED VERSUS UNEXPECTED RETIREMENT

Age at retirement	Retired when planned	Retired unexpectedly
Under age 56	$4,950 (8%)	$3,500 (12%)
56-64	3,830 (10%)	2,850 (16%)
65	3,900 (11%)	2,520 (5%)
66 or older	3,500 (12%)	2,200 (14%)

Note: The figures in parentheses indicate the proportion of all retired people in each group. They add to less than 100 percent because retired people for whom planned versus unexpected retirement could not be ascertained are excluded from the table.

TABLE 5-9

SUBJECTIVE EVALUATION OF DIFFERENCES
BETWEEN CURRENT AND PRERETIREMENT INCOME,
BY PLANNED VERSUS UNPLANNED RETIREMENT

(In percent)

Current ratio of income to preretirement income	Retired when planned	Retired unexpectedly
Less than one-fourth	5	11
About one-fourth	24	32
Smaller, don't know how much	5	4
About one-half	30	26
About three-fourths	5	5
Nearly as large	17	12
Larger	5	4
Not ascertained	9	6
Total	100	100

relatively younger retirees are due primarily to their having received larger incomes before retirement. Recalling, though, that planning to retire before age 65 is becoming more prevalent, and believing that future retirees are more likely to resemble current younger retirees in their employment and earnings history, we may also conclude that the financial situation of future retirees will be, if not adequate, at least less inadequate than currently.

Income represents one indicator of the economic position of the retired, and their subjective evaluation of the living standard another. A third is their available assets. While no measure of current asset levels was obtained, respondents were asked whether they had accumulated savings at the time of retirement; overall about two-thirds reported having savings, with the major differences in this proportion occuring between those who had retired as planned versus those who had retired unexpectedly. Age at retirement seemed a relevant factor in savings accumulation only for those who had retired quite early—before age 56. (See Table 5-10).

II. Improvement in the Income of Retired People
   During the Last Few Years

Data on the income of retired people a few years ago may provide the proper perspective for the discussion presented in the previous section. To be sure, the available data, taken from the 1960 Survey of Consumer Finances,

TABLE 5-10

RELATION OF AGE AND PLANNING FOR RETIREMENT
TO SAVINGS AVAILABLE WHEN RETIRED[a]

(In percent)

	Had savings	No savings	Not ascertained	Total
Retired before age 56				
Expectedly	56	40	4	100
Unexpectedly	45	55	-	100
Retired between ages 56-64				
Expectedly	83	16	1	100
Unexpectedly	70	29	1	100
Retired at age 65				
Expectedly	94	6	0	100
Unexpectedly	52	49	0	100
Retired after age 65				
Expectedly	80	20	0	100
Unexpectedly	71	29	0	100
Not ascertained or don't know when retired or whether retirement was expected	36	18	46	100
All retired	66	28	6	100

[a]The question asked was: "Did you have any savings put away when you retired?"

are based on a very small sample (273 retired people). Nevertheless, they indicate a substantial improvement in the income of the retired during the six years prior to 1965.

The median income of retired people was $2,200 in 1959 as against $3,140 in 1966 (Table 5-11).[8] An upward adjustment of the 1959 income data by approximately 10 percent, needed because of the greater purchasing power of the dollar in 1959, does not alter the comparison greatly. (The consumer price index stood at 101.5 in 1959, and 109.9 in 1965 and at 113.1 in 1966.) In 1959 close to one-half of all retired had a family income of less than $2,000 while in 1966 only one-third of the retired fell in this income bracket. The difference between the retired in a very favorable economic position (income of more than $7,500) and those in a highly unfavorable position appears to have been even larger in 1959 than in 1966.

[8]The definition of the retired was the same in 1959 and in 1966. In complete families only the retirement of the family head was considered and the total family income was taken into account.

The lower half of Table 5-11 is indicative of income differences in 1959 and in 1965 among younger and older retired people. In 1959 a smaller proportion of all retired than in 1966 were 64 years of age or younger. It appears that a pronounced income differential by age prevailed in 1959 as well.[9]

TABLE 5-11

FAMILY INCOME OF RETIRED PEOPLE IN 1959, 1966, AND 1968

(In percent)

Income	1959	1966	1968
Less than $2,000	46	33	36
$2,000-2,999	19	18	19
$3,000-7,499	24	33	36
$7,500 or more	11	16	9
Total	100	100	100
Median	$2,200	$3,140	a

	Percent with less than $2,000 income[b]		
Age			
Under age 65	37 (17)	23 (27)	10 (16)
65-74	40 (52)	26 (45)	⎡ 41 (84)
75 or older	60 (31)	44 (28)	⎣
All retired	46 (100)	33 (100)	36 (100)

—————

[a]Not available for 1968.

[b]The figures in parentheses represent the proportion of all retired families in each age group, in percent.

—————

[9]For purposes of comparison, relevant statistics derived from the 1968 survey are included in Table 5-11. The reader should recall, however, that the number of retired family heads in this survey was so small as to call into some question the validity of such comparisons. Thus, while the rather substantial income improvements apparent from 1959 to 1966 were not so evident in the 1968 data, a shift of only a few cases from a lower income to a higher income category would have essentially duplicated the 1966 distribution. And, the less-than-$2,000-income distribution is based on only 65 cases.

FIGURE 5-1

MEDIAN INCOME OF THE NONRETIRED (BY AGE GROUPS) AND OF THE RETIRED

(Expressed as percent of median income of all families, 1957 and 1965)*

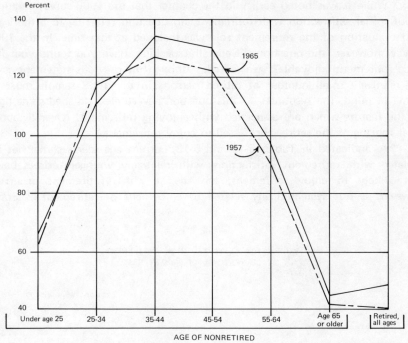

AGE OF NONRETIRED

*Income of spending units in 1957 and of family units in 1965.
Source: 1958 Survey of Consumer Finances and 1966 Survey of Consumer Finances.

The relative income position of the retired is compared with that of the nonretired in different age groups in Figure 5-1. The relation of the median income of the various groups to the median income of all family units is shown for 1957 and 1965. Thereby the absolute growth of income and the effects of inflation are disregarded.

While the income of the retired is lower than the income of the nonretired, it is only slightly lower than the income of people aged 65 or more who are not retired.[10] Figure 5-1 shows that the relative income position of the retired improved considerably in the last few years. In 1965 their median income was 47 percent of the overall median; in 1959 it was 42 percent, in 1957, 37 percent. To be sure, the income position of all age groups (except those under 35 years of age) improved in this period, but the proportion of improvement was greatest among the retired.

_____

[10]Many of those age 65 or older and not retired are not in the labor force either (being widows).

III. Satisfaction with Retirement

While it was noted earlier in the chapter that the 1966 survey inquired about initial satisfaction with retirement, no question referring to a more recent evaluation of the retirement role was included at that time. In the 1968 survey, however, the question, "Generally speaking, have you found your life since retirement enjoyable?" was asked. Although the previous statement as to the relatively small number of retired persons in the 1968 sample must be borne in mind, the responses to this question nevertheless do shed some light on the factors which are associated with enjoying retirement. (Overall, about three-fourths of the retirees professed to enjoy retirement.)

As indicated in Tables 5-12 and 5-13, current age seems somewhat associated with retirement satisfaction, with relatively younger retirees being more likely to enjoy retirement; the age at which retirement occurred, however, is not systematically related to enjoyment of retirement.[11] Some

TABLE 5-12

PROPORTION SATISFIED WITH RETIREMENT,
BY CURRENT AGE OF FAMILY HEAD

Age	Percent who enjoy retirement
Under age 65	82
Age 65 or older	73

TABLE 5-13

PROPORTION SATISFIED WITH RETIREMENT,
BY AGE AT RETIREMENT

Age at retirement	Percent who enjoy retirement
50-59	72
60-64	79
65	75
66-69	68
70 or older	79

---

[11]But if the sample is divided into two groups—those who retired early and those who retired at or after age 65—it happens that the early retirees were a little better satisfied with retirement.

fairly substantial differences in enjoyment emerge when this variable is tabu-
lated against planning for retirement and preretirement health status. It was
noted before that initial satisfaction with retirement was dramatically lower
for those persons who had retired unexpectedly; here, though the differences
are much less clear-cut, it remains true that those retirees who had retired as
planned were more likely to report that their life since retirement has been
enjoyable (Table 5-14). It will be noted subsequently in this report that automobile workers who retired on a disability pension (and who presumably had
rather severe problems with their health) were less likely to be satisfied with
retirement than other retirees. Here, a somewhat related variable was measured; and persons who reported preretirement illness or difficulty in keeping
up with their work were similarly less likely to be enjoying their retirement
experiences (Table 5-15).

TABLE 5-14

PROPORTION SATISFIED WITH RETIREMENT,
BY WHETHER RETIREMENT WAS PLANNED

Whether retirement planned	Percent who enjoy retirement
Retired as planned	88
Retired unexpectedly	67

TABLE 5-15

PROPORTION SATISFIED WITH RETIREMENT,
BY PRERETIREMENT HEALTH STATUS

Preretirement health status	Percent who enjoy retirement
Experienced illness or difficulty in keeping up with the job	68
Did not have significant health problems	80

The effect on retirement satisfaction of two financial factors was investigated (Tables 5-16 and 5-17). The respondent was asked "Considering income and expenses, are you living about as well as before you retired, not
quite as well, or what?" As one might have expected, persons who had experienced no decline in living standard were substantially more likely to be
enjoying retirement than were those who were less well off. Reported family

TABLE 5-16

PROPORTION SATISFIED WITH RETIREMENT,
BY CHANGE IN THE STANDARD OF LIVING

Present standard of living compared with preretirement standard	Proportion who enjoy retirement
Better	100
Same	85
Worse	66

TABLE 5-17

PROPORTION SATISFIED WITH RETIREMENT,
BY 1967 FAMILY INCOME

Family income in 1967	Proportion who enjoy retirement
Less than $2,000	65
$2,000-2,999	79
$3,000-3,999	64
$4,000-4,999	88
$5,000-5,999	83
$6,000 or more	85

income for the year 1967 was also related to satisfaction with retirement, though the association was not as strong as that between satisfaction and change in the living standard; on the whole, retirees whose family income was $4,000 or more were more likely to be satisfied than the others.

Finally, the effect on satisfaction of two demographic factors—marital status and education—was assessed. Retirees who had been separated from their spouse, by either death or legal decree, were somewhat less likely to be enjoying retirement than their married or single peers (Table 5-18). (The especially high likelihood of satisfaction for the single group is perhaps surprising, and it should be noted that the number of single retirees in the sample is quite small.) As is evident from Table 5-19, relatively higher educational attainment (high school diploma or better) was associated with a larger proportion enjoying retirement, though some writers have suggested that the more educated might find retirement less satisfying.

TABLE 5-18

PROPORTION SATISFIED WITH RETIREMENT,
BY MARITAL STATUS

Marital status	Percent who enjoy retirement
Married	76
Single	88
Widowed	69
Divorced or separated	67

TABLE 5-19

PROPORTION SATISFIED WITH RETIREMENT,
BY EDUCATION OF RETIRED FAMILY HEAD

Education	Percent who enjoy retirement
0-5 grades	54
6-8 grades	74
9-11 grades	65
12 grades	89
12 grades plus other noncollege training	92
Some college, less than Bachelor's degree	100
College, Bachelor's or advanced degree	83

IV. Perceived Reasons for Retirement Plans and Behavior

Non-retired respondents were asked why they planned to retire at the age they stated, why they thought their wife wanted them to retire or to remain at work, and why they thought other people were retiring before age 65. Retired respondents were asked why they retired when they did.

The retired overwhelmingly mentioned health reasons for retiring when they did (48 percent of those who gave reasons), with family reasons (14 percent) a poor second, and with job reasons (11 percent) and financial reasons (10 percent) trailing.

Non-retired persons commonly thought other people retired early because they could afford it (36 percent), but health reasons (28 percent) were also often given. Job considerations (16 percent) and the desire to do other things such as traveling or playing golf (14 percent) were less frequently mentioned. When speaking about their own situations and giving reasons for their own retirement plans, the most common response for those planning to retire at some age was financial ability (24 percent), followed by health (16 percent), dislike of the job (10 percent), and the lure of other things to do (8 percent). Finally, when the family head was asked why he thought his wife felt as she did about his retirement, the most common response was that she looked forward to the possibility of his doing other things than work (19 percent); presumably these were mostly family activities, such as travel, visiting relatives, and the like. Health and financial reasons (both 15 percent) were also seen as salient to the wife.

The importance of financial considerations in the reasons given by the family head for his (anticipated) and other's (accomplished) retirement was shown by the previously discussed multivariate analyses, which implied that economic factors provide the basic enabling framework for the retirement decision. If one can afford to retire, then his decision will be affected by his health and by his attitudes toward work and retirement. But if one feels economically unable to retire, only rather severe problems with (say) health or work may induce retirement. Financial considerations, indeed, seem to create the environment within which the other relevant variables are able to influence behavior.

That retired persons mention health overwhelmingly as a reason for their decision to leave work is, we think, not incompatible with this analysis. Finances are mentioned less often in retrospect (1) because they merely enabled retirement when health became a problem or the job less bearable and/or (2) because such considerations seemed obvious to the respondent. We infer the importance of finances from correlations, rather than from expressed reasons, and are not deterred from this inference by the fact that those who have retired focus on health (or other) reasons.

Chapter 6

AUTOMOBILE WORKER RESPONSE TO THE AVAILABILITY OF EARLY RETIREMENT

Somewhat in contrast to the heterogeneity of incomes, occupations, and retirement provisions inherent in the representative national sample heretofore analyzed, the second part of the retirement decision study focused on a more homogeneous group: a sample of older workers—those around 60 years of age—in the automobile industry.[1] Such persons were generally working-class and blue-collar, and their incomes from work fell into a more restricted range than those obtained from the national sample. Because of this homogeneity and the expectation that most workers in this age group would be actively involved in making a decision on early retirement, it was felt that the auto worker group would be particularly relevant for the purposes of the study. It was found, however, that the range of available retirement incomes for auto workers (stated as an actual amount by retirees and as an expected sum by those still working) was quite large, though not as large as that for workers in general. Thus, our earlier hope that a study of such persons would contribute more to the clarification of the relationship between early retirement and attitudes toward work and leisure than was possible in the analysis of the national sample (where financial differences tended to overshadow this relationship) was not completely realized.

Almost all auto workers are members of a single industrial union, the United Automobile, Aerospace & Agricultural Implement Workers of America (UAW). During the 1964 contract negotiations, the union and the automobile companies (as well as the agricultural implement companies) agreed to liberalize an early retirement provision which was part of a previously established retirement program. Briefly, this provision made it possible for a qualified worker to retire as early as age 60 with a pension of up to $400 per month or at ages between 55 and 60 with lesser pension amounts; in either event the

---

[1]Actually, about seven percent of the respondents in the final personal interview sample were employed by agricultural implement manufacturers (who were eligible for the same retirement benefits as those persons employed in the automobile industry); nevertheless, we shall continue to characterize this group as "auto workers."

71

STUDY OF RETIREMENT PLANS

1. When will you first become eligible to retire and get supplemental early retirement benefits?_____
   ___(year)___

   ( ) Already eligible

   ( ) Already retired: fill in back of this page and return

   ( ) Not eligible before I'm 65

2. Will you retire within the next twelve months? (Check one.)

   ( ) I definitely plan to retire within the next twelve months.

   ( ) I probably will retire within the next twelve months.

   ( ) I won't retire within the next twelve months.

3. When do you plan to retire? (Check one.)

   ( ) I will probably retire before I am 65.

   ( ) I will probably retire at 65

   ( ) I plan to work as long as I can. I don't plan to retire.

4. Which of the following are important to you in deciding when to retire? (Check as many as you please in both columns.)

   I'm thinking of retiring because: I'm thinking of staying at work because:

   ( ) I expect to have enough money to   ( ) Not enough to live on comfortably
       live on comfortably if retired.   if I retire early.

   ( ) I'd like to do many things if I had   ( ) Don't know what I would do with
       more time.   my time

   ( ) Poor health   ( ) Good health

   ( ) Job doesn't pay well enough   ( ) Job pays too well to quit

   ( ) Too much pressure on the job,   ( ) I need money for unusual expenses.
       hard to keep up with the work.

   ( ) Work is unsteady, irregular.   ( ) I enjoy the work.

                                                ( ) I'm able to keep up with the work
                                                    easily.

5. Do you organize your own work or vary its pace?

   ( ) Yes, I have some chance to vary the work or the speed.

   ( ) No, it's all determined by a production line or a crew that has to keep together.

6. What is your job title:

   (Assembler, inspector, toolmaker, etc.)_____

7. What is your current hourly wage (including cost-of-living allowance)?

                    ( ) $3.25 or less   ( ) more than $3.25

8. How long does it take you to get from your home to where you work?

   ( ) Less than   ( ) 15 to 30   ( ) more than
       15 minutes   minutes   30 minutes

9. How long have you worked for the company (if retired, how long had you worked before retirement)?_____
    (years)

10. In what year were you born?_____
    (year)

11. Did you finish high school?   ( ) YES   ( ) NO

12. Sex: ( ) Male   ( ) Female

13. Are you married: ( ) Yes, Married   ( ) No, Single, widowed, divorced,
                                                      separated

14. Does your wife (husband) work?
    ( ) Yes, full time   ( ) Yes, part time   ( ) No   ( ) Not married

15. Do you own your own home?
                            ( ) Yes   ( ) No   ( ) Buying home on
                                                                     a land contract

16. Write here the name and address of the person most likely to know how to find you in
    case you move:

    _____
    (name)

    _____
    (address)

17. If we did not use your correct name and address in sending this to you, please
    indicate the corrections we should make:

    _____
                                                    ( ) Name and address
    _____   are correct

18. If you want to make any comments, please write them here:

    _____
                                                    ( ) No comments
    _____

19. Please mail this page to Survey Research Center, University of Michigan, Ann Arbor,
    using the envelope, which requires no postage.

Project 753   1966

benefit was subject to reduction at age 65. (The employment situation of automobile workers and their pension program is described in detail in Appendix B.) The early retirement provision became operational in the fall of 1965 and had been in effect somewhat over six months when the auto worker sample was initially contacted.

With the cooperation of the UAW, which obtained employee records from the four corporations involved, a simple random sample of one-fourth the 58 through 61 year-old workers employed by General Motors, Ford, Chrysler, and International Harvester within coterminous United States was obtained. (The sample and sampling procedures are discussed in Appendix C.) The approximately eight thousand members (one-in-four of the sample) were contacted initially via a short mail questionnaire (reproduced on pp. 72-73), to obtain some basic demographic data for each worker and information on the time of his expected retirement. These data were then to be used to select a subsample of about one thousand workers with whom personal interviews would be arranged. In response to the initial and one follow-up mailing, some five thousand replies were received (62 percent of the one-in-four sample).

While a major purpose of the mail questionnaire was to facilitate selection of a personal interview sample, enough background information was obtained to permit a multivariate analysis of individual retirement planning. The search-technique analysis used revealed that only two factors, seniority and home ownership, were important for the retirement decision (see Figure 6-1). Since seniority was known to correlate closely with the pension income to which a worker would be entitled upon retirement, these results provided early evidence that the salience of economic factors observed in the national sample analyses might also be manifested in the sample of auto workers.

Mail questionnaire data on personal retirement plans and eligibility for the early retirement provision formed the basis on which a personal interview sample was selected. After ascertaining that over 80 percent of workers in the original one-in-four sample resided in a four-state "Midwest" area (Michigan, Ohio, Indiana, and Illinois) and that these did not differ significantly in rate of response or in retirement expectations from workers in the rest of the United States, it was decided for reasons of economy to restrict the personal interview sample to the four-state area. The number of persons included in this sample was 1336; after deducting those persons whose correct address could not be ascertained and those who had died since the sample was drawn, approximately 90 percent of the sample was interviewed. (The sampling procedure is discussed further in Appendix C.)

Analysis of the data collected during the Summer of 1967 from personal interviews with the auto workers revealed that the workers could be divided into three almost equal groups: (1) those who responded promptly to the availability of the early retirement program and were retired when interviewed

FIGURE 6-1

AUTOMOBILE WORKERS' RESPONSE TO EARLY RETIREMENT PROVISION

(For 3,811 respondents, including those working and those
retired as of Summer 1966; mail questionnaire data)

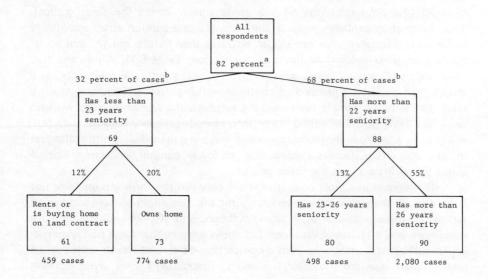

[a]This percentage relates the number of auto workers retired or planning to retire before
age 65 at the time of the mail contact to the total number in the subgroup defined in
the box.

[b]This percentage relates the number of auto workers who are in the subgroup specified in
the lower box to the number of all auto workers included in the analysis.

in 1967 (32 percent), (2) those who were working when interviewed but
planned to retire before age 65 (35 percent), and (3) those who planned to
continue working until age 65 or later (subject to a compulsory retirement
age)—thus making no use of the early retirement provision (33 percent). The
balance of this chapter is devoted to a discussion of simple distributions of
various demographic, financial, and attitudinal variables within the three
groups; subsequent chapters will detail the results of multivariate analyses.

Demographic Factors

Contrasted with working respondents, the retired were considerably more likely to be older than 61 years of age and less likely to be younger than 60 (the proportion age 61 was quite similar across the three groups). This distribution probably reflects the facts (1) that pension arrangements are much more favorable after one's 60th birthday than before and (2) that social security benefits become available at age 62 (see Table 6-1). Within the two "working-now" groups, those who planned to retire early were younger, as a group, than those who planned to continue working. Retired respondents were more likely to be female than working respondents. Nonwhite auto workers were less likely to have retired when interviewed, probably because they generally have lower paying jobs and/or less seniority than their white colleagues in this age group, factors contributing to lower pension amounts.[2] Marital status varied little across the three groups.

Differences in educational attainment between the three groups were not large, though there was a slight tendency for the nonretired to have progressed farther up the educational scale. Some differences existed *vis-à-vis* the religious preference and attendance variables, but these were neither large nor systematic. The differences associated with a comparison of current health with that of several years ago are, however, revealing. Respondents who were working when interviewed and who planned to retire early were much more likely to see their health as having deteriorated than were those who planned to continue work, while retired persons were more likely to state that their health had improved. The implication here seems to be that health problems are a contributing factor in the early retirement decision but that, when the pressures of work are removed by that retirement, a significant improvement in physical well-being is felt. The former point is supported by the information on disability; the "planned-early-retirers" were a little more likely to report the presence of a work-limiting disability. Finally, both the retired and those who plan early retirement were more likely to have worked for a company which has, in association with the UAW, been most actively involved in a program of retirement preparation classes for its employees.

---

[2]About 35 percent of nonwhite respondents reported earned income of less than $7,000 during the last calendar year in which they were employed, while about 8 percent reported earnings of $10,000 or more. The relevant proportions for white workers are 24 percent and 25 percent. Similarly, only 21 percent of nonwhite respondents had accumulated 30 years or more seniority when interviews were taken in 1967, as compared with 35 percent of whites.

TABLE 6-1 (Sheet 1 of 3)

EXTENT OF AUTO WORKER RESPONSE TO AVAILABILITY OF EARLY RETIREMENT,
WITHIN VARIOUS DEMOGRAPHIC GROUPS

(In percent)

Demographic factor	Retired respondents	Working respondents who plan to retire early	Working respondents who do not plan to retire early
Age			
Under age 59	0.2	0.9	1.5
59	3.9	26.2	16.3
60	22.9	29.4	21.9
61	24.0	25.4	24.2
62	30.2	12.8	24.9
63	18.1	4.9	10.4
64 or more	0.7	0.4	0.2
Not ascertained	0.0	0.0	0.6
Total	100.0	100.0	100.0
Sex			
Male	88.7	94.7	91.2
Female	11.3	5.3	8.8
Total	100.0	100.0	100.0
Race			
White	90.7	81.3	79.2
Negro, Latin American	8.6	18.7	20.6
Not ascertained	0.7	0.0	0.2
Total	100.0	100.0	100.0
Marital status			
Married	84.9	87.5	86.1
Single	5.7	4.0	3.8
Widowed	3.9	4.9	4.8
Divorced; separated	5.5	3.6	5.3
Total	100.0	100.0	100.0

TABLE 6-1 (Sheet 2 of 3)

EXTENT OF AUTO WORKER RESPONSE TO AVAILABILITY OF EARLY RETIREMENT,
WITHIN VARIOUS DEMOGRAPHIC GROUPS

(In percent)

Demographic factor	Retired respondents	Working respondents who plan to retire early	Working respondents who do not plan to retire early
Educational attainment			
0-5 grades	8.9	11.0	10.7
6-8 grades	42.9	37.6	38.0
9-11 grades; 0-11 grades plus other noncollege training	30.8	29.9	29.1
12 grades	9.5	10.0	9.3
12 grades plus other non-college training	4.6	5.0	5.0
Some college, less than Bachelor's degree	2.8	5.0	5.8
College, Bachelor's or advanced degree	0.5	0.6	1.8
Not ascertained	0.0	0.9	0.3
Total	100.0	100.0	100.0
Religious preference			
Baptist	18.0	22.9	27.7
Other Fundamentalist Protestant	9.0	11.0	8.0
Roman Catholic; Eastern churches	31.1	29.3	22.2
Lutheran	8.1	9.4	10.3
Agnostic; atheist; non-Christian except Jewish; preference not ascertained	3.3	3.4	4.6
Methodist	14.6	10.3	15.1
Other Protestant[a]	6.2	9.0	7.6
Presbyterian	7.9	3.2	2.6
Jewish	0.2	0.0	0.9
Episcopalian	1.6	1.5	1.0
Total	100.0	100.0	100.0

---

[a]Christian Science; Congregational; Disciples of Christ; Dutch Reformed;
Evangelical United Brethren; Friends; Latter Day Saints; Unitarian; United
Church of Christ; Protestant, denomination not ascertained.

TABLE 6-1 (Sheet 3 of 3)

EXTENT OF AUTO WORKER RESPONSE TO AVAILABILITY OF EARLY RETIREMENT,
WITHIN VARIOUS DEMOGRAPHIC GROUPS

(In percent)

Demographic factor	Retired respondents	Working respondents who plan to retire early	Working respondents who do not plan to retire early
Religious attendance			
More than once a week	8.6	10.1	7.9
Once a week	34.5	37.1	32.2
2-3 times a month	10.4	8.2	13.2
Once a month	6.9	7.1	5.0
A few times a year	24.8	23.2	25.7
Never	13.6	13.1	15.0
Not ascertained	1.2	1.2	1.0
Total	100.0	100.0	100.0
Comparison of current health with that of several years ago			
Better now	20.5	4.7	7.5
Same	34.1	29.4	44.9
Worse now	34.3	54.4	34.0
Not ascertained	11.1	11.5	13.6
Total	100.0	100.0	100.0
Presence of a work-limiting disability			
Yes	b	20.6	16.8
No	b	79.3	83.2
Not ascertained	b	0.1	0.0
Total		100.0	100.0

---

[b]This question was not asked of retired automobile workers.

Financial Factors

Various income data, involving both retirement income and income from work, were requested in the personal interviews. A summation of the negotiated pension and social security income to which the respondent reported himself entitled at the time of the interview revealed substantial differences among the three groups (see Table 6-2). Retired respondents were found to be eligible for significantly larger pension amounts than working respondents, and within the still-at-work group, those who planned to retire early were eligible for larger amounts than the others. Data on post-retirement earned income were obtained (actual earnings for the retired; expected earnings for the non-retired). In this respect the proportion not earning (expecting to earn) money after retirement was similar in the three groups. Yet there were sizable differences in the amounts earned (expected to be earned). Post-retirement earnings of $2,000 were quite frequent among the retired. Among the preretired their expected earnings were often not ascertained and were then assigned a small amount; the assignment procedure probably accounts for the sizeable proportion in the $1 - 499 category. The potential income available from asset holdings (including the respondent's equity in his house, if owned)[3] was similar across the three groups.

The respondent's wage income during the last full year of auto-company employment (1966 for those who were working when interviewed, as early as 1964 for the retired) was somewhat lower for the retired auto workers than for both still-working groups. No adjustment was made, however, for wage increases which resulted during the period of the study from cost-of-living and "improvement factor" provisions of the negotiated contract; and these call into question the relevance of the observed differences in wage income for the retirement decision. These wage adjustments were shared, though, by workers who did not retire; here, the mean wage income of those working respondents who planned to retire early was a little higher than that of those who expected to continue working. A similar distribution existed for the respondent's family's total income in the last full year before his retirement, with workers who did not plan early retirement having received somewhat less on average than those planning to retire before age 65 and somewhat more on average than the retired group. But, again, no adjustment was made for the secular income trend.

Two ratios involving the respondent's and spouse's (expected or actual) retirement income were calculated, one comparing pension and social security income with preretirement wage earnings and the other comparing pension,

---

3"Potential asset income" was calculated as six percent of asset holdings. Six percent was chosen as a compromise between the return available as interest on principal and that available if an amount equal to the asset holdings was placed in a life annuity.

TABLE 6-2 (Sheet 1 of 5)

EXTENT OF AUTO WORKER RESPONSE TO AVAILABILITY OF EARLY RETIREMENT,
WITHIN VARIOUS FINANCIAL GROUPS

(In percent)

Financial factor	Retired respondents	Working respondents who plan to retire early	Working respondents who do not plan to retire early
Pension and social security income to which respondent and spouse entitled when interviewed			
Less than $1,000	0.3	24.3	47.9
$1,000-1,999	0.8	6.0	7.0
$2,000-2,999	4.6	10.4	10.9
$3,000-3,999	10.8	15.4	15.1
$4,000-4,999	41.9	38.1	16.1
$5,000-7,499	36.9	5.6	3.0
$7,500 or more	4.7	0.2	0.0
Total	100.0	100.0	100.0
Expected or actual post-retirement earned income (whole family)			
None	62.7	66.6	61.4
$1-499	3.2	20.9	24.8
$500-999	1.0	1.9	2.6
$1,000-1,999	3.6	9.8	8.6
$2,000 or more	29.5	0.8	2.6
Total	100.0	100.0	100.0
Potential income from assets which respondent held when interviewed			
None	7.8	11.1	12.3
$1-499	17.6	20.8	21.3
$500-999	34.1	32.3	25.9
$1,000-1,999	30.8	33.7	31.4
$2,000-2,999	6.0	6.8	7.7
$3,000 or more	3.7	4.3	1.4
Total	100.0	100.0	100.0

TABLE 6-2 (Sheet 2 of 5)

EXTENT OF AUTO WORKER RESPONSE TO AVAILABILITY OF EARLY RETIREMENT,
WITHIN VARIOUS FINANCIAL GROUPS

(In percent)

Financial factor	Retired respondents	Working respondents who plan to retire early	Working respondents who do not plan to retire early
Respondent's wage income during last full year of employment			
Less than $4,000	2.1	0.7	0.8
$4,000-4,999	3.1	0.7	1.2
$5,000-5,999	11.9	2.8	5.4
$6,000-6,999	22.7	17.8	25.4
$7,000-7,999	19.0	24.1	16.0
$8,000-9,999	23.2	29.1	25.4
$10,000-14,999	14.1	20.9	20.3
$15,000 or more	0.3	1.2	0.6
Not ascertained	3.6	2.7	4.9
Total	100.0	100.0	100.0
Respondent's total family income during last full year of his employment			
Less than $5,000	2.7	0.7	0.8
$5,000-5,999	6.0	1.5	2.4
$6,000-6,999	11.0	7.8	14.2
$7,000-7,999	11.8	11.2	11.2
$8,000-9,999	19.8	26.7	16.3
$10,000-14,999	28.0	27.1	27.5
$15,000 or more	5.4	9.6	6.0
Not ascertained	15.3	15.4	21.6
Total	100.0	100.0	100.0
Ratio of respondent's (and spouse's) available pension and social security income to his pretirement wage earnings			
.00 (no available pension income)	0.2	20.6	43.1
.01-.19	0.3	5.7	7.8
.20-.29	1.8	7.9	5.4
.30-.39	4.6	10.3	9.8
.40-.49	11.0	17.4	11.8
.50-.59	14.5	13.6	9.4
.60-.69	20.1	13.5	4.9
.70-.79	16.0	5.0	0.6
.80 or more	28.0	3.2	2.2
Not ascertained	3.5	2.8	5.0
Total	100.0	100.0	100.0

TABLE 6-2 (Sheet 3 of 5)

EXTENT OF AUTO WORKER RESPONSE TO AVAILABILITY OF EARLY RETIREMENT,
WITHIN VARIOUS FINANCIAL GROUPS

(In percent)

Financial factor	Retired respondents	Working respondents who plan to retire early	Working respondents who do not plan to retire early
Ratio of respondent's (and spouse's) available pension and social security income and his expected or actual retirement earnings to his family's total preretirement income			
.00 (no available pension income)	0.2	12.5	25.6
.01–.19	0.3	10.0	17.5
.20–.29	2.1	11.1	8.4
.30–.39	6.4	15.7	8.4
.40–.49	9.2	12.1	7.2
.50–.59	12.5	10.2	7.1
.60–.69	14.9	8.0	2.8
.70–.79	12.7	2.5	1.0
.80 or more	26.3	2.2	0.6
Not ascertained	15.4	15.6	21.4
Total	100.0	100.0	100.0
Family income change during last full year of his employment			
Substantial increase	11.2	15.2	10.7
Some increase	34.5	27.4	33.6
No change	34.0	19.8	21.4
Some decrease	10.4	21.7	19.9
Substantial decrease	9.2	14.0	11.3
Not ascertained	0.7	1.9	3.1
Total	100.0	100.0	100.0
Income earned by respondent's spouse during last full year of his employment			
Less than $1,000	73.9	77.1	74.1
$1,000–1,999	3.3	3.1	2.2
$2,000–2,999	2.3	4.4	4.8
$3,000–3,999	3.8	3.3	1.8
$4,000–4,999	4.1	2.0	3.2
$5,000–7,499	7.8	5.7	7.4
$7,500 or more	1.5	2.6	0.2
Not ascertained	3.4	1.8	6.3
Total	100.0	100.0	100.0

TABLE 6-2 (Sheet 4 of 5)

EXTENT OF AUTO WORKER RESPONSE TO AVAILABILITY OF EARLY RETIREMENT,
WITHIN VARIOUS FINANCIAL GROUPS

(In percent)

Financial factor	Retired respondents	Working respondents who plan to retire early	Working respondents who do not plan to retire early
Respondent's age at which any mortgage on home was/will be paid off			
Under age 61; no mortgage	67.0	60.8	53.5
61-62	2.4	2.4	3.4
63-64	2.3	4.9	2.6
65-67	3.6	3.1	7.2
68-70	1.6	3.4	2.2
71 or older	5.1	5.1	6.3
Does not own home	14.3	15.0	18.3
Not ascertained	3.7	5.3	6.5
Total	100.0	100.0	100.0
Respondent's equity in his home at time of interview			
None (including non-owners)	15.1	17.6	18.7
$1-2,499	1.3	2.5	2.4
$2,500-4,999	4.1	5.3	1.8
$5,000-7,499	9.0	10.7	10.7
$7,500-9,999	10.6	7.4	9.2
$10,000-12,499	17.4	14.2	13.7
$12,500-14,999	7.2	4.6	5.2
$15,000-19,999	17.4	15.1	12.1
$20,000 or more	9.8	13.7	12.6
Not ascertained	8.1	8.9	13.6
Total	100.0	100.0	100.0
Number of dependents of respondent (including spouse)			
None	14.0	10.7	10.3
One	69.8	66.0	59.2
Two	10.8	15.1	20.5
Three	3.6	4.0	5.6
Four	0.7	1.3	2.6
Five or more	0.5	2.5	1.2
Not ascertained	0.6	0.4	0.6
Total	100.0	100.0	100.0

TABLE 6-2 (Sheet 5 of 5)

EXTENT OF AUTO WORKER RESPONSE TO AVAILABILITY OF EARLY RETIREMENT,
WITHIN VARIOUS FINANCIAL GROUPS

(In percent)

Financial factor	Retired respondents	Working respondents who plan to retire early	Working respondents who do not plan to retire early
Total amount of savings and investments (excluding house equity) of respondent's family			
Less than $100	19.0	7.4	9.2
$100-499	4.2	6.4	7.0
$500-1,999	12.0	10.1	17.9
$2,000-4,999	16.1	23.6	18.5
$5,000-9,999	18.8	18.8	14.6
$10,000-24,999	18.8	17.8	15.5
$25,000-49,999	5.4	7.9	2.6
$50,000 or more	1.6	1.0	1.0
Not ascertained	4.1	7.0	13.7
Total	100.0	100.0	100.0
Whether respondent plans to make a major purchase before retirement			
Yes	a	49.7	50.3
Doesn't know	a	6.3	15.3
No	a	44.0	32.9
Not ascertained	a	0.0	1.5
Total		100.0	100.0
Subjective retirement financial outlook			
Very favorable	a	25.2	16.1
Favorable	a	45.4	34.1
Pro-con response	a	2.8	3.6
Unfavorable	a	14.6	25.4
Very unfavorable	a	0.6	2.2
Doesn't know	a	9.6	15.0
Not ascertained	a	1.8	3.6
Total		100.0	100.0

---

[a] These questions were not asked of retired auto workers.

social security, and earned retirement income with the family's total preretirement income. The distributions of both ratios were quite similar; the retired were much more likely than either working group to enjoy a ratio of 0.5 or better, and those working respondents who planned to retire early had larger ratios than the non-early-retirers. There was little difference between the two working groups in the amount and direction of income change in the last full calendar year of their employment; the retired group, though, was rather more likely to have experienced no income change in that period.

Several other financial variables were investigated; their distributions may be summarized as follows: the three groups were similar in income earned by the respondent's spouse and in equity possessed in his house; retired persons were least likely to have a mortgage on their house after age 60, with the planned-early-retirers being less likely than the remaining group to have a mortgage; retired workers were least likely, and nonretired workers who did not plan early retirement most likely, to have two or more dependents. Distributions of savings and investments (excluding house equity) were roughly similar across the groups, though retired respondents were more likely to have very small savings. Finally, two financial variables were asked only of nonretired workers; here, those not planning early retirement were less certain about plans for major purchases before retirement and less sanguine about their retirement financial outlook.

Retirement-related Factors

Five retirement-related variables were coded for the three auto worker groups, with an additional two being available for those respondents who were working when interveiwed (see Table 6-3). Auto worker attendance at retirement information programs was found to be very much as expected; the retired group contained the largest proportion who had participated in such programs, followed by the working respondents who planned to retire early and, with the smallest proportion, by the non-early-retirer group.[4] Retired persons were most likely to express satisfaction with the negotiated early retirement provision; and those who planned to continue work until the regular retirement age (65) were the least satisfied (though even here almost 60 percent viewed the program in a favorable light).

---

[4]Of the respondents who attended at least one retirement information meeting, 41 percent were employed by the company which, with the UAW, has undertaken a "retirement preparation" program which offers employees a series of retirement-related discussion sessions. (About one-quarter of all workers interviewed for the study were employed by this company.)

TABLE 6-3 (Sheet 1 of 2)

EXTENT OF AUTO WORKER RESPONSE TO AVAILABILITY OF EARLY RETIREMENT,
BY VARIOUS RETIREMENT-RELATED FACTORS

(In percent)

Retirement-related factor	Retired respondents	Working respondents who plan to retire early	Working respondents who do not plan to retire early
Attendance at retirement information programs			
Attended more than one session	19.2	9.9	4.6
Attended one session	8.7	4.0	2.8
Attended no session	72.1	85.9	92.0
Not ascertained	-	0.2	0.6
Total	100.0	100.0	100.0
Evaluation of the negotiated early retirement provision			
Very favorable	29.4	23.0	11.0
Favorable	55.3	53.6	48.9
Pro-con response	5.4	8.7	13.5
Unfavorable	2.6	2.4	7.0
Very unfavorable	-	0.1	1.0
Not ascertained; depends	7.3	12.2	18.6
Total	100.0	100.0	100.0
Whether respondent is spending/ plans to spend time on hobby activities after retirement			
Yes	59.0	80.4	75.7
No	41.0	19.5	23.3
Not ascertained	-	0.1	1.0
Total	100.0	100.0	100.0
Whether respondent is/will be doing charitable or other volunteer work after retirement			
Yes	34.5	46.8	39.5
No	65.5	53.2	60.5
Total	100.0	100.0	100.0

TABLE 6-3 (Sheet 2 of 2)

EXTENT OF AUTO WORKER RESPONSE TO AVAILABILITY OF EARLY RETIREMENT,
BY VARIOUS RETIREMENT-RELATED FACTORS

(In percent)

Retirement-related factor	Retired respondents	Working respondents who plan to retire early	Working respondents who do not plan to retire early
Whether respondent plans to give/is giving financial aid to relatives after retirement			
Yes	21.4	21.8	17.1
No	78.6	78.2	82.9
Total	100.0	100.0	100.0
Whether respondent knows someone who has retired under the negotiated early retirement provision			
Yes	a	74.7	61.1
No	a	25.1	38.9
Not ascertained	a	0.2	0.0
Total		100.0	100.0
Extent to which respondent has talked with others about retirement			
Much	a	39.0	23.8
Some	a	15.8	10.9
Little	a	28.2	30.4
None	a	15.1	33.6
Not ascertained	a	1.9	1.3
Total		100.0	100.0

---

[a]These questions were not asked of retired respondents.

There were interesting differences in the distributions of variables which measured participation in post-retirement activities. While, as expected, working respondents who planned early retirement were more likely to plan to spend time on hobbies and volunteer work after retirement than were the non-early-retirers, a larger proportion of both working groups expressed *plans* for such activity than the proportion of retired respondents actually participating in it. Apparently good intentions are often not realized after retirement. There was little difference between groups in the proportion planning to give financial aid to relatives after retirement, though the difference that did appear was somewhat surprising. One might have thought that expecting to give such aid would retard retirement plans, but the data did not support this view.

Finally, the two factors whose distributions are available only for the working respondents both revealed that those who planned to retire early were more aware of and involved with the idea of retirement; these people were more likely both to know other early retirees and to have talked with someone outside the family about retiring.

Job-related Factors

Rather in contrast with the retirement-related variables, several factors which have been broadly categorized as "job-related" were not found to operate as expected (see Table 6-4). Various observers have suggested that the following characteristics may be associated with a desire for early retirement:

—having a repetitive job
—being unable to control the pace of one's job
—being dissatisfied with one's place of work
—not getting along with one's foreman
—working primarily with younger colleagues
—having to spend considerable time traveling to work.

In fact, however, the univariate relationships between these factors and having retired or planning to retire early did not support such hypotheses. For example, retired respondents were a little less likely to see their job as repetitive, about as likely to be able to control the pace of their work, and about as likely to be dissatisfied with their place of work as were working respondents. And there were no significant differences between the two working groups with respect to these variables. Similarly, the retired were less likely to have worked with younger colleagues than both working groups, and less likely to have spent over 30 minutes in getting to work than those not planning early retirement.

However, some expectations were supported by the data. There was some evidence that persons who had experienced recent change in the nature of their job (for example, through automation) were more likely to undertake and to plan early retirement. The feeling that the trip to work was annoying was also associated with early retirement. There was a small tendency for the proportion of respondents dissatisfied with their job to be larger among those who had undertaken or planned early retirement. Further, a rather substantial correlation between having difficulty keeping up with one's work, while also being unable to control the pace of one's work, and undertaking or planning

TABLE 6-4 (Sheet 1 of 4)

EXTENT OF AUTO WORKER RESPONSE TO AVAILABILITY OF EARLY RETIREMENT,
BY VARIOUS JOB-RELATED FACTORS

(In percent)

Job-related factor	Retired respondents	Working respondents who plan to retire early	Working respondents who do not plan to retire early
Whether work is/was repetitious			
Yes	54.2	54.9	58.5
No	45.2	44.0	40.9
Not ascertained	0.6	1.1	0.6
Total	100.0	100.0	100.0
Ability to control the pace of own work			
Could control pace	57.7	62.6	58.0
Could not control pace	42.3	37.1	40.8
Not ascertained	-	0.3	1.2
Total	100.0	100.0	100.0
Feelings about the physical work environment			
Pleasant	58.3	60.1	60.2
Pro-con response	18.3	19.9	18.2
Unpleasant	19.6	17.5	19.0
Not ascertained	3.8	2.5	2.6
Total	100.0	100.0	100.0
Influence of recent change in nature of respondent's job (e.g., automation) on his retirement decision			
Job change influenced him to retire earlier	16.8	13.0	7.4
Job change had no such influence on retirement decision; no job change	83.2	86.4	91.4
Not ascertained	-	0.6	1.2
Total	100.0	100.0	100.0

TABLE 6-4 (Sheet 2 of 4)

EXTENT OF AUTO WORKER RESPONSE TO AVAILABILITY OF EARLY RETIREMENT,
BY VARIOUS JOB-RELATED FACTORS

(In percent)

Job-related factor	Retired respondents	Working respondents who plan to retire early	Working respondents who do not plan to retire early
Age of co-workers			
Most same as respondent	11.7	10.7	8.4
Some same, some younger	49.9	41.2	42.4
Most younger than respondent	38.4	47.7	49.2
Not ascertained	-	0.4	0.0
Total	100.0	100.0	100.0
Ease or difficulty of getting along with foreman			
Easy	68.8	63.0	68.3
Pro-con response	20.6	28.1	20.9
Difficult	9.9	6.9	6.7
Not ascertained	0.7	2.0	4.1
Total	100.0	100.0	100.0
Time consumed in traveling to work			
Less than 15 minutes	17.1	21.8	22.1
15-30 minutes	57.0	51.8	46.2
More than 30 minutes	25.5	25.7	30.0
Not ascertained	0.4	0.7	1.7
Total	100.0	100.0	100.0
Feelings about the trip to work			
Annoying	23.6	19.5	15.5
Pro-con response	35.9	32.3	29.8
Enjoyable	39.1	46.6	52.7
Not ascertained	1.4	1.6	2.0
Total	100.0	100.0	100.0

TABLE 6-4 (Sheet 3 of 4)

EXTENT OF AUTO WORKER RESPONSE TO AVAILABILITY OF EARLY RETIREMENT,
BY VARIOUS JOB-RELATED FACTORS

(In percent)

Job-related factor	Retired respondents	Working respondents who plan to retire early	Working respondents who do not plan to retire early
Ability to keep up with the work physically			
Has/had trouble keeping up and is/was not able to control pace of own work	22.5	7.8	1.8
Has/had no trouble keeping up or is/was able to control the pace of work	77.5	92.2	98.2
Total	100.0	100.0	100.0
Satisfaction with job			
Very satisfied	7.5	5.1	9.2
Satisfied	51.4	56.8	55.3
Pro-con response	25.1	23.4	24.4
Dissatisfied	6.6	7.5	4.2
Very dissatisfied	8.6	6.9	5.8
Not ascertained	0.8	0.3	1.1
Total	100.0	100.0	100.0
Opinion as to whether younger workers want older workers to retire to make jobs available			
Thinks most feel this way	a	80.2	66.6
Thinks some feel this way	a	4.1	8.6
Mixed response	a	2.1	3.2
Thinks few or none feel this way	a	7.2	12.2
Doesn't know	a	4.4	8.0
Not ascertained	a	2.0	1.4
Total		100.0	100.0

_____

[a]These questions were not asked of retired respondents.

TABLE 6-4 (Sheet 4 of 4)

EXTENT OF AUTO WORKER RESPONSE TO AVAILABILITY OF EARLY RETIREMENT,
BY VARIOUS JOB-RELATED FACTORS

(In percent)

Job-related factor	Retired respondents	Working respondents who plan to retire early	Working respondents who do not plan to retire early
Feelings about working more with a proportionate pay increase			
Strongly desires more work	a	15.4	22.0
Desires more work	a	8.0	10.5
Pro-con response	a	1.6	3.5
Does not want more work	a	3.2	1.6
Strongly does not want more work	a	70.7	61.8
Not ascertained	a	1.1	0.6
Total		100.0	100.0

---

[a]These questions were not asked of retired respondents.

early retirement was noted. Finally, two other characteristics were found to be associated with planning to retire before age 65: believing that most younger workers want older workers to retire to make more jobs available and wanting no more work than one is now doing.

Some profiles emerge from these distributions of auto workers:

The Auto Worker Early Retiree.—This married white male in his early sixties likely is eligible for a reasonably comfortable retirement income which will be a substantial proportion of his preretirement income. His financial situation is improved by the likelihood that he owns his house outright and has only one dependent—his wife—other than himself. He enjoys good health now, though he may have found it difficult keeping up with his work before retirement. While he was not particularly dissatisfied with his work, the daily grind of driving to and from the plant was perhaps becoming annoying. He may have prepared for retirement by attending educational meetings on the retirement provisions; his general satisfaction with life since retirement is implied by the overwhelmingly favorable evaluation he gives for the early retirement program.

The Prospective Early Retiring Auto Worker.—This typical auto worker who plans to retire early is similar in many respects to his retired colleague, though there are important differences. The pension income to which he was entitled when interviewed is somewhat lower than that received by the average retiree; in fact, his deferment of retirement is likely based on the expectation that a few more years' work will lead to a financially more comfortable retirement. He is somewhat less likely to own his house mortgage-free and more likely to have three or more persons dependent on him for support. His health is much more likely than the retiree's to have declined during the last few years, though he is less likely to be having difficulty keeping up with his job. His evaluation of the early retirement program is only slightly less favorable than that of the retiree.

The Prospective Late Retiring Auto Worker.—Rather in contrast to those who have responded positively to the availability of the early retirement program is the person who plans to continue work until the regular retirement age. A most important area of difference is in available pension and social security income; here the planned-late-retirer was much less likely to be eligible for a substantial amount at the time of interview. Frequently this difference seems to derive from his having worked fewer years for a given auto company than those planning early retirement (pension amounts are dependent primarily on seniority). He is more likely to be still paying on a mortgage and to have three or more dependents. His health seems better than that of his colleague who is planning early retirement but worse than that of his colleague who actually has retired; he is much less likely than either colleague to be having trouble keeping up with his job. Indeed, he seems rather more committed to working than the others; he is a little more likely to be satisfied with his work and to desire more work than he is now doing. He is less likely to have attended even one retirement information meeting than his peers; he is less interested in post-retirement leisure activities. While he probably feels that the early retirement plan is a "good thing for UAW members," he really hasn't thought too much about retirement himself, as indicated by the likelihood that he neither knows someone who has taken advantage of the plan nor has talked much with anyone else about retirement.

*   *   *

The next three chapters discuss the results of multivariate analyses of the auto worker data. The analysis scheme was as follows: the entire personal interview sample of 1,123 persons was analyzed with respect to initial prompt response to the availability of the early retirement provision. Two subgroups were produced by this analysis: the retired and the nonretired. Subsequently the nonretired group was analyzed with respect to plans for early retirement; the retired group, with respect to satisfaction or dissatisfaction with the retirement experience. This scheme is diagrammed on the following page.

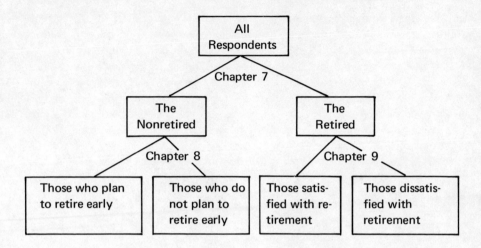

Chapter 7

FACTORS INFLUENCING AUTOMOBILE WORKER RETIREMENT BEHAVIOR

I. Search-Technique Analysis of Retirement Response

A two-stage analysis of automobile workers' response to the availability of early retirement was carried out by using the search-technique multivariate analysis, with economic and demographic factors in the first stage, attitudinal and expectational factors in the second. The analysis indicated that economic factors are predominantly important in deciding whether or not to retire, with other more or less "objective" variables being generally of little importance. More subjective (or potentially circular) variables, used in the second stage of analysis, were of much less importance than the economic ones; and, indeed, they frequently did not operate in accordance with some widely-supported assumptions.

The total sample of 1,090 nondisabled auto workers was used in the investigation (33 respondents who had retired because of disability[1] were excluded in the belief that their health problems were the factor of primary relevance for their retirement). The dependent variable was dichotomous with a value of one for those who were retired as of the time of interview[2] and of zero for the others; 32 percent of the respondents were retired. Variables used in the first stage of the analysis are listed in Table 7-1 (ordered by their ability to explain the variance in retirement behavior by a single division of the whole sample), with their (univariate) relation to retirement indicated in the third column of the table. The results of the first-stage computer analysis is

---

[1]The disability retirement provision is discussed briefly in Appendix B.

[2]It is quite likely that all such persons had retired early (that is, before age 65), since only one retiree was older than age 64 when interviewed. The auto worker sample was to have been limited to persons age 58 through 61 as of January 1, 1966 (in which case all retirees would certainly have been younger than age 65); but errors in the records from which the sample was selected caused the inclusion of a few persons younger and older than that range.

TABLE 7-1 (Sheet 1 of 4)

PROPORTION OF AUTO WORKERS WHO HAD RETIRED AT TIME OF INTERVIEW,
BY VARIOUS PREDICTORS[a]

Predictor	Number of cases	Proportion retired (in percent)
Pension and social security income to which respondent and spouse are entitled when interviewed[b]		
Less than $1,000	180	0.5
$1,000-1,999	35	1.3
$2,000-2,999	87	17.6
$3,000-3,999	134	23.5
$4,000-4,999	431	41.8
$5,000-7,499	202	80.0
$7,500 or more	21	96.3
Ratio of respondent's (and spouse's) available pension and social security income and his expected or actual retirement earnings to his family's total preretirement income		
.00 (no available pension income)	93	0.5
.01-.19	76	0.6
.20-.29	76	10.0
.30-.39	117	20.3
.40-.49	118	30.1
.50-.59	134	41.3
.60-.69	107	53.7
.70-.79	66	76.5
.80 or larger	128	89.3
Family income change during last full year of his employment[b]		
Substantial increase	143	29.2
Some increase	341	35.6
No change	288	44.4
Some decrease	178	19.7
Substantial decrease	124	24.0

---

[a] For 1,090 nondisabled respondents.

[b] These variables could explain more than 0.5 percent of the total sum of squares by a single division of the whole sample.

TABLE 7-1 (Sheet 2 of 4)

PROPORTION OF AUTO WORKERS WHO HAD RETIRED AT TIME OF INTERVIEW,
BY VARIOUS PREDICTORS[a]

Predictor	Number of cases	Proportion retired (in percent)
Race[b]		
White	952	35.2
Negro, Latin American	133	16.5
Number of dependents (including spouse)[b]		
None	123	38.7
One	739	34.9
Two	160	22.2
Three	39	26.7
Four or more	27	18.2
Place of residence of children[b]		
Same state as respondent	509	35.8
Midwest[c] but not respondent's state	72	20.7
Some outside midwest	193	26.1
All outside midwest	63	28.7
No children	244	35.0
Age of co-workers[b]		
About same as respondent	113	36.7
Some same, some younger	469	36.5
Mostly younger	507	27.5
Age at which any mortgage on home was/will be paid off[b]		
Under age 65	60	23.4
65-70	77	19.7
71 or older	58	31.8
No mortgage at time of interview	849	34.9

---

[a] For 1,090 nondisabled respondents.

[b] These variables could explain more than 0.5 percent of the total sum of squares by a single division of the whole sample.

[c] The "midwest" was defined as Illinois, Indiana, Iowa, Michigan, Minnesota, Ohio, and Wisconsin.

TABLE 7-1 (Sheet 3 of 4)

PROPORTION OF AUTO WORKERS WHO HAD RETIRED AT TIME OF INTERVIEW,
BY VARIOUS PREDICTORS[a]

Predictor	Number of cases	Proportion retired (in percent)
Religious preference[b]		
Fundamentalist Protestant	316	26.1
Roman Catholic; Eastern churches	301	37.2
Other Protestant	430	34.8
Non-Christian; not ascertained	42	27.3
Potential income from assets which respondent held when interviewed.[b]		
No such income	101	22.8
$1-499	191	27.7
$500-999	311	40.3
$1,000-1,999	362	31.7
$2,000-2,999	83	29.0
$3,000 or more	42	38.1
Educational attainment[b]		
0-5 grades	98	26.7
6-8 grades	428	35.7
9-11 grades	338	32.7
12 grades	109	33.0
12 grades plus noncollege training	55	30.6
Some college, less than Bachelor's degree	48	21.2
College, Bachelor's or advanced degree	10	18.8

---

[a] For 1,090 nondisabled respondents.

[b] These variables could explain more than 0.5 percent of the total sum of squares by a single division of the whole sample.

TABLE 7-1 (Sheet 4 of 4)

PROPORTION OF AUTO WORKERS WHO HAD RETIRED AT TIME OF INTERVIEW,
BY VARIOUS PREDICTORS[a]

Predictor	Number of cases	Proportion retired (in percent)
Time consumed in traveling to work		
Less than 15 minutes	228	27.3
15-30 minutes	573	35.6
More than 30 minutes	283	30.8
Income earned by respondent's spouse during last full year of his employment		
Less than $1,000	822	32.0
$1,000-1,999	37	37.3
$2,000-2,999	37	19.4
$3,000-3,999	34	35.1
$4,000-4,999	37	44.9
$5,000-7,499	74	38.0
$7,500 or more	14	26.9

[a]For 1,090 nondisabled respondents.

diagrammed in Figure 7-1.[3] It is immediately apparent from both the table and the figure that retirement income, expressed either as an absolute level or as a ratio to preretirement income, was of crucial—one might even say of singular—importance in determining the initial prompt response to early retirement. The proportion who had retired increased monotonically as both the absolute pension level and the pension ratio increased; the differences evident in the first two rows of Figure 7-1 are of a size seldom realized with the search-technique analysis. The first split in the analysis divided the sample into two roughly equal parts: those eligible for less than $4,000 in pension income, of whom only 10 percent had retired; and those eligible for $4,000 or more, of whom 55 percent had retired.[4] This rather dramatic difference well illustrates the overriding importance of financial considerations in the auto worker retirement decision. A third broadly financial factor which was found to be important by the analysis was the respondent's number of dependents; both overall and in the subgroup which split on this variable the effect of having more dependents was generally to decrease the likelihood of early retirement.

Generally the economic predictors operated in expected directions in the first-stage analysis, but some generally-held assumptions were contradicted. Those persons who had all of their children living outside the four-state midwest area within which interviewing was carried out were not more likely to have retired, though retirement would enable them to move nearer their children. The relation between retirement and potential income from assets was not systematic, though this had been an important factor in the retirement plans for our national sample of respondents. There was no evidence that respondents who worked primarily with younger people, and who thus might be more subject to pressure to retire and make room for younger workers than would those working with their age-peers, were more responsive to the availability of early retirement. We had expected that persons who had to spend

---

[3]It should be noted here that in this (and in all subsequent figures summarizing the results of a search-technique analysis) the percentages which designate the proportion of the sample contained in the various subgroups refer to the *weighted* number of cases, while the numbers given for all final groups refer to the actual (unweighted) number of cases contained in those groups. On average, the weighting process generates 3.2 cases per actual respondent. (For a discussion of the weighting procedure necessary for the analysis of auto worker data, see Appendix C.)

[4]Interestingly, this first split was the same as that in our analyses of the retirement plans of national-sample respondents. There, too, the single most important factor in retirement plans was pension and social security income, and the split occurred at the $4,000 mark. It is worth noting here that a labor department survey of living costs in urban areas of the United States revealed that the cost of maintaining a "moderate standard of living" for a self-supporting retired couple was $3,869 in the autumn of 1966. [See Bureau of Labor Statistics Bulletin No. 1570-4: "Retired Couple's Budget for a Moderate Standard of Living" (Autumn 1966).]

FIGURE 7-1

PROPORTION OF AUTO WORKERS WHO HAD RETIRED AT TIME OF INTERVIEW

(For 1,090 nondisabled respondents)

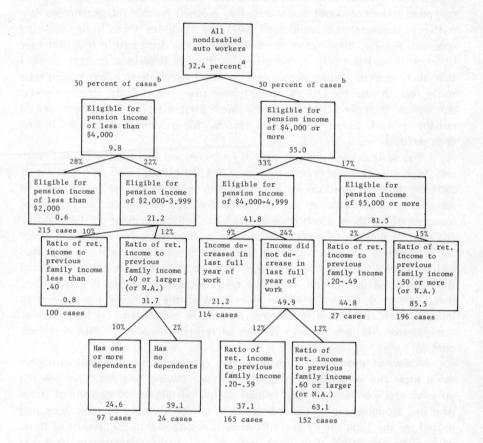

[a]This percentage relates the number of auto workers already retired at the time of the interview (Summer 1967) to the total number in the subgroup defined in the box.

[b]This percentage relates the weighted number of auto workers who are in the subgroup specified in the lower box to the weighted number of all non-disabled auto workers.

large amounts of time in getting to work might be more anxious to retire, but such was not apparent here. And, there was no tendency for those respondents having spouses who earned substantial income from their own jobs to postpone retirement until the spouse had reached normal retirement age (admittedly, however, the number of cases are small for those having working spouses). Finally, those respondents whose income decreased in their last year of work were less likely to have retired, though it seemed at least possible that such persons, being discouraged by the income decline and having relatively less to lose by retiring, would have been more likely to retire early. Apparently the counter-argument—that such persons would feel it necessary to remain at work longer in order to recoup this income loss—is more in line with reality.

The second-stage analysis had as its dependent variable the pooled residuals from the nine end-groups of Figure 7-1. In effect, much of the effect of differing financial position at retirement was removed by the first stage; and we attempted at this point to investigate the additional effects on retirement response of variables which depended on subjective judgment by the respondent (e.g., evaluation of health) or posed a problem by being potentially circular in effect (e.g., attendance at a retirement preparation class). As indicated earlier, several of the variables used here worked in directions opposite to those expected (or had no net effect on retirement behavior). It may suffice, then, to list in Table 7-2 all variables used in the residuals analysis and to indicate their relation to retirement response in two forms: (1) univariate or "unadjusted" (column 3) and (2) net of retirement income differences (column 4).

A few of the second-stage predictors retained some independent importance after the economic-factors adjustments. Having had difficulty keeping up with the job was strongly related to having retired; 54 percent of those who had trouble keeping up and did not control the pace of their work had retired by the time they were interviewed, as opposed to 30 percent of those who *either* controlled their work pace *or* had no trouble keeping up. Good health was found to have a strong positive correlation with early retirement after the first-stage adjustments. On the surface this finding seems to contradict that from our national sample data, which indicated that persons whose health is poor are more likely, other things equal, to plan early retirement. And, the observed association between having difficulty keeping up with work and retiring early seems somewhat at variance with the finding. But, since this question concerns, in part, the current health of retirees, the result here is consistent with other findings that health (or at least health feelings) may improve after retirement.[5] Further investigation of the importance of health for

---

[5]It should be noted also that the availability to auto workers of disability retirement, at any age, may have eliminated from the sample many persons who would otherwise have been classed as early retirees.

TABLE 7-2 (Sheet 1 of 2)

PROPORTION OF AUTO WORKERS WHO HAD RETIRED AT TIME OF INTERVIEW,
BEFORE AND AFTER ADJUSTMENT FOR DIFFERENCES IN ECONOMIC POSITION,
BY VARIOUS PREDICTORS[a]

Predictor	Number of cases	Unadjusted proportion (in percent)	Proportion net of economic differences (in percent)[c]
Ability to keep up with the work physically[b]			
Has/had trouble keeping up and is/was not able to control pace of own work	141	68.8	53.8
Has/had no trouble keeping up or is/was able to control the pace of work	949	27.7	29.7
Whether respondent is/will be doing charitable or other volunteer work after retirement[b]			
Yes	375	16.2	22.1
No	715	41.2	38.0
Comparison of current health with that of several years ago[b]			
Much better now	7	100.0	74.1
Better now	130	62.2	49.3
Same	389	32.8	33.0
Worse now	433	24.0	28.8
Much worse now	17	44.0	34.5
Whether is spending/plans to spend time on hobby activities after retirement[b]			
Yes	786	27.1	29.1
No	300	47.2	41.5
Attendance at retirement information meetings[b]			
Attended such meetings	221	55.2	42.8
Did not attend such meetings	869	27.6	30.2
Feelings about the trip to work			
Very annoying	19	31.9	27.7
Annoying	206	39.7	36.3
Pro-con response	383	35.5	34.4
Enjoyable	455	27.2	29.7
Very enjoyable	14	43.8	37.0

---

[a] For 1,090 nondisabled respondents.

[b] These variables could explain more than 0.5 percent of the residual sum of squares by a single division of the whole sample.

[c] The "economic factors" were pension income to which respondent was entitled, ratio of retirement income to family income when respondent was working, change in income during respondent's last full year of employment, and number of dependents of respondent; they accounted for 42 percent of the variance.

TABLE 7-2 (Sheet 2 of 2)

PROPORTION OF AUTO WORKERS WHO HAD RETIRED AT TIME OF INTERVIEW,
BEFORE AND AFTER ADJUSTMENT FOR DIFFERENCES IN ECONOMIC POSITION,
BY VARIOUS PREDICTORS[a]

Predictor	Number of cases	Unadjusted proportion (in percent)	Proportion net of economic differences (in percent)[c]
Ease or difficulty of getting along with foreman			
Very easy	170	34.8	33.7
Easy	549	33.2	32.8
Pro-con response	259	28.3	31.1
Difficult	70	40.0	35.4
Very difficult	21	44.8	37.4
Satisfaction with job			
Very satisfied	77	34.4	35.2
Satisfied	584	30.5	31.8
Pro-con response	264	33.5	32.1
Dissatisfied	74	34.5	28.9
Very dissatisfied	83	39.0	37.6
Feelings about the physical work environment			
Pleasant	636	31.8	32.2
Pro-con response	211	31.5	31.3
Unpleasant	206	34.1	35.2
Ability to control pace of own work			
Could control pace	664	31.3	32.6
Could not control pace	422	34.4	32.3
Whether work is/was repetitious			
Yes	589	31.6	31.9
No	493	33.7	33.1

---

[a]For 1,090 nondisabled respondents.

[c]The "economic factors" were pension income to which respondent was entitled,
ratio of retirement income to family income when respondent was working, change
in income during respondent's last full year of employment, and number of
dependents of respondent; they accounted for 42 percent of the variance.

the retirement decision will be discussed in Chapter 8. Attendance at the retirement information meetings remained somewhat correlated with initial prompt response to early retirement after the economic-factors adjustment, though its effect was attenuated.

Taken together, the variables which measured participation in post-retirement activities—hobbies and charitable work—were second in importance, after ability to keep up with the job, in explaining the response to the early retirement program. As in the univariate distributions discussed in the previous chapter, however, the two variables did not work as expected after the first-stage financial adjustments; again, actual behavior in these respects was different from intentions. (As will be shown later, plans for hobbies and/or charitable work retain some importance for the retirement *plans* of nonretired auto workers.)

None of the other predictors utilized in the second-stage analysis—satisfaction with job and with place of work, relative ease or difficulty in getting along with the foreman, extent to which the work was repetitive, and ability to control the pace of the work—were systematically related to early retirement response. Since all these variables seemed likely to be influential in making a decision about retirement, it is interesting to speculate why they in fact did not appear important. We should first mention that the nature of the interviewing procedure has probably led to some anomalous results. For retired respondents it was, of course, necessary to give retrospective answers to questions about their work experience and environment, while nonretired respondents could talk about current events. Although no person in the sample had been retired for as long as two years when interviewed, it seems likely that some biases resulted from this difference in perspective. The importance of the ability-to-keep-up variable and the relative unimportance of such things as the difficulty of getting along with the foreman may derive from the former's being more consonant with the maintenance of a good self-image, as opposed to the latter, which might conjure up the image of a vindictive, blame-it-on-the-other-guy personality. (And, of course, it is quite possible that work seems more appealing when seen retrospectively.) On the other hand, some psychological theories would suggest that workers might be expected to exaggerate job-related problems as a means to justifying retirement; see, for example, Leon Festinger's *A Theory of Cognitive Dissonance* (Evanston, Ill.; 1957).

Another possibility is that the second-stage predictors were so correlated with first-stage income differences that their true effects were masked by our two-stage analysis procedure. In view of the fact, however, that some of the same noneconomic predictors retain importance (after financial-differences adjustments) in the analysis of retirement plans of nonretired workers, this does not seem particularly likely.

The third possibility—and the one which seems most probable here—is that, in the face of the rather overwhelming differences in retirement financial situation uncovered in the first-stage analysis, noneconomic considerations were in fact of relatively minimal importance for the retirement decision. An auto worker tended to retire if his available retirement income was of a size to enable reasonably comfortable living; he remained at work—perhaps for only a couple more years—if this were not so.

II. Regression Analysis of the Predictive Value of Mail Questionnaire and Personal Interview Variables

It was mentioned earlier that a certain amount of demographic and attitudinal data were obtained via the initial mail contacts with the automobile workers. After data from the personal interviews had been processed, the mail questionnaire information was integrated with it; and an analysis of the retirement response of those workers who had been in the labor force when the mail contact was initiated was undertaken, using variables from both the personal and the mail questionnaires. Here, the dependent variable reflected whether this group of workers had retired in the interval between mail and personal contacts (the variable was again dichotomous, with a value of one for those who had retired after the mail contact and of zero for others); thus, it was possible to obtain some measure of the importance for the retirement decision of preretirement attitudes and situation. Additionally, supplemental data on retirement during the year following the personal interviews was obtained in Summer 1968 with the cooperation of the UAW; it was then possible to compare an analysis of initial prompt retirement response with one incorporating workers who had retired only after some delay. Multiple regression techniques were used for all these analyses; their results are reported below.

The following variables were utilized in the investigation of the importance of mail questionnaire data for the retirement decision; they are listed in order of their importance in the regression analysis (Table 7-3).

The usual financial variables retain their primary importance in this regression, but three mail-questionnaire predictors demonstrate a reasonably strong correlation with early retirement response. Two of these are retirement-income related; the third refers to the respondent's health. The initial question on the mail schedule asked "When will you first become eligible to retire and get supplemental early retirement benefits?" Responses to this question were distributed as follows:

TABLE 7-3

VARIOUS PREDICTORS BY THEIR IMPORTANCE IN THE REGRESSION

Predictor	Index of relative importance (Square of partial beta coefficient)
Ratio of pension and social security income to respondent's earned income	0.094
Available pension and social security income	0.044
Eligibility for negotiated pension[a]	0.039
Income change during last calendar year before retirement	0.027
Expectation of an inadequate retirement income[a]	0.026
Poor health experience[a]	0.024
Number of dependents (including spouse)	0.011
Potential income from assets	0.010
Income earned by respondent's spouse during calendar year before his retirement	0.006
Attendance at religious services	0.006
Age at which mortgage will be paid off	0.004
Ability to control the pace of own work[a]	0.004
Educational attainment	0.004
Marital status	0.003
Satisfaction with one's work[a]	0.002
Expectation of an adequate retirement income[a]	0.002
Lack of difficulty in keeping up with the work[a]	0.001
Good health experience[a]	0.001
Plans to participate in leisure activities after retirement[a]	0.001
Race	0.001
Sex	*
Multiple correlation coefficient (R^2)	0.397

---

*Less than 0.0005

[a]Variables from the mail questionnaire. As is evident from the reproduction of the questionnaire (pp. 72-73), many of these are coded from simple check-the-box statements relating to reasons for retiring and reasons for staying at work; thus the inclusion of such factors as good and poor health and adequate and inadequate pension.

Year in which respondent expected to be eligible for benefits	Percent who had retired at time of personal interview (multivariate relationship)
1966 or before	31.5
1967	14.1
1968	11.0
1969 to 1972	19.7
1973 or after	19.5

Apparently, then, many auto workers had a good understanding of the eligibility requirements of the early retirement program. From the 20 percent who retired within a year after having said that they would not be eligible for benefits until 1969 or later, however, it seems that a substantial fraction of the workers contacted became acquainted with the requirements only after the mail questionnaire had brought them to their attention. The other income-related mail questionnaire variable which retained some importance in the regression was the expectation of "not enough [income] to live on comfortably if I retire early." Here, after maintaining "other things equal" with the regression, 16 percent of those who shared this outlook had retired when interviewed, contrasted with 30 percent of the others. The final mail-questionnaire variable which demonstrated a significant association with the retirement decision was an awareness of poor health; 37 percent of those checking the "poor health" box had retired by the summer of 1967, while about 21 percent of those for whom health was not such a problem had retired. All other mail-questionnaire variables were of trivial importance in the multivariate analysis.

Generally, then, the mail-questionnaire variable only confirmed the previously documented importance of financial factors in the retirement decision; attitudinal differences were again revealed to be of secondary importance.

To take advantage of the additional retirement data which became available in Summer 1968, two regression analyses were undertaken. In one, the dichotomous dependent variable had a value of one for those auto workers who had been retired at the time of interviewing (Summer 1967) and of zero for the nonretired; in the second, the dependent variable had a value of one for auto workers who were retired as of Summer 1968 and of zero for the remaining nonretired. As stated before, 32 percent of the 1,090 workers contacted were retired when interviewed; an additional 11 percent were found to have retired during the subsequent year. Both regressions utilized identical predictor variables; these are listed in Table 7-4 in order of their relative importance in the first analysis (as measured by the square of their partial beta coefficient).

It is clear from the list that there was substantial correspondence in predictor rank within the two regressions; indeed, the four most important variables were the same for both analyses. The retirement income variable

TABLE 7-4

VARIOUS PREDICTORS BY THEIR IMPORTANCE IN TWO REGRESSIONS

	Index of relative importance (Square of partial beta coefficient)	
Predictor	Dependent: whether retired by Summer 1967	Dependent: whether retired by Summer 1968
Ratio of pension and social security income to respondent's earned income	0.2305	0.2560
Ability to keep up with one's work	0.0374	0.0260
Comparison of current health with that of several years ago	0.0338	0.0153
Plans for, or participation in, post-retirement charitable work	0.0178	0.0123
Income change during last calendar year before retirement	0.0167	0.0080
Plans for, or participation in, post-retirement hobby activities	0.0117	0.0013
Potential income from assets	0.0088	0.0085
Whether trip to work was annoying	0.0078	0.0054
Ability to control the pace of own work	0.0066	0.0046
Satisfaction with one's work	0.0053	0.0011
Number of dependents (including spouse)	0.0044	0.0110
Age at which mortgage was/will be paid off	0.0035	0.0068
Ease or difficulty in getting along with foreman	0.0033	0.0038
Time consumed in traveling to work	0.0029	0.0042
Whether work repetitious	0.0021	0.0002
Age of co-workers	0.0015	0.0061
Effect of change in nature of job on retirement decision	0.0008	0.0032
Satisfaction with the physical work environment	0.0007	0.0009
Sex	*	*
Partial correlation coefficient (R^2)	0.447	0.410

* Less than 0.00005.

TABLE 7-5

COMPARATIVE EFFECTS OF THREE PREDICTOR VARIABLES
ON EARLY RETIREMENT RESPONSE

(Multivariate relationships)

Predictor	Number of cases	Percent retired by 1967	Percent retired by 1968
Family income change during last year before retirement			
Substantial increase	143	32.6	41.6
Some increase	341	33.7	42.7
No change	288	40.2	49.8
Some decrease	178	26.6	40.6
Substantial decrease	124	23.0	43.4
Whether respondent is spending/plans to spend time on hobby activities after retirement			
Yes	786	29.4	43.2
No	300	40.7	45.2
Number of dependents of respondent (including spouse)			
None	123	38.5	54.3
One	739	32.2	42.9
Two	160	29.7	39.1
Three or more	66	31.9	44.6

(here, the pension-income-to-working-income ratio) again evinced its dominance, with measures of ability to keep up with one's work, current health status, and (projected or actual) participation in charitable work following rather distantly.

A few fairly important changes were engendered by the inclusion of the delayed retirees in the analysis. The tendency for those who had experienced income declines in their last working year to postpone retirement was virtually eliminated; the discrepancy between plans for and participation in post-retirement hobby activities nearly disappeared, so that the "hobby" predictor became unimportant; the relation between retirement and number of dependents became more U-shaped, with both those having no dependents and those having three or more dependents being more likely to have retired. But, generally, the results of the parallel analyses indicated that the explanatory power of most work-related and retirement-related variables would not be enhanced merely by extending the period in which response to the early retirement program was possible. And, this conclusion is reinforced by the fact that the partial correlation coefficient was actually a little lower for the delayed response regression than for the prompt-response one.

Chapter 8

RETIREMENT PLANS OF NONRETIRED AUTOMOBILE WORKERS

This chapter comprises two sections; in the first we discuss the results of a multivariate analysis of the plans for retirement of those workers who were still employed during the interview period (Summer 1967); in the second we summarize a comparative regression analysis of the effects on retirement plans and on actual prompt retirement of the various psychological or attitudinal factors measured in the study.

I. The Retirement Plans Analysis

Undertaken here was a two-stage multivariate analysis of the retirement plans of the 646 non-retired respondents. The analysis was analogous to that discussed in the previous chapter; the dependent variable was dichotomous, with a value of one for those who reported plans to retire before age 65 (defined throughout the study as "early") and a value of zero for all others. Again, the effect on retirement plans of economic and demographic variables was examined in the first stage; psychological and attitudinal variables were utilized in the second.

The (univariate) relation between planned retirement age and all predictors used in the first-stage analysis is detailed in Table 8-1; predictors are listed in order of their ability to explain the variance in retirement plans by a single division of the whole sample. Generally the economic variables operated here as they did in our analyses of the representative national sample; the reader will recall that plans for retirement were correlated quite highly with such economic factors as expected retirement income, number of dependents expected around retirement age, the age at which any mortgage on one's home would be paid off, etc. In addition, this analysis revealed that persons having a relatively high *ratio* of available retirement income to current income (this ratio calculated by us from income and pension figures obtained from respondents) as well as those with relatively high *levels* of pension income were much more likely to plan early retirement. Those few auto workers with

113

TABLE 8-1 (Sheet 1 of 3)

PROPORTION PLANNING TO RETIRE EARLY, BY VARIOUS PREDICTORS[a]

Predictor	Number of cases	Proportion (in percent)
Ratio of expected retirement income to current family income[b]		
.00 (no available pension income)	92	39.8
.01-.19	75	43.9
.20-.29	65	64.3
.30-.39	91	71.8
.40-.49	77	69.6
.50-.59	70	66.2
.60-.69	40	79.6
.70 or more	26	80.0
Not ascertained	110	49.2
Pension and social security income to which respondent and spouse entitled when interviewed[b]		
Less than $1,000	178	40.7
$1,000-1,999	34	53.9
$2,000-2,999	70	56.3
$3,000-3,999	91	58.0
$4,000-4,999	235	76.2
$5,000 or more	38	72.2
Spouse's earned income in 1966[b]		
Less than $1,000 (including non-married respondents)	493	58.4
$1,000-1,999	20	65.6
$2,000-2,999	28	55.6
$3,000-3,999	19	71.4
$4,000-4,999	17	45.8
$5,000-7,499	38	51.3
$7,500-9,999	9	94.7
Not ascertained	22	27.3
Potential income from assets which respondent held when interviewed[b]		
None	76	54.9
$1-499	126	56.9
$500-999	160	54.9
$1,000-1,999	209	59.2
$2,000-2,999	53	54.4
$3,000 or more	22	80.8

---

[a] For 646 non-retired auto workers.

[b] These variables could explain more than 0.5 percent of the total sum of squares by a single division of the whole sample.

TABLE 8-1 (Sheet 2 of 3)

PROPORTION PLANNING TO RETIRE EARLY, BY VARIOUS PREDICTORS[a]

Predictor	Number of cases	Proportion (in percent)
Amount of life insurance[b]		
None	108	49.5
$1-1,500	46	53.0
$1,501-3,500	103	60.7
$3,501-5,500	72	55.1
$5,501-7,500	74	63.2
$7,501-9,500	68	68.2
$9,501-14,499	66	55.2
$14,500 or more	21	67.7
Doesn't know amount	71	58.1
Number of dependents (including spouse)[b]		
None	67	58.4
One	419	60.1
Two	112	49.9
Three	27	49.1
Four or more	19	57.8
Type of environment in which respondent grew up		
Farm	275	56.1
Other than farm	371	58.6
Sex		
Male	608	58.4
Female	38	45.0
Expected earnings from post-retirement work		
None	423	59.5
$1-999	149	52.9
$1,000 or more	74	56.4
Place of residence of children		
Same state as respondent	287	56.9
Midwest[c] but not respondent's state	52	41.3
Some outside midwest	125	61.3
All outside midwest	39	73.6
No children	137	57.8

---

[a] For 646 non-retired auto workers.

[b] These variables could explain more than 0.5 percent of the total sum of square by a single division of the whole sample.

[c] The "midwest" was defined as Illinois, Indiana, Iowa, Michigan, Minnesota, Ohio, and Wisconsin.

TABLE 8-1 (Sheet 3 of 3)

PROPORTION PLANNING TO RETIRE EARLY, BY VARIOUS PREDICTORS[a]

Predictor	Number of cases	Proportion (in percent)
Age at which any mortgage on home will be paid off		
Under age 65	41	60.5
65-70	51	48.4
71 or older	39	52.6
No mortgage at time of interview	482	59.0
Income change in 1966		
Substantial increase	84	65.7
Some increase	186	52.4
No change	142	55.6
Some decrease	132	59.6
Substantial decrease	90	62.5
Religious preference		
Baptist	147	52.8
Other Fundamentalist Protestant	66	65.1
Roman Catholic; Eastern churches	159	64.1
Non-Fundamentalist Protestant	273	54.7
Jewish	1	00.0
Marital status		
Married	561	57.9
Single	28	58.7
Widowed	29	57.9
Divorced; separated	28	48.1
Race		
White	544	58.1
Negro, Latin American	101	55.1
Education		
0-5 grades	59	58.1
6-8 grades	241	57.2
9-11 grades	200	58.2
12 grades	65	59.4
12 grades plus noncollege training	37	57.6
Some college, less than Bachelor's degree	33	54.0
College, Bachelor's or advanced degree	7	30.8

---

[a]For 646 non-retired auto workers.

large asset holdings—enough to produce a potential income of $3,000 or more per year, using a 6 percent rate of return[1] were quite likely to plan to retire before age 65. Similarly, those with more than $1,500 in life insurance, those with one or fewer dependents, and those with no mortgage (or with one which would be paid before age 65) were rather more likely to express such plans.[2] Persons whose income had increased substantially in recent years were also more likely to plan early retirement, although one may have thought that recent increases are correlated with future increases and therefore that such people would want to continue working. Finally, expecting to earn money after retirement was not importantly related to retirement plans.

The relationship between retirement plans and first-stage non-economic variables was not so clear-cut as that involving the economic predictors. The type of environment in which the respondent grew up (farm versus nonfarm) was little associated with retirement plans. The univariate sex-related difference in retirement plans is large, but an investigation of the effect of sex in subgroups of Figure 8-1 implies that much of this difference is associated with women's lower current earnings and available retirement income. (It should be noted, though, that the lower earnings and expected retirement income of women stem from the fact that they generally hold lower-paying jobs and have less seniority than men. There is no within-job discrimination against women in the automobile industry.) There is some evidence that workers whose children live relatively far away find more acceptable the idea of early retirement, perhaps because retirement will enable them to move nearer these children.[3] The relationship between religious preference and early retirement plans follows closely that observed from the national-sample analysis; finally, neither marital status nor race nor education seem to matter very much.

Results of the first-stage search procedure are summarized in Figure 8-1. Divisions of the sample diagrammed here are straightforward and consistent with the relationships inferred from Table 8-1; generally, people with a

---

[1] Recall that 6 percent was chosen on the assumption that it lay somewhere between the rate available solely from interest on the principal and the rate available if the principal were converted into an annuity to be consumed entirely by the time of the annuitant's death.

[2] The high rank of spouse's current income among the predictors derives not from a systematic relationship between retirement plans and amount of such income, but from the fact that the relatively few persons for whom such income was not ascertained were very much different from the rest (i.e., they were much less likely to plan early retirement). The reason for this is unclear, but it is worth noting that a similar association between not ascertained cases and delayed retirement obtains in the retirement-income-to-current-income ratio variable.

[3] But recall from the previous chapter that there was no such relation between this variable and actual early retirement.

relatively favorable retirement financial position are more likely to plan retirement before age 65. Note, in addition, that only four economic predictors were powerful enough to cause sample divisions; apparently the other predictors, both economic and demographic, were so correlated with those on which the sample divided that, after the Figure 8-1 splits occurred, they were not able to make a significant additional contribution to the explanation of retirement plans. The seven groups based on four variables used in Figure 8-1 increased our ability to predict early retirement by about 15 percent.

FIGURE 8-1

PROPORTION OF AUTO WORKERS WHO PLAN TO RETIRE BEFORE AGE 65

(For 646 auto workers who were not retired at time of interview)

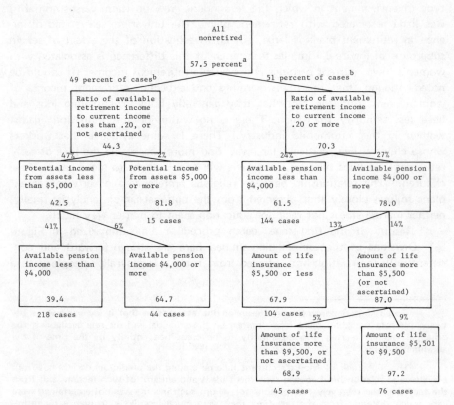

[a]This percentage relates the number of auto workers planning early retirement at the time of the interview (Summer 1967) to the total number in the subgroup defined in the box.

[b]This percentage relates the weighted number of auto workers who are in the subgroup specified in the lower box to the weighted number of all nonretired auto workers.

The dependent variable used in the second-stage analysis was the pooled differences from the end-group averages of Figure 8-1; the effects of some rather sizeable differences in retirement financial situation were, then, removed from this analysis. Table 8-2 lists the various predictors investigated in the second-stage analysis, with their relation to retirement plans indicated both before and after the economic-differences adjustment.[4] A perusal of the table will confirm that most predictors operated in a manner consistent with some generally-held hypotheses, though often the observed relationships were not particularly strong ones. The following circumstances, for example, were all associated with a significantly larger proportion planning retirement before age 65:

—being in relatively poor, or declining, health
—having a favorable retirement financial outlook, subjectively expressed (this predictor retained considerable importance even after the first-stage adjustments)
—having talked about "the question of when to retire" with persons outside the immediate family
—thinking that most younger people feel that older workers should retire to provide job openings
—planning to change place of residence after retirement
—preferring less work than one is now doing, or not preferring more work
—having attended at least one retirement information session.

Some other variables were also associated with planning early retirement, though the differences here were not so large: planning to spend time on hobbies and/or charitable work after retirement; finding the trip to work annoying, or at least not enjoyable, and having a work-limiting disability.

A closer look at the predictors whose effects were not as expected is interesting. While it had been thought that persons who planned to make major purchases before retirement might be forced thereby to postpone the retirement age, the data indicate only a slight difference in retirement plans between those who expect definitely either to buy or not to buy (though, to be sure, those who plan to buy are a little less likely to plan early retirement). The major difference here is associated with being uncertain about possible purchases, though one might have thought that this group would lie somewhere between the two groups with definite plans. On the other hand, this correlation between lack of information and plans to remain at work is consistent with that found in some first-stage economic variables, as discussed in

---

[4]Again, predictors are listed in order of their ability to explain the variance in the pooled residuals by a single division of the whole sample.

TABLE 8-2 (Sheet 1 of 4)

PROPORTION[a] PLANNING TO RETIRE EARLY - BEFORE AND AFTER ADJUSTMENT
FOR DIFFERENCES IN ECONOMIC AND DEMOGRAPHIC SITUATION

Predictor	Number of cases	Unadjusted proportion (in percent)	Proportion net of economic & demographic differences (in percent)
Comparison of current health with that of several years ago[b]			
Better now	38	46.0	45.8
Same	226	47.0	48.0
Worse now	315	68.4	67.5
Retirement financial outlook as expressed by respondent[b]			
Very favorable	147	67.9	67.1
Favorable	279	64.3	61.4
Pro-con	17	51.4	54.3
Unfavorable	112	42.7	46.0
Extent to which respondent has talked with others about retirement[b]			
Very much; much	221	69.0	65.8
Some	90	66.2	64.0
A little	188	55.6	55.3
Not at all	134	37.8	44.3
Respondent's opinion as to whether young people feel that older workers should retire early[b]			
Thinks that most feel this way	472	62.0	61.3
Thinks that some or "quite a few" feel this way	41	39.4	44.0
Mixed response	18	46.7	46.3
Thinks that few or none feel this way	64	44.5	46.5
Plans for change of residence after retirement[b]			
Plans to move	198	64.2	64.1
Plans to remain in current residence	434	53.8	53.9

---

[a] For 646 non-retired auto workers.

[b] These variables could explain more than 0.5 percent of the residual sum of squares by a single division of the whole sample.

TABLE 8-2 (Sheet 2 of 4)

PROPORTION[a] PLANNING TO RETIRE EARLY - BEFORE AND AFTER ADJUSTMENT
FOR DIFFERENCE IN ECONOMIC AND DEMOGRAPHIC SITUATION

Predictor	Number of cases	Unadjusted proportion (in percent)	Proportion net of economic & demographic differences (in percent)
Plans for major purchase(s) before retirement[b]			
Plans to make such purchase(s)	323	57.2	57.7
Does not plan to make purchase(s)	264	64.4	61.8
Is not sure whether will make purchase(s)	56	35.8	42.5
Whether wants less work than now doing[b]			
Yes	103	68.4	70.8
Pro-con	9	70.5	71.9
No	523	54.4	55.1
Whether wants more work than now doing[b]			
Yes	169	49.4	48.9
Pro-con	11	38.6	48.1
No	462	61.2	60.8
Ability to keep up with the work physically			
Has/had trouble keeping up and is/was not able to control pace of own work	36	74.8	79.8
Has/had no trouble keeping up or is/was able to control the pace of work	610	56.9	56.3
Whether plans to give help to relatives after retirement[b]			
Yes	138	63.2	64.7
No	508	56.1	55.7

---

[a] For 646 non-retired auto workers.

[b] These variables could explain more than 0.5 percent of the residual sum of squares by a single division of the whole sample.

TABLE 8-2 (Sheet 3 of 4)

PROPORTION[a] PLANNING TO RETIRE EARLY - BEFORE AND AFTER ADJUSTMENT
FOR DIFFERENCES IN ECONOMIC AND DEMOGRAPHIC SITUATION

Predictor	Number of cases	Unadjusted proportion (in percent)	Proportion net of economic & demographic differences (in percent)
Attendance at retirement information meeting(s)[b]			
Yes	84	70.5	66.8
No	562	55.7	56.3
Satisfaction with job			
Very satisfied	41	43.2	47.6
Satisfied	350	58.1	58.8
Pro-con	156	56.5	55.5
Dissatisfied	48	70.8	67.6
Very dissatisfied	47	61.8	58.0
Ease or difficulty of getting along with foreman			
Very easy	102	56.0	56.1
Easy	320	55.3	56.2
Pro-con	162	64.5	61.3
Difficult	45	58.4	61.5
Whether plans to do more charitable work after retirement			
Yes	287	61.6	60.7
No	359	54.4	55.0
Ability to control pace of own work			
Could control pace	401	59.5	59.8
Could not control pace	241	55.1	54.4
Whether knows someone who has retired under negotiated early retirement provision			
Yes	467	62.3	59.3
No	178	46.7	53.4

---

[a] For 646 non-retired auto workers.

[b] These variables could explain more than 0.5 percent of the residual sum of squares by a single division of the whole sample.

TABLE 8-2 (Sheet 4 of 4)

PROPORTION[a] PLANNING TO RETIRE EARLY - BEFORE AND AFTER ADJUSTMENT
FOR DIFFERENCES IN ECONOMIC AND DEMOGRAPHIC SITUATION

Predictor	Number of cases	Unadjusted proportion (in percent)	Proportion net of economic & demographic differences (in percent)
Whether plans to spend time on hobbies after retirement			
Yes	506	58.9	58.8
No	136	53.0	53.4
Feelings about the trip to work			
Annoying	122	62.9	60.5
Pro-con response	213	59.5	58.4
Enjoyable	302	54.4	55.8
Whether has disability which limits amount or kind of work respondent can do			
Yes	115	61.2	61.8
No	523	56.3	56.4
Age of co-workers			
About same as respondent's age	63	63.3	62.5
Some, same, some younger	255	56.8	54.9
Mostly younger	327	56.8	58.6
Whether work is repetitious			
Yes	355	55.9	56.6
No	286	59.3	58.4
Feelings about the physical work environment			
Pleasant	383	57.5	57.7
Pro-con	124	59.6	57.9
Unpleasant	119	55.5	56.7

---

[a] For 646 non-retired auto workers.

[b] These variables could explain more than 0.5 percent of the residual sum of squares by a single division of the whole sample.

Footnote 1, p. 117. Auto workers who plan to give financial aid to relatives after retirement were found to be more likely to plan early retirement, even though one might expect them to be less likely so to plan. A possible objection to this assumption—that such persons might also be those with relatively favorable financial positions, and that the observed correlation with retirement plans might then derive from this latter condition—seems obviated by the fact that the correlation becomes stronger after the adjustment for economic differences.

Satisfaction with one's auto company job was mildly but positively related to planning early retirement. Furthermore, the few persons who reported having a foreman who was difficult to get along with were a little more likely to plan early retirement. One might expect, in addition, that those workers who were not able to control the pace of their own work would find that work more difficult and perhaps less satisfying than others who could exercise control, and that this difficulty and dissatisfaction would lead to a greater desire to leave the job. Yet, in fact, such difference as can be observed is in the opposite direction. Apparently, then, the factor that matters is inability to keep up with the work *in conjunction with* inability to control the work pace, and not this latter factor *per se*.

As in the prompt response analysis, auto workers who worked primarily with younger people were no more likely to plan early retirement than others who worked mainly with their age-peers. Finally, neither reports of repetitive work nor of an unpleasant place of work were at all positively correlated with planning to retire before age 65.

The results of the second-stage search procedure are summarized in Figure 8-2. The diagrammed divisions are consistent with the whole-sample relationships indicated in Table 8-2 and discussed before. The first division separates those whose health was worse now as compared with that of several years ago[5] (who were more likely to plan early retirement) from those whose health had not declined (who were less likely to plan early retirement). For the former group the proportion planning early retirement was variously further enhanced by expecting a relatively favorable retirement financial position, by having hobbies to pursue after retirement, by seeing the work-place as not unpleasant, by not planning to make a major purchase before retirement, and/or by having talked with others about retirement. For persons whose health had not declined, a further *decrease* in the proportion planning early retirement was associated with reporting little or no talk about retirement with others, expecting a relatively unfavorable financial position, viewing one's work-place as unpleasant, not planning to move after retirement, not feeling

---

[5]This group also included a sizeable fraction—about one-quarter—for whom the health comparison was not ascertained.

that young people want older people to retire early, and/or controlling the pace of one's work. The predictors used in the second-stage analysis increased our ability to predict early retirement plans by an additional 22 percent (over that afforded by the first-stage predictors).

FIGURE 8-2

PROPORTION OF AUTO WORKERS WHO PLAN TO RETIRE BEFORE AGE 65:

ANALYSIS OF DIFFERENCES FROM END-GROUP AVERAGES OF FIGURE 8-1

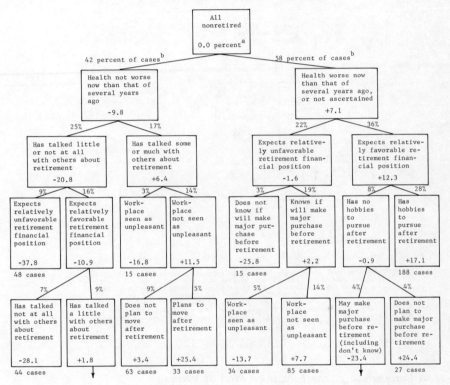

(Continued on next sheet)

PROPORTION OF AUTO WORKERS WHO PLAN TO RETIRE BEFORE AGE 65:

ANALYSIS OF DIFFERENCES FROM END-GROUP AVERAGES OF FIGURE 8-1 - Continued

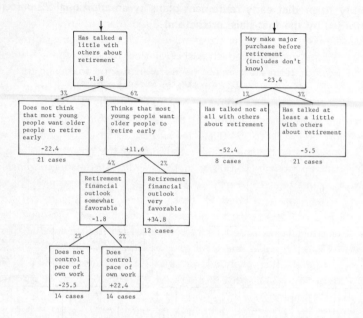

---

[a]This percentage indicates the deviation from the overall mean proportion planning early retirement (57.5 percent) associated with the various sub-groups produced by the analysis procedure. For all respondents the deviation is, of course, zero. For the first two subgroups produced by the analysis, the figures may be interpreted as follows: the mean proportion planning early retirement of those whose health was not worse at interview time than that of several years ago is 9.8 percent lower than the proportion for all respondents (and is thus 47.7 percent); the mean proportion planning early retirement for those whose health was worse is 7.1 percent higher than the overall proportion (and is thus 64.6 percent).

[b]This percentage relates the weighted number of auto workers who are in the subgroup specified in the lower box to the weighted number of all nonretired auto workers.

II. A Comparison of the Effects on Prompt Versus Delayed Retirement Response of Psychological and Attitudinal Variables

We summarize here the results of an analysis which compared the effects on initial prompt retirement and on retirement plans of various economic, demographic, and attitudinal variables. In the previous separate analyses of prompt and of delayed response to the negotiated early retirement provision, it was noted that these variables which generally have been subsumed under the heading "attitudinal" were more likely to be correlated with plans for early retirement than with actual early retirement; for example, persons who had hobbies on which to spend time after retirement were more likely to plan early retirement, but the proportion of early retirees actually pursuing hobbies was smaller than that of the delayed-reponse group *planning* to spend time on hobbies after retirement. This situation resulted then, in a negative correlation between spending or planning to spend time on hobbies and actual early retirement. It was hypothesized that the relation between the attitudinal variables and prompt retirement might be different in the following three groups: (1) the group formed by those eligible for a relatively small retirement pension income (less than $4,000), in which economic barriers would prevent most people from retiring early; (2) the group eligible for a relatively favorable pension ($4,000 to $4,999), in which other-than-economic variables would have a greater chance to operate; and (3) the group eligible for a very favorable pension income ($5,000 or more), in which the economic incentive to leave work would tend to overshadow other factors. Accordingly, the analyses herein reported were restricted to those auto workers eligible for a pension income of $4,000 to $4,999; for purposes of comparison, the dependent variable in one analysis measured retirement *behavior* (with a value of one for those who were retired at the time of interview and a value of zero for the others) and in the other analysis measured retirement *plans* (with a value of one for those nonretired auto workers who planned to retire before age 65 and of zero for the others).

The predictor variables, used in both regressions, are listed below (Table 8-3) in the order of their importance in accounting for the variance of the dependent variable (indicated by the square of their beta coefficient). (The relative rank of the same predictors in a "prompt-retirement" regression including respondents in *all* income groups is included in the final column.)

Since the focus of this analysis is on the importance of the non-economic/demographic predictors, we shall touch only on these in the following discussion. There is little evidence from the beta-squared values as to the relative ability of the predictors to explain prompt retirement as against retirement plans; in some cases this value is higher in the retirement behavior regression; in others, in the retirement plans regression. A more detailed comparison of their effects is given in Table 8-4, in which the adjusted deviations from the grand mean proportion who had retired and from the grand mean proportion who planned to retire before age 65 are listed for each predictor category (not ascertained cases are excluded from this table). On balance, again, no clear-cut differences in importance emerge; some predictors operate more in accord with conventional views in the retirement behavior regression; others, in the retirement plans regression. In both analyses having experienced a change in the nature of one's job (for example, automation or other technological change) seems associated with having retired or planning to retire early. But the same problem with interpretation of the charitable work and hobbies

TABLE 8-3

VARIOUS PREDICTORS BY THEIR IMPORTANCE IN THREE REGRESSIONS

(As measured by the square of their partial beta coefficient)

Predictor	Beta squared (prompt retirement regression)	Beta squared (retirement plans regression)	Beta squared (prompt retirement - all income groups)
Comparison of current health with that of several years ago	0.078	0.048	0.034
Extent to which income changed in last full year before retirement	0.070	0.032	0.017
Ratio of available pension and social security income to respondent's income earned from auto company job	0.047	0.055	0.230
Ability to keep up with the job, for those who did not control the pace of their work	0.047	0.002	0.037
Plans for, or participation in, post-retirement charitable work	0.035	0.014	0.018
Potential income from assets which respondent held at time of interview	0.023	0.017	0.009
Plans for, or participation in, post-retirement hobby activities	0.019	0.028	0.018
Number of dependents (including spouse)	0.014	0.075	0.004
Time consumed in traveling to work	0.014	0.035	0.003
Ease or difficulty in getting along with foreman	0.012	0.046	0.003
Ability to control the pace of own work	0.011	a	0.007
Feelings about the trip to work	0.010	0.078	0.008
Sex	0.010	a	a
Satisfaction with job	0.009	0.010	0.005
Age at which any mortgage on respondent's house will be paid off	0.006	0.062	0.003
Feelings about the place of work	0.006	0.064	0.001
Repetitiveness of the work	0.005	0.009	0.002
Influence of any change in the nature of respondent's job on his retirement decision	0.005	b	0.001
Age of co-workers	0.003	0.012	0.002

---

[a] Less than 0.0005.

[b] Atypically large because of small number of extreme not ascertained cases.

TABLE 8-4 (Sheet 1 of 2)

ADJUSTED DEVIATIONS FROM THE PROPORTION HAVING RETIRED
AND THE PROPORTION PLANNING EARLY RETIREMENT,
FOR AUTO WORKERS INTERVIEWED IN 1967, BY VARIOUS PREDICTORS

Predictor	Whether retired promptly		Whether plans to retire	
	Number of cases	Adjusted deviation	Number of cases	Adjusted deviation
Whether a change in the nature of the job has changed respondent's retirement decision				
Yes	60	+.077	28	+.025
No	358	-.012	201	+.013
Whether plans to do/is doing charitable work after retirement				
Yes	138	-.128	100	+.057
No	281	+.066	130	-.045
Whether plans to spend time on hobbies after retirement				
Yes	311	-.037	186	+.029
No	107	+.121	43	-.154
Whether work is repetitive				
Yes	228	-.030	129	-.034
No	190	+.040	100	+.046
Whether can control the pace of own work				
Yes	259	+.041	148	*
No	158	-.058	80	*
Satisfaction with the job				
Very satisfied	27	+.148	12	+.117
Satisfied	216	-.012	129	-.017
Pro-con response	103	+.016	49	+.019
Dissatisfied	30	-.042	19	+.053
Very dissatisfied	39	-.053	20	-.068

---

*Less than .0005.

TABLE 8-4 (Sheet 2 of 2)

ADJUSTED DEVIATIONS FROM THE PROPORTION HAVING RETIRED
AND THE PROPORTION PLANNING EARLY RETIREMENT,
FOR AUTO WORKERS INTERVIEWED IN 1967, BY VARIOUS PREDICTORS

Predictor	Whether retired promptly		Whether plans to retire	
	Number of cases	Adjusted deviation	Number of cases	Adjusted deviation
Feelings about the physical work environment				
Pleasant	234	-.016	130	-.060
Pro-con response	94	-.012	52	-.008
Unpleasant	75	+.081	39	+.231
Age of respondent's co-workers				
Same as respondent	47	-.008	22	-.116
Some same, some younger	181	+.028	87	+.016
Mostly younger	190	-.028	120	+.002
Ease or difficulty of getting along with foreman				
Very easy, easy	277	+.006	151	+.103
Pro-con response	97	*	56	-.029
Very hard, hard	39	+.014	18	-.153
Ability to keep up with the job				
Has trouble keeping up <u>and</u> does not control pace of own work	57	+.269	10	-.075
All other cases	101	-.153	70	+.011
Amount of time consumed in traveling to work				
Less than 15 minutes	76	+.027	41	+.009
15 to 30 minutes	235	+.010	128	+.058
More than 30 minutes	106	-.022	59	-.127
Feelings about the trip to work				
Annoying	85	+.091	43	-.032
Pro-con response	157	-.011	82	-.082
Enjoyable	171	-.029	100	+.063
Comparison of current health with that of several years ago				
Better now	56	+.336	12	+.282
Same	152	+.025	84	-.099
Worse now	171	-.109	113	+.050

---
*Less than .0005.

variables mentioned before occurs again within the subgroups utilized here; retired persons actually spend less time on charitable work and on hobbies than non-retired persons *plan* to spend; thus, while planning to spend more time on charitable work and/or hobbies is associated with planning to retire early, the relationship is reversed for the whether-retired regression. It had been expected that persons whose work was repetitive and those who did not control the pace of their work would be more likely to have retired and to plan early retirement, but such a relationship is not observable in either of the regressions. Similarly, those who reported dissatisfaction with their jobs were not, as a whole, more likely to opt for early retirement. On the other hand, workers who found their work-place unpleasant were somewhat more likely to want to leave work.

While, as has been suggested before, one might expect that persons who found their foreman difficult to get along with would be more likely to undertake or plan early retirement, this is evident only in the whether-retired regression—and here the relation is very weak. And, though retirement was encouraged by difficulty in keeping up with the job, the same relationship does not obtain for the nonretired group (the number of cases here is, however, small). There is evidence of a slight tendency for those having relatively long trips to work to be more likely to undertake or plan early retirement, but finding the trip annoying apparently encouraged only early retirement behavior, not plans.

Finally, the strong positive correlation between relatively good health and having retired early was not unexpected. Previous multivariate analyses have, as stated before, indicated that those auto workers who had retired early were substantially more likely to view their health as having improved during the past few years than were those still at work. The previously-noted relationship between declining health and early retirement *plans,* however, is repeated here.

The importance of economic factors for retirement decisions, affirmed repeatedly in earlier multivariate analyses, seems reinforced by the fact that several hypotheses relating to noneconomic predictors received little or no support here, even though this inquiry was limited to those auto workers whose level of available retirement income was expected to maximize the consideration given to such factors.

Chapter 9

AUTOMOBILE WORKER
SATISFACTION WITH RETIREMENT

This chapter presents the results of a two-stage multivariate analysis of satisfaction with retirement, as expressed by the 477 automobile workers who were retired when interviewed in 1967. The dependent variable was dichotomous, with a value of one for those who reported being "very satisfied" (25 percent of all retirees) or "satisfied" (50 percent) with their life since retirement and a value of zero for the less satisfied (25 percent). Analogous to the procedure in other analyses, the effect on satisfaction of economic and demographic variables was examined in the first stage; more subjective and/or retrospective variables were utilized in the second.

The relation between satisfaction with retirement and all predictors used in the first-stage analysis is detailed in Table 9-1. (Predictors are listed in order of their ability to explain the variance in retirement satisfaction by a single division of the whole sample.) Having to meet mortgage payments, especially after age 65; having more than one dependent; having a low pension and social security income; and having little or no life insurance were all associated with a relatively lower level of satisfaction. But, the objective current-income-to-preretirement-income ratio (calculated by us from income figures obtained from the respondents) was erratically related to satisfaction with retirement (only those whose ratio was not ascertained were significantly different from the others). No systematic relation between satisfaction and income earned after retirement was apparent. The relatively few auto workers who had received some educational training beyond the high school level were very satisfied with retirement, though some observers have suggested that the better-educated may find retirement less fulfilling. Place of residence of the respondent's children was not highly correlated with retirement satisfaction; those who lived far away from their children were not less satisfied.

The effects of two other variables, while not unexpected, are worth noting. Fundamentalist Protestant respondents were observed to be a little less satisfied with retirement; this finding is consistent with our earlier one that such people are less likely to plan early retirement and are, apparently, more committed to the "work ethic" than non-Fundamentalists. And, the high level

TABLE 9-1 (Sheet 1 of 3)

SATISFACTION WITH RETIREMENT, BY VARIOUS PREDICTORS[a]

Predictor	Number of cases	Proportion satisfied, (in percent)
Age mortgage (if any) paid off[b]		
No mortgage at time of interview (including renters)	388	77.7
Under age 65	22	75.4
65-70	32	56.3
70 or older	19	64.5
Ratio of current income to previous (i.e., preretirement) income[b]		
Less than .30	14	87.5
.30-.39	27	64.1
.40-.49	44	75.0
.50-.59	66	75.0
.60-.69	74	81.2
.70-.79	58	79.4
.80 or larger	124	80.3
Not ascertained	70	55.9
Potential income from assets[b]		
None	29	62.1
$1-499	75	61.7
$500-999	162	79.0
$1,000-1,999	160	75.9
$2,000-2,999	32	83.6
$3,000 or more	20	95.6
Marital status[b]		
Married	412	77.6
Single	24	49.3
Widowed	18	66.7
Separated, divorced	23	59.7
Number of dependents[b]		
None	60	57.6
One	341	78.7
Two	53	74.0
Three or more	23	66.7

---

[a]For 477 auto workers who were retired when interviewed.

[b]These variables could explain at least 0.5 percent of the total sum of squares if used to make a single division of the whole sample.

TABLE 9-1 (Sheet 2 of 3)

SATISFACTION WITH RETIREMENT, BY VARIOUS PREDICTORS[a]

Predictor	Number of cases	Proportion satisfied (in percent)
Pension and social security income of respondent and spouse[b]		
Less than $3,000	23	57.1
$3,000-3,999	53	66.4
$4,000-4,999	207	71.6
$5,000-7,499	172	82.6
$7,500 or more	22	78.6
Amount of life insurance[b]		
None	23	59.3
$1-1,500	41	61.0
$1,501-3,500	51	79.3
$3,501-5,500	16	95.0
$5,501-7,500	130	73.4
$7,501-9,500	118	77.9
$9,501-14,499	61	73.3
$14,500 or more	16	75.7
Sex[b]		
Male	430	76.0
Female	47	63.8
Housing status[b]		
Owns house	420	75.2
Owns trailer	10	83.3
Rents	31	72.4
Neither owns nor rents	15	57.9
Religious preference[b]		
Fundamentalist Protestant	117	71.4
Roman Catholic	148	75.7
Other Protestant	211	75.7
Jewish	1	100.0
Earned income[b]		
None	297	76.7
$1-999	18	72.5
$1,000-1,999	18	81.8
$2,000-2,999	16	68.2
$3,000-3,999	61	67.7
$5,000-7,499	44	75.2
$7,500-9,999	17	57.1
$10,000 or more	6	87.5

---

[a]For 477 auto workers who were retired when interviewed.

[b]These variables could explain more than 0.5 percent of the total sum of squares by a single division of the whole sample.

TABLE 9-1 (Sheet 3 of 3)

SATISFACTION WITH RETIREMENT, BY VARIOUS PREDICTORS[a]

Predictor	Number of cases	Proportion satisfied (in percent)
Education[b]		
0-5 grades	44	66.7
6-8 grades	200	75.5
9-11 grades; 0-11 grades plus noncollege training	150	72.8
12 grades	45	74.8
12 grades plus noncollege training	20	82.1
Some college	18	90.0
Place of residence of children[b]		
No children	116	69.2
Same state as respondent	238	78.1
Midwest[c] but not respondent's state	22	80.8
Some outside midwest	73	67.0
All outside midwest	25	88.9
Race		
White	436	74.0
Nonwhite (including Latin American)	37	81.0

---

[a] For 477 auto workers who were retired when interviewed.

[b] These variables could explain more than 0.5 percent of the total sum of squares by a single division of the whole sample.

[c] The "midwest" was defined to include these states: Illinois, Indiana, Iowa, Michigan, Minnesota, Ohio, and Wisconsin.

FIGURE 9-1

PROPORTION SATISFIED WITH RETIREMENT

(For 477 auto workers retired at time of interview)

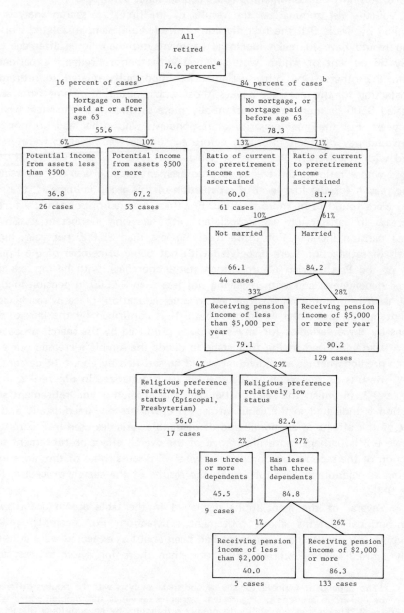

---

[a]This percentage relates the number of auto workers who expressed satisfaction with retirement to the total number in the subgroup defined in the box.

[b]This percentage relates the weighted number of auto workers who are in the subgroup specified in the lower box to the weighted number of all retired auto workers.

of reported satisfaction for nonwhites may be due merely to the often-observed tendency of such persons to express general satisfaction with things and to refrain from complaining (the "acquiescence syndrome").

Figure 9-1 summarizes the results of the first-stage search analysis. As implied by Table 9-1, the first division of the (whole) sample isolated workers who would have to make mortgage payments on their home after age 62—only 56 percent of whom were satisfied with their retirement experience—from the others. One other variable was importantly related to retirement satisfaction for the mortgage payees; those whose potential income from assets totaled $500 or more were substantially more satisfied than their less well-to-do peers. For the great majority of respondents who either had no mortgage or would pay off their mortgage before age 63, several variables were associated with relatively high levels of satisfaction. After a split which set aside those whose ratio of retirement to preretirement income was not ascertained (the reason for the low level of satisfaction of this group is unclear), the married were found to be more satisfied. For these married respondents, a further increase in satisfaction was associated with receiving a substantial ($5,000 plus) pension income. For those receiving less than $5,000 per year, higher levels of satisfaction were associated with not being a member of the Episcopal or the Presbyterian Church (high status churches), with having less than three dependents, and with receiving not less than $2,000 in pension income. The relative unimportance of earned income, education, place of residence of children, and race—inferred from Table 9-1—is confirmed by the lack of divisions by these variables for any subgroups produced by the search procedure.

Variables used in the first stage to divide the sample increased our ability to predict whether an individual would be satisfied by about 14 percent.

Results of the second-stage analysis are summarized in Figure 9-2 and in Table 9-2, in which the relation between the predictors and retirement satisfaction is indicated in the usual forms: (1) univariate or "unadjusted" and (2) net of the effects of economic and demographic variables used in Figure 9-1.[1] Table 9-2 is perhaps more illustrative of the overall effect on retirement satisfaction of the second-stage predictors; we shall discuss some of the more interesting associations before turning to the results of the search procedure (Figure 9-2).

Several of the associations displayed in the table are in accord with conventional notions about retirement satisfaction. For example, retirees whose experiences since retirement had been about as expected were considerably more likely to express satisfaction than those for whom at least some

---

[1] The dependent variable for the second-stage analysis was the pooled differences from the end-group averages of Figure 9-1. Variables on which the sample divided (those in Figure 9-2) increased our ability to predict satisfaction by an additional 35 percent, for a total explanation of 44 percent of the original variance.

TABLE 9-2 (Sheet 1 of 4)

SATISFACTION WITH RETIREMENT, BEFORE AND AFTER ADJUSTMENT
FOR SOME ECONOMIC AND DEMOGRAPHIC DIFFERENCES,
BY VARIOUS PREDICTORS[a]

Predictor	Number of cases	Unadjusted proportion satisfied (in percent)	Proportion satisfied net of economic & demographic differences (in percent)
Whether life since retirement generally as expected[b]			
Yes	384	82.4	80.9
Some things as expected, some things not	25	54.8	65.5
No	41	45.7	50.9
Stated reason for retirement[b]			
Health	121	67.4	69.7
Finances	77	87.3	83.7
Job	42	72.2	69.5
Family	16	75.0	76.3
Recreation	36	91.0	94.5
Qualification for negotiated pension plan	48	81.1	79.6
Being tired of working	74	82.3	77.4
Other	15	76.5	81.9
Evaluation of health[b]			
Better than that of several years ago	102	87.6	84.2
Same	163	81.7	80.7
Worse	160	60.4	63.5
Type of pension received[b]			
Disability	32	30.0	40.1
Non-disability	441	77.6	76.5
Attendance at retirement information meetings[b]			
Attended more than one meeting	96	89.7	85.0
Attended one meeting	41	87.7	88.6
Attended no meetings	338	68.9	70.0

[a]For 477 auto workers who were retired when interviewed.

[b]These variables could explain at least 0.5 percent of the residual sum of squares by a single division of the whole sample.

TABLE 9-2 (Sheet 2 of 4)

SATISFACTION WITH RETIREMENT, BEFORE AND AFTER ADJUSTMENT
FOR SOME ECONOMIC AND DEMOGRAPHIC DIFFERENCES,
BY VARIOUS PREDICTORS[a]

Predictor	Number of cases	Unadjusted proportion satisfied (in percent)	Proportion satisfied net of economic & demographic differences (in percent)
Comparison of current living standard with that before retirement[b]			
Better now	28	100.0	95.7
Same	360	77.4	76.3
Worse now	72	56.4	63.5
Time of retirement[b]			
Before 1966	119	81.0	80.0
1/66 through 6/66	136	80.4	76.2
7/66 through 12/66	114	73.8	76.6
1967	105	61.9	65.2
Whether retirement planned or unexpected[b]			
Planned	324	83.2	80.9
Unexpected	114	64.5	68.0
Change in savings since retirement[b]			
Decreased, unexpectedly	53	61.3	63.5
Decreased, but as planned	62	78.1	79.7
Did not decrease	359	76.7	76.0
Spouse's feelings about respondent's retirement[b]			
Very favorable	50	91.6	86.4
Favorable	226	78.2	75.9
Pro-con	67	89.1	87.1
Unfavorable	20	83.7	76.7
Not married	61	60.7	71.2
Feelings about foreman of previous job[b]			
Very easy to get along with	68	72.0	79.1
Easy to get along with	229	81.6	78.1
Pro-con	97	73.1	73.0
Hard to get along with	35	81.4	79.7
Very hard to get along with	11	61.6	62.4

[a]For 477 auto workers who were retired when interviewed.

[b]These variables could explain at least 0.5 percent of the residual sum of squares by a single division of the whole sample.

TABLE 9-2 (Sheet 3 of 4)

SATISFACTION WITH RETIREMENT, BEFORE AND AFTER ADJUSTMENT
FOR SOME ECONOMIC AND DEMOGRAPHIC DIFFERENCES,
BY VARIOUS PREDICTORS[a]

Predictor	Number of cases	Unadjusted proportion satisfied (in percent)	Proportion satisfied net of economic & demographic differences (in percent)
Work-weeks lost because of illness during two years before retirement[b]			
None	298	79.5	77.9
1-2 weeks	14	60.0	53.3
3-4 weeks	15	83.2	86.9
5-8 weeks	33	80.0	73.7
9-12 weeks	27	70.7	79.0
More than 12 weeks	40	75.8	79.9
Whether doing volunteer work for church or charity[b]			
Yes	176	83.1	80.9
No	801	70.1	71.2
Whether pursuing hobbies[b]			
Yes	293	79.7	78.6
No	184	67.3	68.8
Feelings about the (previous) trip to work			
Annoying	103	81.3	80.4
Pro-con	170	78.4	77.3
Enjoyable	167	76.3	75.4
Knowledge of pattern of negotiated pension payments			
Knows payments will decline at age 65	425	75.8	75.2
Thinks payments will continue at same level	39	63.3	67.7
Subjective comparison of current income with preretirement income			
Ratio of current to previous less than .30	44	65.0	71.0
Ratio .30 - .39; "smaller", how much not ascertained	33	65.3	67.9
Ratio .40 - .59	191	74.1	73.3
Ratio .60 - .79	112	80.7	79.8
Ratio .80 or more	86	78.2	75.9

---

[a] For 477 auto workers who were retired when interviewed.

[b] These variables could explain at least 0.5 percent of the residual sum of squares by a single division of the whole sample.

TABLE 9-2 (Sheet 4 of 4)

SATISFACTION WITH RETIREMENT, BEFORE AND AFTER ADJUSTMENT
FOR SOME ECONOMIC AND DEMOGRAPHIC DIFFERENCES,
BY VARIOUS PREDICTORS[a]

Predictor	Number of cases	Unadjusted proportion satisfied (in percent)	Proportion satisfied net of economic & demographic differences (in percent)
Whether foreman urged retirement			
Yes	15	90.5	91.0
No	429	77.4	76.6
Whether union urged retirement			
Yes	42	86.3	81.4
No	401	77.4	76.9
Whether co-workers urged retirement			
Yes	94	85.1	83.0
No	349	76.0	75.6
Whether received social security when interviewed			
Yes	232	79.7	76.5
No	245	69.9	72.8
Optional survivors' benefit			
Chosen	151	74.6	72.6
Not chosen	230	79.8	77.3
Not married	63	58.0	68.5
Change in place of residence			
Changed	45	78.9	84.4
Did not change	431	74.1	73.5
Whether giving financial aid to relatives			
Yes	103	80.6	80.0
No	373	76.3	73.5
Whether controlled pace of preretirement work			
Yes	263	80.6	75.2
No	181	80.7	79.2

---

[a]For 477 auto workers who were retired when interviewed.

[b]These variables could explain at least 0.5 percent of the residual sum of squares by a single division of the whole sample.

things had not turned out as planned. In general, persons who mentioned as reasons for retiring health or the job (a substantial part of the latter reasons centered around having trouble keeping up with the work, which is itself health-related) were more likely to be dissatisfied though, as will be apparent from Figure 9-2, this did not obtain for all subgroups of retired auto workers. Similarly, those who reported that their health had declined during recent years and those who were receiving a disability pension (and whose health was presumably very bad indeed) were substantially dissatisfied with retirement. Retirees who had attended none of the retirement information sessions were rather less satisfied than those who had attended at least one session. But there was little difference between those who attended one meeting and those who attended more than one. Further, for a few subgroups of the sample, attendance at such meetings was not at all systematically related to retirement satisfaction (persons who had not attended were slightly *more* likely to be satisfied). In view of the not insignificant amount of time and resources which both the union and the industry have spent to facilitate understanding of the early retirement provision and (in some cases) planning for retirement, these findings seem disturbing.

As expected, retirees who viewed their current living standard as equal to or better than their preretirement standard were well satisfied (and this variable retained its importance even after the first-stage adjustment for differences in economic situation), as were those who reported that their retirement had been planned (rather than unexpected) and those who had not had an unexpected decrease in their savings since retirement. But the effect of time of retirement was somewhat surprising; while one might have thought that the great enthusiasm for retirement expressed by so many respondents derived from the newness of their situation, the data indicate that the most recent retirees are the *least* satisfied. (Planned reinterviews with a subsample of the auto workers contacted in 1967 should aid in clarifying this point.) The feelings of the respondent's spouse about his retirement, the respondent's feelings about his foreman, and the number of work weeks lost because of illness before retirement were all relatively unimportant for retirement satisfaction. Persons who were spending time on hobbies and/or charitable work were, though, somewhat more satisfied than their less active counterparts.

The pattern of negotiated pension payments are of interest in an analysis of retirement satisfaction. The program is so structured that beneficiaries receive a constant monthly negotiated pension (comprising a "supplementary early retirement benefit" and a basic pension) from the time of (early) retirement until age 65, at which time the early retirement supplement ends and the basic pension continues. Union officials who devised the plan assumed that retirees would elect to take unreduced social security benefits at age 65; the resulting life-time income stream would then be reasonably constant from point of retirement to death (though some dip would occur at age 65). Two obvious questions then arise: (1) are persons who do not realize that the negotiated pension will decrease substantially at age 65 more satisfied than the others, and (2) are persons who have elected to take reduced social security benefits (between age 62 and 65)—and who will thus experience a substantial income decrease at 65—more satisfied than those who are waiting for un-reduced benefits? Two variables which investigated these points were included in the analysis. It appears that respondents who realize that negotiated benefits will decline—these being the overwhelming majority—are rather more satisfied than their less informed colleagues. But it is also true that persons who have elected to receive reduced social security benefits (almost half the sample) are a little more satisfied (even after the adjustment for economic differences) than the others; it would be interesting, then, to see whether this difference continues after age 65.[2] (Hopefully, we shall contact some of these people at or after the age 65 break during reinterviewing late in 1969.)

Some final comments on the data shown in Table 9-2: persons who say they were urged to retire—by union, management, or co-workers—were somewhat more satisfied than those who were not so urged, though one might have thought that such persons, feeling themselves pushed out of the job, might be less satisfied. Retirees who had not chosen to provide survivors' benefits for their spouse were a little more likely to be satisfied, though such benefits presumably would serve to reduce anxiety about the future. But those who had changed their place of residence (and so presumably were nearer an equilibrium position) and those who had escaped from a job over which they had little control were, as anticipated, rather more likely to be satisfied.

Results of the second-stage search procedure are summarized in Figure 9-2. We recall from Table 9-2 that the most important factor here was whether the retiree's experiences since retirement had been generally as expected. Those whose experiences had not been as expected were substantially below the overall mean proportion in satisfaction, but even here some factors were associated with being relatively well satisfied. The few respondents who had attended at least one retirement information session were above the overall average in satisfaction; for those who did not attend such meetings, mentioning other than health-related reasons for retirement was associated with more satisfaction; and those who subjectively estimated their current income as 60 percent or more of their preretirement income were not dissimilar from the overall average in proportion satisfied.

---

[2]While overall the proportion of auto workers who expected the negotiated benefits to continue unabated was quite small, it is perhaps worth noting here that this proportion was twice as high for those receiving reduced social security benefits as for those drawing only the negotiated pension (12 percent versus 6 percent).

FIGURE 9-2

PROPORTION SATISFIED WITH RETIREMENT: ANALYSIS OF DIFFERENCES

FROM END-GROUP AVERAGES OF FIGURE 9-1

(For 477 auto workers retired at time of interview)

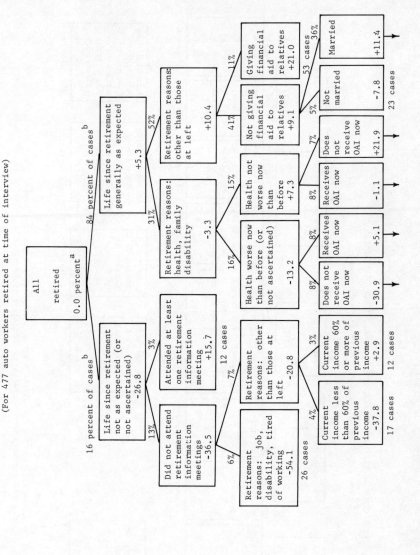

PROPORTION SATISFIED WITH RETIREMENT: ANALYSIS OF DIFFERENCES
FROM END-GROUP AVERAGES OF FIGURE 9-1 - Continued

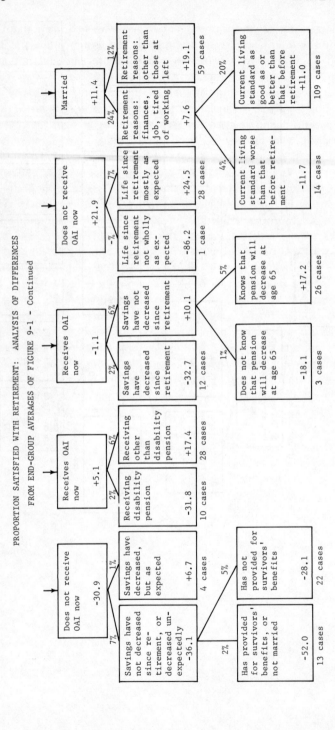

[a] This percentage indicates the deviation from the overall mean proportion satisfied with retirement (74.6 percent) associated with the various subgroups produced by the analysis. For all respondents the deviation is, of course, zero.

[b] This percentage relates the weighted number of auto workers who are in the subgroup specified in the lower box to the weighted number of all retired auto workers.

For the large majority whose retirement experiences had been about as expected, numerous other factors were isolated by the search process as importantly related to retirement satisfaction. Again, those who did not give health-related (or, for a few, family-related) reasons for retirement were more likely to be satisfied; the proportion satisfied of this group was variously enhanced by being able to afford financial aid to relatives, by being married, and by reporting a current living standard as good as or better than that before retirement. The group who did give health- or family-related reasons were happier if their health had not deteriorated during the last few years. Depending on whether current health was worse now, receiving social security payments had an opposite effect on retirement satisfaction: for those with declining health, persons currently receiving social security were more likely to be satisfied, while for those whose health had not declined, persons waiting for unreduced benefits were more satisfied. Perhaps this striking difference results from the former's need for additional resources with which to purchase medical services. Additional sample divisions (detailed on the second page of the figure), while they sometimes involve relatively few cases, are generally consistent with the overall relationships inferred from Table 9-2 and discussed above.

It is worth noting, finally, that the apparent importance of some predictors for retirement satisfaction nevertheless did not result in any divisions of the sample. It appears then that such things as time of retirement, whether retirement was planned or unexpected, time spent on hobbies or charitable work, etc., were substantially correlated with those predictors on which the sample did divide and that this intercorrelation accounted for a large part of the observed differences.

Chapter 10

THE AUTOMOBILE WORKER
AND RETIREMENT:
SUMMARY AND CONCLUSIONS

We have seen that approximately two-thirds of the auto workers contacted in 1967 responded positively to the availability of the negotiated early retirement provision. Of those who responded, about half retired promptly (that is, within 18 months of the program's inception) and half expressed plans to retire sometime before the usual retirement age. The pattern of situational and attitudinal factors associated with actual retirement was somewhat different from that associated with retirement plans.

Generally, economic factors—such as available retirement income, the ratio of this income to earned income, number of dependents, potential income from assets—were of more importance for actual than for planned early retirement; about 42 percent of the variance in actual retirement was attributable to the economic factors, as opposed to about 15 percent of the variance in expected retirement plans. Conversely, the relation between retirement plans and the psychological variables (those which measured attitudes and expectations) was at once stronger and more in accord with conventional ideas than that between actual retirement and the same variables. Several possible reasons for this difference were discussed: that the nature of the interviewing procedure may have led to response differences between the retired and the nonretired, that the playing down of difficulties with the work situation may have been consonant with a heightened self-image, that the two-stage analysis scheme may have masked the importance of some second-stage predictors. It is worth noting here, in addition, that the history of Survey Research Center studies of consumer behavior strongly implies that psychological variables generally correlate better with planned behavior than with past behavior. Attitudes mainly influence behavior that is discretionary. Plans to retire early, or to buy cars, reflect discretionary decisions, while an actual early retirement, or the actual purchase of a car, may be necessitated by unforeseen developments (e.g., the deterioration of health, or the breakdown of one's car).[1] This observation is consistent with our auto worker findings.

---

[1] For further development of these ideas, see George Katona, *The Powerful Consumer* (New York, 1960).

Whatever the relative significance of economic and psychological factors in the retirement decision, the findings from the auto worker survey which seem to us most important are these: that a substantial majority of the workers either have responded or plan to respond positively to the availability of an early retirement program, and that a preponderance of those who have already retired seem eminently satisfied with their retirement. Despite the naysaying and the doubting speculation of many observers,[2] then, these two findings would seem to indicate that, at least for certain mass-production-industry workers, early retirement is both strongly desired and (initially, at least) largely enjoyable.

The following responses to "Generally speaking, how do you feel about your life since retirement?" well illustrate the dominant auto worker sentiment about retirement:

"I am very happy and glad about it. I have time for myself and my wife for just enjoying living."

"I feel very happy because I don't worry about time. I used to have to run, run, run. I have been relieved of the pressures of doing things on the minute."

"I keep busy and I enjoy my life. It is heaven not to have to go to the plant every day."

"It's good—oh boy, it is! I tell all my friends."

"Great—I couldn't say more about it. I don't have to wake at five a.m."

"It's been so full. I'm doing all of the things I've wanted to do."

". . . I feel I can do things now that I didn't have time for. Happier. Not obligated to anyone—can go and come as I please."

"Fine. Life is wonderful. I'm enjoying it, every minute."

"I enjoy myself. My life is much fuller than it was when I was working. Leading a different life now; I can go and come as I please. Call my life my own."

---

[2]Merton C. Bernstein in particular has criticized the automobile industry early retirement program. Several of his major points—that early retirement will lead to substantial economic deprivation, that workers will be driven from their jobs by coercion from fellow workers, and that an inevitable loss of purpose and status will follow retirement—received little if any support from our study. See Bernstein, "The Arguments Against Early Retirement," *Industrial Relations* (May 1965), pp. 29-38.

"... I am getting to do things that I was looking forward to doing and couldn't do when I worked. I'm really enjoying being free to do what I want."

"Happy! Believe me I am! I would advise anyone to retire."

From the responses to the same question by those who were dissatisfied with their retirement experience, it appears that illness—on the part of either the auto worker or other family members—was the factor making for discontent in the great majority of cases. A sample of such responses follow:

"Illness—to date retired life has been hospitals and slow convalescence—don't drive much."

"To be honest, I feel lost. With my heart bothering me and the arthritis, I don't want to work. But it's a hard thing; there's nothing left."

"Disgusted. I can't do anything because of my lungs. Have to watch every step I make."

"What should I say? I'm sick, can hardly get up and down the steps. I can't even dress myself."

"I never feel good since I had this stroke. I've developed a pretty bad case of nerves and depression and things like that."

"My health keeps me from doing things. I am not enjoying it; it's not the retirement, it's the health."

"To tell you the truth it's been kind of rotten—have to spend so much time in bed."

"Miserable—feel terrible and lost and hopeless."

On the other hand, a few people were dissatisfied for particular personal reasons, as witnessed this unfortunate gentleman:

"All upset! Had my place all set up to enjoy—apple trees, garden, house in good shape. Now, this spring, the highway department comes along and needs my property. I'm getting ready to move the house to a new location."

And, to be sure, there were those who had trouble adjusting for conventional reasons:

"To tell you the truth I feel lost. I have to get used to it."

"It's just lonesome like. I listen to radio and TV and visit my children now and then."

But it is certainly true that the major source of automobile worker dissatisfaction with retirement was health problems, and these are difficulties which cannot be charged against retirement *per se.* Indeed, this finding indicates that, for the worker who remains healthy after retirement, his life experiences are quite likely to be generally enjoyable. And this is, we hold, important to know.

Appendix A

MULTIVARIATE TECHNIQUES

I. Introduction

Two techniques of multivariate analysis have been used in this volume. One, referred to generally herein as the "search technique" provides an unusually flexible analysis procedure. The other, a type of regression analysis, affords a more conventional way of investigating the interrelationships often existing between the various factors associated with a particular behavioral state. The former procedure is flexible in the following ways:

(1) It does not assume that the predictor variables are properly scaled or that their effects are linear or additive.

(2) It allows for more than one stage in the causal process, so that a clearly prior set of variables may be introduced first, and whatever variation they do not explain may then be analyzed against a second set of variables.

The investigative technique itself is a searching process that looks for structure, that is, for the definition of a set of population subgroups such that each differs from the rest as much as possible in terms of the dependent variable, is homogenous within itself, and is large enough to matter.[1]

Since the technique is sequential, both within one analysis and even more in the analysis of residuals at the second stage, it can provide firmer answers to such questions as "Once we take account of current and expected retirement income, do attitudes toward work and leisure matter?"

The technique combines formal statistics with the common sense of an experienced researcher, since it simulates the procedures of a researcher investigating a body of data but, being tireless, does it systematically and with computation at each stage of the proper measurements on which the choices of next steps are based. It is the only multivariate procedure that does not impose the assumption of additivity, and any observer of the world knows that it is full of interaction effects. The effect of education on earnings

---

[1]For a complete explanation, see John Sonquist and James Morgan, *The Detection of Interaction Effects* (Ann Arbor: Survey Research Center, The University of Michigan, 1964).

depends on one's age, the effect of age on hospital utilization depends on sex, and so forth. More important here, non-economic motivation may affect only those not dominated by economic constraints and motivations. And, sometimes any one of several factors may have a similar impact: expecting to have mortgage payments or dependents after age 65, expecting a low potential income from assets, or anticipating low (or no) postretirement earnings can lower the likelihood of a person planning early retirement.

II. The Computer Program Used

The program operates as follows. For each potential explanatory classification it examines the explanatory power (reduction in error variance) achievable by using that classification. It examines the means of the dependent variable against each explanatory classification in turn. In each case it finds the best way to use that explanatory classification to divide the sample into two parts—best in terms of the variance explained ("between sum-of-squares").

If the predicting classification has a natural order, the order is preserved, and the number of possible divisions is one less than the number of classes. The machine examines the fruitfulness of isolating the first group from the rest, the first two groups from the rest, the first three, and so on. If the classification has no natural ordering, all *feasible* splits are examined. (It can be shown that if the classes are arranged in order according to the size of the mean of the dependent variable, then there is never any other more powerful division than one of those preserving that order.)

Keeping in store the best division on that variable, the process proceeds to the next predictor, repeats the process, compares the explanatory power of the better of the two, and preserves that. Then it proceeds to the third explanatory characteristic and repeats the process. In any case, the means of the dependent variable for each class of each predictor are preserved for the printed output at the end.

Having swept through all the predictors and found the best way to use the best one to divide the sample, the computer then divides the sample that way, finds the part with the largest remaining unexplained variability, and repeats the process, examining that part against all the explanatory variables again.

At each stage after that, the group with the largest remaining variance is examined and, if possible, divided again. The process stops when no way can be found to divide any of the groups so as to reduce the unexplained variance by enough to matter (and to provide some assurance that the result is not fortuitous). In the present volume with the sample sizes involved, this has usually been set at 0.5 percent of the original total sum of squares (variance).

Where the sample used is smaller and/or the number and flexibility of the predictors greater, even higher cut-off points are and should be used. For safety, the program also refuses to look at a group that contains less than 1.5 percent of the total original sum of squares, or fewer than 25 cases; and it refuses to generate more than 50 final groups.

Since the printed output contains, for each subgroup examined, the means of the dependent variable for each class of each predictor, and the explained sum of squares from the best use of that predictor, it is possible to see whether any of the divisions made of the sample had close competition from some other predictor. In that case, the two competing predictors are likely to be highly correlated, and a different sample might well allow the other one to be used.

Since at least k - 1 divisions are tried for each variable (k is the number of classes of that variable) at each step, it is easy to see that the total branching finally developed is selected from a very large number of possible ones, and cannot be thought of as testing any hypotheses. There are no "degrees of freedom" left in a statistical sense, and no way to estimate the stability of the results over different samples.[2]

This problem is not unique to the procedure used here, but arises whenever a body of data is subjected to a large number of analyses, or a large number of explanatory variables are used and then scanned for the "significant" ones. The present formalization of the process merely makes the problem more obvious.

The results of the process are independent of the order in which the variables are introduced, but they do depend on *which* variables are used, and on the precision with which they measure what we hope they represent. It is always possible that introducing a new variable, or a better measure of one already tried, would lead to new conclusions.

The greatest power of the procedure is its ability to conclude that a particular variable, as measured, does not matter. If that variable is not able to account for any substantial fraction of the variance of the dependent variable, either over the whole sample or over any of its widely different subgroups, then it really does not matter and can be discarded.

---

[2]Tests with the program indicate that the first divisions made in a set of data remain reasonably stable over different samples of the same population, and that the final groups developed tend to be more stable than the particular order of divisions by which they are generated.

Where the dependent variable has a large variance or has extreme cases, the use of reduction-in-unexplained-sum-of-squares as a criterion leads to the isolation of groups with very few cases. We have generally applied the rule that groups of fewer than 25 cases should not be allowed, since they might well be idiosyncratic. Another sample might well lead to a different result. Hence, the figures were truncated, focusing attention on the differences that were both important and likely to exist in the total population.

A final question is how the process is affected by intercorrelations among the explanatory variables. Multiple regression is frequently described, inaccurately, as "holding other variables constant." The interaction-detecting process used here, since it operates sequentially, actually does take out the effects of variables as it uses them to divide the sample, and analysis of the groups farther down the diagram can show whether the second variable still matters within subgroups divided according to the first. In most cases with correlated variables the answer is no. Hence, whichever of the correlated predictors is the most powerful is actually used, and the other one then drops from sight. We regard this as better, in most cases, then the multiple regression procedure, which can best be described as allowing the correlated variables to "share the credit."

If the predictors are having effects at different stages in the causal process, and particularly if there is one clearly prior set that can affect the other predictors but cannot be affected by them, then a two-stage analysis is called for in which we make sure that the effects of the first set are removed first, and the residuals run only against the second set. It is sometimes possible to argue that there is a whole chain of causes operating sequentially, and that the analysis should operate the same way. We have not constructed it to do so, chiefly because there are often uncertainties, because some of our estimates of earlier variables are current responses possibly affected by later events, and because interaction effects may well mean that the prior variables do affect the way later factors work. Generally, we have put attitudinal variables in the second stage, on the assumption that economic and demographic factors, utilized in the first stage, provide the framework within which other forces were able to operate.

III. The Regression Procedure

Where it seemed appropriate, a relatively flexible regression-type analysis technique has been used in this volume. Even here, by using "dummy variables" representing membership in the subclasses of each predictor, we avoided the assumption that the effects of each variable were linear. Thus, the regression was able to develop its own scaling of each predictor at the same time that it assessed their importance.[3]

Where a variable is assigned to membership in a subgroup, the regression coefficient is an estimate of the effect of belonging to that subgroup if the

---

[3]For a complete explanation, see Frank Andrews, James Morgan, and John Sonquist, *Multiple Classification Analysis* (Ann Arbor: Survey Research Center, The University of Michigan, 1967).

members of that subgroup were like the total population in their distribution on all the other variables. If the coefficients for any set of subclasses which exhausts the population are constrained so that their weighted mean is equal to the overall average of the dependent variable, then we can compare the actual average effect of each subclass on the dependent variable with this multiple regression estimate of what that average effect would be if one adjusted the group for the effects of its abnormality on all the other variables. And the difference between the actual and adjusted average is a measure of the amount of intercorrelation among the predictors. If the predictors were completely uncorrelated with one another, the two sets of numbers would be identical, and the unadjusted subgroup average would become an optimal estimate of the effect of belonging to that subgroup.

Clearly, some intercorrelation among predictors must almost always be taken into account. Multiple regression takes account of it by adjusting the estimated mean for any subgroup to take into account disproportionate distributions within the group on other factors, but using estimates of those effects simultaneously adjusted for the composition of groups defined by the other factors. Hence all the adjustments are attenuated, and a variable which would have no relation to a genuine set of residuals is given a weak relation through this procedure.

Appendix B

AUTO WORKER RETIREMENT AND EMPLOYMENT CONDITIONS

This appendix provides background information describing the retirement options available to the auto worker studied,[1] as well as their pension and other retirement benefits. The type of work and facilities, wages, location of employment, etc. of the auto workers from which the study sample was drawn are also specifically considered.

The retirement arrangements are a result of the collective bargaining process, and thus are subject to revisions every few years. The effect this may have had upon employee retirement planning is also discussed briefly.

I. Retirement Options and Worker Preparation for Retirement

Under the terms of the collective bargaining agreements which were in effect between the UAW and each of the four companies at the time of the study, an employee had to retire no later than the end of the month in which he attained age 68.[2]

Any employee with at least 10 years of credited service[3] could retire voluntarily as early as age 60, although—as discussed below—this would reduce

---

[1]Most employees in the bargaining units at General Motors, Ford, Chrysler, and International Harvester are members of the Union—The International Union, United Automobile, Aerospace and Agricultural Implement Workers of America, UAW. With the exception of plants in certain "Right to Work" States, employees are required (by the terms of the contract between the employer and the Union) to join the Union within a specified period of time after being hired. Whether or not an employee actually belongs to the Union, if his job is in the collective bargaining unit his pre- and post-retirement benefits, working conditions, etc. are determined by the terms of the contract. Thus, union membership, as such, does not influence the economic forces acting upon a given employee, but it may affect social or other forces acting upon him.

[2]At the Ford Motor Company, as a result of the 1964 negotiations, the compulsory retirement age was gradually lowered for those with 25 or more years of service: to age 66 in 1966 and to age 65 in 1967 or later.

[3]A year of "credited service" is defined somewhat differently at each of the companies, but is essentially intended to measure a full year's active employment.

the pension benefit to which he would be entitled. Most employees age 60 or over have the necessary service, and thus are in a position to retire with immediate eligibility for a lifetime pension if they choose to do so. Some long service employees have the option of retiring between ages 55 and 60.[4]

There is also provision for retirement between ages 55 and 65, with higher lifetime pensions than for voluntary retirement, if the employee is disabled or meets certain special criteria.[5] In each of these cases, the only choice the employee has is whether or not to apply for this type of retirement; his eligibility is then determined in accordance with the contractually specified retirement criteria.

Thus, the basic retirement decision facing an auto worker is whether to retire voluntarily or wait until his compulsory retirement age. Furthermore, if voluntary retirement is selected, the employee can choose any date within a span of 8 to 13 years.

The companies and the union have made extensive educational efforts in order to inform the employees of their retirement options and other aspects of retirement. These efforts have been both unilateral (by one of the companies or the union) and joint (company-union projects). In each of the companies, jointly prepared literature describing the retirement benefits and options is widely distributed to the employees. In addition, formal meetings and informal discussion groups have been held to go over these subjects. One of the companies and the union have teamed in an extensive "retirement preparation" program which offers employees a series of seven 2-hour discussion sessions covering subjects such as financial aspects of retirement, health considerations, choice of living accommodations, and retirement activities.

II. Retirement Benefits

In accordance with the collective bargaining agreement between each company and the union, the auto workers are covered by non-contributory pension plans, life insurance, and hospital-surgical-medical insurance programs which are essentially the same at all four companies.[6]

---

[4]Their "credited service" (as defined in the collectively bargained pension plan) must equal the difference between 85 and their age at the time of retirement. Below age 60, benefits are reduced as described below, so that retirement income is considerably less than if the worker retires past age 60.

[5]A totally and permanently disabled employee is eligible for disability retirement at any age, if he has 10 years of credited service.

[6]The non-contributory character of the benefit plans assures that all active workers in the bargaining unit are covered by them.

Changes in the pension and benefit programs covering bargaining unit members are negotiated every few years along with wages and working conditions. Though reaction to and anticipation of such changes may be relevant to the retirement decision (this feature will be discussed further in the next section), the benefits described here are those which were applicable to those retiring during the period of October 1964 to September 1967.[7]

The amount of the monthly lifetime pension was calculated as the product of (a) years of credited service and (b) the following age related factor:

Age at which benefits start*	Lifetime benefit factor	Percentage of maximum factor
55	$2.46	58
56	2.70	64
57	2.95	69
58	3.20	75
59	3.43	81
60	3.68	86
61	3.97	93
62 or older	4.25	100

*For ages other than an exact number of years, an interpolated factor applies.

Illustrative lifetime pensions are shown in Appendix Table B-1.

At time of retirement, the employee could choose a reduced pension in order to assure a spouse's survivor pension. The reduction factor (the cost in foregoing pension to the worker) was

10 percent + ½ percent (Age of retiree − Age of spouse)

The spouse's survivor benefit (Survivor Pension) would be 55 percent of the reduced amount which had been payable to the retiree while living. This provision is also illustrated in Table B-1.

Early Retirement

For employees retiring prior to age 65, in the fall of 1965 or later,[8] an additional supplemental allowance was payable until the retiree attained age 65. The supplemental allowance was calculated as the difference between the

[7]These benefits are payable to employees whose retirement eligibility is based solely on meeting the necessary age and service requirements. As indicated above, there are other benefit provisions applicable to disabled workers or those meeting other special criteria. Specific provisions also apply to workers who terminate employment at a relatively early age but have sufficient service for a deferred "vested" pension. None of these cases was considered relevant to this study.

[8]The exact starting date varied between September 1 and October 1.

monthly lifetime benefit described above (before any reduction for survivor protection) and the product of:

(a) years of credited service (subject to a maximum of 30) and
(b) the following age-related temporary benefit factor:

Age at which benefits start*	Temporary benefit factor	Percentage of maximum factor
55	$ 6.67	50
56	7.41	56
57	8.33	62
58	9.52	71
59	11.11	83
60 or older	13.33	100

*For ages other than an exact number of years, an interpolated factor applies.

These benefits are illustrated in Table B-1.

The total monthly benefit payable before age 65 (before calculating the reduction for survivor protection) is subject to a maximum of 70 percent of the worker's monthly straight-time base earnings prior to retirement. This maximum is not pro-rated for service. Thus, a combination of a relatively low wage and long service must exist for the maximum to affect a retiree's benefit.

A worker retiring prior to age 65 would thus receive a higher total benefit prior to age 65 than after that age. However, this decline could be at least partially offset by commencing receipt of Social Security at age 65.[9] On the other hand, the retiree could further accentuate the difference between pre- and post-age 65 benefits by commencing, prior to age 65, receipt of (lifetime) reduced Old-Age benefits under Social Security.

The lifetime benefits are payable without regard to other earnings or employment (except that in some of the companies the benefits would be suspended if the retiree were reemployed by the same company; this is a relatively rare occurrence). On the other hand, the supplemental allowance is specifically designed to encourage early retirement from the labor force. Therefore, its continued payment is subject to the retiree limiting his earnings after retirement to the basic annual amount specified in the retirement test of the Social Security Act; in 1965 through 1967, this amount was $1,500.

In addition to these cash benefits, retirees had certain life insurance and hospital-surgical-medical expense protection.

---

[9]In general, the pensions described above are payable independently (i.e., in addition to) Old Age benefits under Social Security, although the Supplemental Allowances are subject to adjustment if the retiree becomes eligible for Disability Benefits under Social Security or if the law is changed to provide full Old Age benefits prior to age 65.

TABLE B-1

REPRESENTATIVE MONTHLY PENSIONS FOR AUTO WORKERS
1964-1967

		Lifetime pension		Total payable[a] prior to age 65[c]	
Age at which benefits start	Years of service	No survivor protection	With survivor protection[b]	No survivor protection	With survivor protection[b]
62	40	$170.00	$149.60	$400.00	$379.60
	30	127.50	112.20	400.00	384.70
	25	106.20	93.40	333.30	320.50
	20	85.00	74.80	266.70	256.50
60	40	147.40	129.70	400.00	382.30
	30	110.50	97.20	400.00	386.70
	25	92.10	81.00	333.30	322.20
	20	73.70	64.80	266.70	257.80
58	40	127.80	112.50	285.70	270.40
	30	95.90	84.40	285.70	274.20
	27[d]	86.30	75.90	257.10	246.70

Note: Amounts have been rounded off to the nearest $0.10.

[a] "Early Retirement Supplement" (included in Total Payable Prior to Age 65) effective for retirements in the fall of 1965 and after.

[b] If the retiree dies first the spouse receives 55 percent of the amount shown on this line under "lifetime pension with survivor protection." Assumes typical spouse to be 4 years younger than worker. (See *Survivor Benefits: A Study of Auto Workers and Their Survivors,* by Eugene L. Loren and Thomas C. Barker, Michigan Health and Social Security Research Institute.)

[c] If base hourly rate is less than $3.30, reduce $400 payable to 70 percent of straight time monthly earnings. If base hourly rate is less than $2.75, reduce $333.33 payable to 70 percent of straight time monthly earnings. Amount payable "with survivor protection" is reduced by same amount. Other amounts shown in this table are not affected by this limit.

[d] Minimum service required for voluntary retirement at this age.

Life Insurance

The life insurance protection available to a retiree was related to his wage prior to retirement: before age 65 the amount approximated one year's earnings; after age 65 the amount was subject to a monthly reduction formula which resulted in a lower level lifetime amount starting approximately at age 68.[10] In addition, prior to age 65, at all except one of the companies, an

---

[10] For example, if the worker's straight-time hourly wage rate at the time of retirement had been $2.97, his life insurance amount would be $6500. Active or retired employees past the age of 65 had their life insurance reduced by 2 percent per month until the amount of coverage (which was then continued) equalled 1½ percent of the

extra Accidental Death or Dismemberment Benefit equal to 50 percent of the regular life insurance amount was available. This protection for retirees differed from that for non-retired employees in the following respects:

(a) Retirees were required to pay a monthly premium of $0.50 per $1,000 of life insurance protection prior to age 65; after age 65 no contribution was required. Nonretired employees were not required at any age to pay monthly premiums for their life insurance.

(b) Nonretired employees were covered for additional survivor benefits providing $100 monthly to certain defined classes of beneficiaries (e.g., wife) for periods ranging from 2 to 12 years as determined by plan provisions. Most retirees did not have any comparable coverage;[11] although as noted above a retiree could elect a reduced pension with provision for benefits to a surviving spouse.

Health Insurance

The hospital-surgical-medical insurance protection for retirees was identical to that for non-retired employees. In both cases, the protection was provided without any payment of premium by the employee or the retiree (except that when an individual became eligible for Medicare, he was required to pay the monthly premium for that coverage). Without describing the benefits in detail, the plan covering the employees studied generally would pay for most hospital-surgical-medical expenses. The major cost items that were not fully covered in the plan were home and office medical visits, prescription drugs, dental care and private duty nursing; in addition, in the event of protracted illness (beyond 365 days per individual) hospital bills were not covered in the basic plan. Since retirement did not result in any reduction in this type of coverage, presumably, the only effect which this benefit may have had upon the retirement decision would result from the lower post-retirement income from which uncovered expenses would have to be paid by the retiree as compared with the active employee's ability to meet these from pre-retirement earnings.

(Footnote 10 Continued)

active (pre-65) amount times the years of service (up to 20) or (at one company) a minimum of $1,500 and a maximum of $3,900. This reduced coverage was non-contributory for active or retired workers. The companies varied somewhat with respect to the minimum and the maximum amounts of continued coverage and the associated wage brackets.

[11] Disability retirees had this coverage continued to age 60.

III. Collective Bargaining Concerning Retirement

As noted above, the retirement alternative and benefits are open to fairly frequent revisions as the result of collective bargaining. For all practical purposes, the first such provisions for the groups of employees covered by this study became effective in 1950; they have subsequently been revised in 1953, 1955, 1958, 1961, 1964, and 1967.

In the previous sections there is a description of these provisions based upon the 1964 collective bargaining agreement. Retirement decisions made between 1964 and 1967 were undoubtedly affected by the substance of the 1964 provisions; they may also have been affected by the extent to which these provisions differed from those previously in effect as well as by the employee's expectations with respect to the provisions which might be bargained in 1967.

Prior to 1964, the retirement options were essentially as described above.[12] However, the level of benefits was substantially lower than described above. There was no supplemental allowance, and the factor multiplied by years of credited service in order to calculate the monthly lifetime benefit was as given below (for comparison the 1964 factor is also shown):

Age at which	Lifetime benefit factor	
benefits start*	1961 plan	1964 plan
60	$1.88	$3.68
61	2.05	3.97
62	2.24	4.25
63	2.43	4.25
64	2.61	4.25
65 or older	2.80	4.25

*For ages other than an exact number of years, an interpolated factor applies. The percentage benefit reduction for early retirement varied slightly at the companies studied.

Thus, for a worker who may have been considering retiring about age 60, the 1964 negotiations resulted in a substantial increase in his pension entitlement. Consider, for example, an employee age 60 with 25 years of service:

Under the 1961 plan, he would be entitled to a monthly lifetime income of $47.00.[13] Under the 1964 plan, he would be entitled to a

---

[12] Voluntary retirement with immediate eligibility for benefits was not available prior to age 60, but the 1964 change only affected long service employees between ages 55 and 60. Also prior to 1964, the compulsory retirement age at Ford was 68 for all employees; the same as at the other companies.

[13] It was possible for the employee to elect to receive a somewhat increased amount prior to his attaining age 62, and a correspondingly lower amount thereafter.

monthly income of $333.33 (or, if less, 70 percent of his pre-retirement pay) until he attained age 65, and $92.00 thereafter.[14]

However, the 1964 plan also introduced a new restriction: in order to collect the supplemental allowance (which accounts for the higher income prior to age 65) the retiree had to limit his earnings.

There were also liberalizations in spouse's survivor pension, life insurance, and hospital-surgical-medical coverage provisions due to the 1964 negotiations.

These changes agreed to in 1964 by the companies and the union, with the heavy emphasis upon substantially improved benefits for early retirees who withdrew from the total work force (not just the company he retired from), reflected attitudes frequently voiced by auto workers in 1963 and 1964: early retirement was a high priority goal, and could be used as a means to reduce unemployment among younger workers.

Turning to expectations which employees considering retirement in late 1966 or early 1967 may have had with respect to 1967 negotiations, it is necessary to understand the historical background. During each of the negotiations after 1950, liberalizations were made in provisions affecting retirement benefits of those who would retire *subsequent* to the time of the negotiations; in no instance, however, had the liberalizations approached the magnitude of those negotiated in 1964. In addition, liberalizations had been negotiated, but with less consistency and liberality, for workers who were *already* retired at the time of the negotiations.[15] Thus, as the period prior to 1967 negotiations (the collective bargaining agreements expired at various dates in the fall of 1967) grew shorter, the possible but uncertain effect of changes to be negotiated probably became more important in any employee's retirement decision making.

(Although the field interviews were completed in 1967, prior to negotiations, it may be of interest to note that the retirement benefits were further improved that year. However, the improvements were not as great as those negotiated in 1964, and the improvements applicable to those already retired were not as great as those applicable to future retirees.)

------

[14]The Supplemental Allowance only applied to retirements in the fall of 1965 or later; if the employee retired under the 1964 Plan prior to that his lifetime monthly benefit would have been $92.00.

[15]The Companies have, on various occasions, expressed their opposition to making any changes in the benefits of those already retired.

IV. Size and Geographical Distribution of the Workforce

As noted in Chapter 6 of this volume, the study sample was drawn from employees of the four companies cited who had been born in the years 1904-07, i.e., those 58 through 61 as of January 1, 1966. During 1966, the total workforce in the bargaining units averaged approximately 700,000 employees, working at nearly 350 units in 34 states in coterminous United States. A large percentage of the plants are located in urban and suburban areas.

Approximately 32,000 employees were within the age group studied. About one in four of the 58 through 61 year old population at the four companies was interviewed by mail questionnaire. Over 80 percent of the 58 through 61 year old group sampled were found to be living in a four state area of the Midwest: Michigan, Ohio, Indiana, and Illinois. During 1966, 76 percent of the total bargaining unit workforce resided in the four state area.

V. The Work Environment

The UAW is an industrial union and thus represents a broad spectrum of the manufacturing employees of the four companies involved, as well as a relatively small number of clerks, technicians, and engineers. While the exact range of jobs included in the bargaining unit is often a matter of controversy, they include unskilled, semi-skilled, and highly skilled activities carried out in facilities which include such diverse environments as offices, warehouses, assembly plants, and foundries—representing a wide range of noise, heat, and other conditions affecting employment.

Similarly, the employee's control over his work pace varies among the workers studied. In the case of an assembly line worker, the employee generally must maintain a fairly steady work pace determined by the flow of work on the line. On the other hand, a stock clerk can generally vary his work pace during the day, in accordance with his own desires subject to certain requirements as to the total amoung of work to be accomplished during the day. An employee's control over work pace also varies to the extent that he works as an individual or as a member of a related work group.

VI. Wages

A major factor in describing the employment characteristics of the universe is the wage rate and earnings of the employees. While the workers interviewed reported their individual and family income, the data below are indicative of the range of wages derived from the primary employment of the universe of covered workers.

Although there is significant variation between the hourly wage of the highest and lowest paid employees in the bargaining unit, the bulk of the employees are actually concentrated in a fairly narrow range of wage rates. Based upon data available for employees of two of the four companies involved in the study, during 1966 approximately 70 percent of the employees in the bargaining units had an hourly wage rate (including the cost of living allowance) between $2.97 and $3.20.[16] It is believed that these data are representative of the situation at all four companies since the collective bargaining applicable to all four companies tends to follow a "pattern" with respect to wages and other benefits.[17]

Based upon the same data, the lowest hourly wage rate was $2.02, but fewer than 10 percent of the employees were earning less than the $2.97 rate previously cited. (In fact, less than 1 percent of the employees were earning under $2.72 per hour.) Similarly, while the highest wage rate was $6.56, fewer than 20 percent of the employees were earning more than the $3.20 previously cited. (Approximately 1 percent of the workers earned more than $3.99 per hour, including the cost of living allowance.) Thus while approximately 70 percent of the workers earned between $2.97 and $3.20 per hour; 98 percent earned between $2.72 and $3.99.

The use of hourly wage rates leaves much to be desired in preparing any comparison of pre- and post-retirement income levels, since earnings prior to retirement will be affected by overtime work, layoff, illness,[18] etc. whereas post-retirement income is mainly made up of fixed monthly Social Security and pension amounts. While no data are available indicating the net effect of these variables on total pre-retirement income, it is reasonable to assume that for those employees near retirement the net effect on income would not be negative, i.e., omission of these variable factors leads to an income underestimate for the workers sampled.

---

[16]The cost of living allowance in 1966 ranged from $0.10 to $0.18 per hour. On a monthly basis (173.3 hours) this difference represents less than $14.00. The wage range used in indicating the wage distribution includes $1.12 cost of living allowance, the allowance in effect between March and June, 1966. 1966 wage rates are used because they are representative of the middle period of the contracts which had been negotiated in September, 1964. The Early Retirement Supplement is based on straight-time monthly earnings.

[17]Analysis of the Collective Bargaining Agreements indicate general consistency of the negotiated provisions, though minor exceptions (some of which have been noted) do exist.

[18]The collective bargaining agreement covering these employees provided some income replacement during layoff or illness.

The above conclusion is based upon the fact that employees nearing retirement age generally have relatively long seniority and are thus subject to minimal (at most) periods of layoff. Thus, overtime work (which has been fairly wide-spread in these companies) would probably provide sufficient additional income to offset the losses (not covered by income replacement programs) during any layoffs or illnesses.[19]

Based on the above assumptions, monthly wage income for those considering retirement probably averaged at least 173.3 times[20] the applicable hourly rate. As noted above, for approximately 70 percent of all the employees, this would be between $515 and $555 per month; for 98 percent of the workers, the monthly income would range from $417 to $691.

[19]While some of these employees suffer substantial income losses due to lengthy illnesses, it is assumed that these employees will generally be eligible for disability or special retirement; thus they are not representative of those who must make a voluntary decision as to date of retirement.

[20]Fifty-two weeks, at 40 hours per week, averaged over the year.

Appendix C

THE AUTOMOBILE WORKER SAMPLE

This appendix comprises two sections: the first discusses the sample of automobile workers with which initial contact was made for the retirement decision study; the second discusses the sample of auto workers (a subset of the initial contact sample) with whom personal interviews were arranged for the in-depth study of auto worker early retirement.

I. The Mail Survey Sample

As stated above, this section describes the procedures used to select the sample of auto workers which was used for the mail survey. The efforts undertaken to obtain a high level of response and cooperation from those in the sample are also discussed.

Raw Data

The UAW receives semi-annually from various companies (including the four whose employees are covered by this study) computer processable data concerning the employees in the bargaining unit represented by the union. The data from each of the four companies involved in this study generally included the following items for each employee: name, address, date of birth, Social Security number, and local union number.[1] However, for some individuals one or more of these items was not available; the number of cases in which this occurred is not known, nor is it possible to estimate what bias, if any, this may have introduced into the sample.[2] (The replies to the mail

---

[1] A "local union" is an organizational unit of the union, and generally corresponds to a single work location, such as a plant.

[2] It was estimated that about 10 percent of the employees' records were missing one or more items, and thus not used. *A priori*, one would expect the records of new workers to be less complete than for longer service workers. If that is correct, these unused records would have little effect upon the sample since it was concerned with older—hence, generally longer service—workers.

survey and the personal interview survey revealed some inaccuracies in the raw data. Presumably this reflects random error that is practically inevitable in any large body of data, and did not produce any bias in the findings.)

For each of these four companies, the data were based on company records as of the fall of 1965 (the exact date varied among the companies).

Initial Sampling Requirements

The initial decision was to use employees with years of birth 1904 to 1907 inclusive. As of the beginning of 1966, this would produce a population age 58 to 61 inclusive. This age span was selected because it was felt that the retirement benefits structure tended to reduce the incentive to retire before age 60 (even though some employees were eligible to retire voluntarily as early as age 55), and because employees closer to age 65 would not provide as clear-cut a basis for analyzing "early" retirement attitudes.

A preliminary analysis of the data by geographic area and by year of birth was considered desirable to see if any "clustering" was present which might affect the procedure to be used in selecting the mail sample. Therefore, a tabulation was made for each year of birth (1904-1907) of the number of employees residing in each zip code sectional center (i.e., identified by variation in the first three digits of the zip code). As was expected, the largest concentrations of employees were in Michigan; Table C-1 shows an extract of the data for the Detroit area.

TABLE C-1

EXTRACT OF ZIP CODE—YEAR OF BIRTH TABULATION

First 3 digits	Year of birth				
of Zip Code	1904	1905	1906	1907	Total
480	792	847	979	1073	3691
481	615	660	719	709	2703
482	2042	2089	2203	2285	8619

(The above Zip Code sectional centers are in the Detroit area.)

In total, 32,266 employees' records were obtained in this preliminary analysis, distributed as follows:

1904	7,007
1905	7,591
1906	8,392
1907	9,276
	32,266

Sample Selection

Based upon the zip code—year of birth tabulation, it was decided that a random 25 percent selection procedure would produce a sample of sufficient size and dispersion for the mail survey.

The selection procedure decided upon was to choose those employees the last two digits of whose Social Security number was a multiple of 4.[3] This produced a sample size of 8,093 or 25.1 percent of the total population.

The following checks were made on the randomness of the sample:

(a) For each company, the ratio of the employees in the sample to those in the population was calculated, and expressed as a percentage; the four values were: 25.1 percent, 25.6 percent, 26.3 percent, and 22.8 percent.[4]

(b) For the companies with the largest and smallest work forces, respectively, the percentage of employees in the sample for each year of birth as compared with the population was calculated:

Year of birth	Sample as percent of population	
	Largest company	Smallest company
1904	25.3	18.5
1905	25.0	24.2
1906	25.9	22.2
1907	24.1	24.3

The sample data for the smallest company did cause some concern as to the randomness of the sample. Since, however, it was such a small fraction of the total group (7.5 percent of the population, 6.7 percent of the sample), and since the other companies' data appeared consistent with the assumption of randomness, this sample selection procedure was retained. Two sets of mailing labels (for an initial and following up mailing), a control listing, and a magnetic computer tape of the sample employees' records were produced.

---

[3]The Social Security Administration was consulted to determine any known bias in the assignment of the last 4 digits of a Social Security number. While no tests of randomness could be cited, it was believed that this portion of the number was assigned essentially on a sequential—and thus probably unbiased—basis.

[4]The greatest deviation from 25 percent occurred in the company with the smallest work force. For that size work force, the probability of obtaining this size sample was less than 1 percent, if the true probability of selection was in fact 25 percent.

Efforts to Increase Response and Cooperation

The mail questionnaire was tested on two groups prior to being mailed to the sample described above. The first group consisted of employees attending one of the retirement preparation classes which was presented under joint sponsorship of the union and one of the companies. A staff member of the union explained the purpose of the questionnaire; the employees then completed the questionnaire and offered comments about the clarity of specific questions. The second group consisted of 42 employees, in the relevant age span, living in zip code sectional center 458 (in Ohio). Contact with these employees was entirely by mail. Their response indicated that the question naire was satisfactory.

The mailing to the test group described above, and subsequently to the entire sample, was done by the Survey Research Center; and all replies were directed to them. The union provided the Survey Research Center with cover letters encouraging cooperation with the study (four versions of the cover letter were used, each by the officer of the union who was directly responsible for bargaining with the company at which the employee worked). It was felt that direct communication with the Survey Research Center would reduce any reservations employees might have about revealing their retirement plans to the union (or the companies), and that the union endorsement would produce a higher level of cooperation than otherwise.

In addition, because the union felt it likely that some employees would check with officials of their local union concerning the study, a letter of explanation was mailed by the union to each of its local unions with members in the sample.[5]

Finally, where the response rate of members of a specific local union was found to be low, the officials of that local union were asked to encourage, in a general way (e.g., notice posted on a bulletin board), the employees to complete and return the questionnaire. In order to avoid biasing the response of any individual, it was not considered desirable to have individual follow-up by the union with any employee.[6]

Of the questionnaires mailed, 4,974 (61.5 percent) were completed and returned to the Survey Research Center.

----

[5]Similar procedures were used in connection with the personal interview phase of the study. At that time a front page article concerning the study was also published in the union's monthly newspaper.

[6]The Survey Research Center, however, did contact approximately 150 Detroit-area nonrespondents to the mail questionnaire in order to ascertain whether such persons differed significantly (in eligibility for the negotiated early retirement provision and in retirement plans) from mail questionnaire respondents. While the nonrespondents were found to be somewhat less likely to be eligible for the early retirement benefits and to plan early retirement, these differences were not sizeable.

II. The Personal Interview Sample

The population represented by this sample was, as previously indicated, a subset of the one-in-four sample of automobile workers with which mail contact was initiated. From a review of the geographical distribution of the 25 percent sample it was clear that national representation in a personal interview survey would be costly because, while about 80 percent of the population concentrated in the four-state area of Michigan, Ohio, Indiana, and Illinois, the other 20 percent was scattered throughout the other 44 coterminous states. Consequently, it was thought efficient and meaningful to restrict the interview study to the four-state area.

The 1967 Sample from the Four-state Area

With respect to retirement plans the 6,581 auto workers in the four-state area who received mail questionnaires in 1966 may be assigned to four classes:

Classification code	Number of persons	Description
1	1,733	Auto worker planned to retire within 12 months, or had already retired
2	1,045	Auto worker was eligible for early retirement benefits but did not plan to retire within 12 months (or retirement plans were not ascertained)
3	1,372	Auto worker was eligible for early retirement benefits only after 1967 (or eligibility was not ascertained) and did not plan to retire within 12 months (or retirement plans were not ascertained)
4	2,431	Auto worker did not respond to mail questionnaire.

Considerations of research objectives and of interviewing costs indicated that a sample of about one thousand interviews would be satisfactory subject to two conditions: (1) that disproportionate sampling be used to give greater chance of selection to members in classes 1 and 2 because they were more important to the research; (2) that some clustering of sample members be effected to keep interviewing costs at an acceptable level. The two conditions were met in the following manner:

—Persons in classes 1 and 2 were sampled at the rate of one in three, while those in classes 3 and 4 were sampled at the rate of one in nine.
—*In the city of Detroit* a systematic selection was made at the appropriate rate within three code classifications: classes 1 and 2, in combination; class 3; class 4.

—In the remainder of the four-state area the general plan was to form geographic clusters of roughly equal size to be sampled at the rate of one in three. Within clusters, all members of classes 1 and 2 were retained for the sample, but only one-third of classes 3 and 4 were designated as eligible for inerviewing. Clusters were formed in such a manner that the four companies were represented approximately in proportion to the number of employees within each retirement classification. The total cluster size varied according to the membership within a local area. In metropolitan Detroit and Chicago the local area was most frequently a group of suburbs, while in the remainder of the interviewing areas a cluster might sometimes be scattered through several counties. Within large cities (other than Detroit) clustering was by postal zones. Clusters of class 1 and 2 members commonly ranged in size from 20 to 40; clusters of class 3 and 4 members were more frequently of size 2 to 12.

The number of selections by major geographic area was as follows:

Geographic location	Number of selections
Michigan	
Detroit city	398
Remainder of Detroit area	364
Other Michigan areas	239
Illinois	
Chicago city	34
Remainder of Chicago area	34
Other Illinois areas	53
Indiana	107
Ohio	102
Places outside the four-state area[7]	5
Total selections	1,336

In order that measures of sampling variability could be calculated, each response and each nonresponse was coded according to the primary cluster with which it was associated. (Each such cluster had been assigned a unique code which was recorded in the sample book for the study.) An analysis of the response rate within the various clusters revealed that only the rate associated with the Cook County, Illinois area was significantly different from (in fact, lower than) the overall mean response rate (84 percent of the 1,336 selections). Accordingly, the weighting procedure which adjusted for differences in the sampling fractions applied to classes 1 and 2 versus classes 3 and 4 was modified to increase the representation of Cook County respondents.

---

[7]This category arose because some workers, who at one time lived within the four-state area, later moved to other places.

Appendix D

THE NATIONAL SAMPLE [1]

I. Sampling Procedures

Data for the analysis of the national population's retirement attitudes and expectations was collected in two surveys during 1966: the January-February annual Survey of Consumers and the August consumer attitudes survey, one of several such surveys conducted regularly by the Survey Research Center. In the former survey information was obtained from personal interviews with 2,419 families; during the August survey 1,228 families were contacted.

The samples of the Survey Research Center represented cross sections of the population living in private households in the United States, excluding Alaska and Hawaii. Transients, residents of institutions, and persons living on military bases are not represented. A multistage area probability sample of dwelling units is drawn, using counties or groups of contiguous counties as primary sampling units. During the survey period covered by this monograph, the number of sample points was 78 (the 12 largest metropolitan areas and 66 other areas selected on the basis of various controls).

In each primary area three to six secondary selections of cities, towns, census tracts, or rural areas are made. In the third stage of sampling, urban blocks or small portions (blocks) of rural areas are chosen. For each survey a new sample of dwelling units, in clusters of about four, is drawn from the block selections.

The basic unit for sampling is the dwelling unit, and for interviewing, the family unit. A family unit is defined as all persons living in the same dwelling unit who are related to each other by blood, marriage, or adoption. A single person who is unrelated to the other occupants of the dwelling, or who lives alone, is a family unit by himself. In some dwelling units there are several family units. The total number of family units in the 48 states can be estimated from survey data and from census data relating to the number of

---

[1]This appendix is derived primarily from G. Katrona *et. al., 1966 Survey of Consumer Finances*(Ann Arbor: Survey Research Center, The University of Michigan, 1967), Chapter 12.

occupied dwelling units. There has been a steady and substantial increase in the number of families. There were approximately 59.1 million families early in 1966, compared with about 50.4 million families 10 years earlier, and 45.7 million families in 1950. Early in 1966, about 2.2 percent of all families were secondary units unrelated to the primary family occupying the dwelling unit.

The head of the family unit is designated as the respondent in the financial surveys, while the head and his wife (if the head is married) are selected alternately in the attitudinal surveys. Five calls, and in some cases more, are made at various times at dwelling units at which no one has been found at home. If a designated respondent refuses to give relevant information, a letter is sent urging him to reconsider. The letter is followed by another visit.

The median interview time in the January-February Survey was 62 minutes. In this survey, 96 percent of the interviews were taken with the head of the family; almost all of the remainder were taken with the wife of the head.

Interviewers were asked to evaluate the quality of the interview. Ninety percent of the interviews were described as extremely satisfactory or satisfactory. The remaining 10 percent were described by the interviewers as involving a respondent who was slow to understand and had some difficulty in answering some of the questions.[2]

The Survey Research Center maintains a national staff of interviewers selected and trained by a staff of traveling supervisors. The interviewers are instructed in the careful and uniform use of the fixed-question open-answer technique. They pay particular attention to the establishment of rapport with respondents. Many questions are answered in the respondent's own words, which the interviewers record verbatim (or as nearly verbatim as possible). Non-directive probes are used to clarify the answers received.

The response rate in the January-February Survey was about 83 percent. About half of the nonresponse results from refusal to be interviewed or to give important data. Most of the remainder results from inability of the interviewer to contact anyone at the dwelling unit.

---

[2]The interviewers were asked "Did the respondent understand the questions and answer readily, or did he have some difficulty understanding and answering (not counting language difficulties)?"

II. Sampling Errors

Data obtained from sample interview surveys are subject to sampling errors. They depend on the magnitude of the reported percentage and on the size of the sample (or the number of respondents in the particular subgroup used). In Table D-1 the number of cases in some major subgroups of the sample from the January-February and the August 1966 surveys are shown.

Sampling errors are presented in two ways; as they relate to survey findings (see Table D-2); second, as they relate to differences in survey findings, either differences between two independent samples or differences between subgroups of the same sample (see Table D-3). Sampling errors are not a measure of the actual errors involved in specific survey measurements. They mean that, except for nonsampling errors, errors greater than those shown in Table D-2 or differences larger than those found in Table D-3 will occur by chance in only five cases out of a hundred.

TABLE D-1

NUMBER OF FAMILY UNITS IN SPECIFIED GROUPS
(January-February and August surveys taken together)

Group characteristic	Number of family units
All family units	3,647
Labor force status	
Working	2,664
Unemployed, sick, or laid off	100
Retired from some job but still in labor force	47
Housewife	220
Student	75
Retired and not in labor force	482
Permanently disabled	55
1966 family income	
Less than $1,000	126
$1,000 - 1,999	277
$2,000 - 2,999	304
$3,000 - 3,999	292
$4,000 - 4,999	321
$5,000 - 7,499	747
$7,500 - 9,999	609
$10,000 - 14,999	568
$15,000 or more	346

(TABLE D-1 Continued)

Group Characteristic	Number of family units
Expected retirement pension income	
Less than $1,000	63
$1,000 - 1,999	403
$2,000 - 2,999	556
$3,000 - 3,999	333
$4,000 - 4,999	219
$5,000 - 5,999	142
$6,000 - 7,499	123
$7,500 - 9,999	91
$10,000 or more	50
Age of family head	
35 - 44	695
45 - 49	383
50 - 54	368
55 - 59	342
60 - 64	289
65 - 69	236
70 - 74	197
75 or older	242
Expected retirement age of family head	
Before age 60	172
60 - 64	461
65 - 69	689
70 or older, some definite age given	93
Head never plans to retire or plans to work as long as possible	290

TABLE D-2

APPROXIMATE SAMPLING ERRORS OF SURVEY FINDINGS

Reported percentage range	Sampling error (in percent), by size of sample or subgroup					
	2000	1000	700	500	300	100
50	3	4	5	6	8	14
30 or 70	3	4	5	6	7	13
20 or 80	2	4	4	5	6	11
10 or 90	2	3	3	4	5	8
5 or 95	1	2	2	3	4	—

Note: The chances are 95 in 100 that the value being estimated lies within a range equal to the reported percentage plus or minus the number of percentage points shown above.

TABLE D-3

SAMPLING ERRORS OF DIFFERENCES

Differences required for significance (in percent)[a]

Size of sample or group	Size of sample or group					
	2000	1000	700	500	300	200
For percentages from about 35 percent to 65 percent						
2000	4	5	6	7	9	10
1000		6	7	8	9	11
700			8	8	10	11
500				9	10	12
300					11	13
200						14
For percentages around 20 percent and 80 percent						
2000	4	4	5	6	7	8
1000		5	6	6	7	8
700			6	7	8	9
500				7	8	9
300					9	10
200						11
For percentages around 10 percent and 90 percent						
2000	3	3	4	4	5	6
1000		4	4	5	6	6
700			4	5	6	7
500				5	6	7
300					7	8
For percentages around 5 percent and 95 percent						
2000	2	2	3	3	4	4
1000		3	3	3	4	5
700			3	4	4	5
500				4	4	5
300					5	6

[a]Differences required for significance (95 percent probability) in comparisons of percentages derived from successive surveys or from two different subgroups of the same survey.

Appendix E

SUMMARY OF REPLIES TO QUESTIONS: THE NATIONAL SAMPLE

The distributions of answers to all questions asked of national sample respondents is given in this appendix, in the order in which the questions were coded. (Generally, this is also the order in which questions were asked, though some reordering was allowed to facilitate coding operations.) The distributions are presented in two parts: Part I contains questions asked of nonretired family heads age 35 to 59, while Part II contains questions asked of retired family heads.

Some questions were asked only of an appropriate subgroup, but the percentages given are always of the total relevant subsample (the nonretired or the retired). Where the appropriate subgroup is less than one-half the relevant subsample, percentages are carried to one-tenth of a percent. Where the subgroup is more than one-half the relevant subsample, however, percentages are rounded to the nearest whole percent.

PART I: THE NONRETIRED

Percent of Nonretired
Family Heads (35-59)

(Questions 1-4 not coded)

5.   LIST ALL PERSONS, INCLUDING CHILDREN, LIVING
      IN THE DWELLING UNIT, BY THEIR RELATION TO
      THE HEAD

FROM QUESTION 5.   AGE OF FAMILY HEAD

35-44	40
45-49	22
50-54	20
55-59	18
Total	100

FROM QUESTION 5.   AGE OF WIFE OF FAMILY HEAD

Under 25	1
25-34	12
35-44	36
45-54	28
55-64	6
Family head is not married	17
Total	100

FROM QUESTION 5.   NUMBER OF ADULTS IN FAMILY UNIT

One	12
Two	64
Three	19
Four or more	5
Total	100

FROM QUESTION 5.   NUMBER OF CHILDREN (UNDER 18)
IN FAMILY UNIT

One	19
Two	17
Three	12
Four	6
Five	3
Six	2
Seven	1
Eight or more	1
Have no children under 18	39
Total	100

SECTION A: GENERAL FINANCIAL ATTITUDES

A1.   WE ARE INTERESTED IN HOW PEOPLE ARE GETTING ALONG
FINANCIALLY THESE DAYS.   WOULD YOU SAY THAT YOU AND YOUR
FAMILY ARE BETTER OFF OR WORSE OFF FINANCIALLY THAN YOU
WERE A YEAR AGO?

Better	39
Same	42
Worse now	18
Uncertain; don't know	1
Total	100

A2.   ARE YOU PEOPLE MAKING AS MUCH MONEY NOW AS YOU WERE
A YEAR AGO, OR MORE, OR LESS?

More now	18.5
About the same	11.7
Less now	3.8
Not ascertained	0.5
Not asked this question	65.5
Total	100.0

A3.   NOW LOOKING AHEAD - DO YOU THINK THAT A YEAR FROM NOW
YOU PEOPLE WILL BE BETTER OFF FINANCIALLY, OR WORSE OFF,
OR JUST ABOUT THE SAME AS NOW?

Better then	40
Same	43
Worse then	8
Uncertain, don't know	9
Total	100

SECTION B: OCCUPATION AND EMPLOYMENT

B1.   NEXT WE WOULD LIKE TO TALK WITH YOU ABOUT YOUR WORK AND
THE EMPLOYMENT OF OTHERS IN THE FAMILY.   HOW ABOUT YOUR PRESENT
JOB.   ARE YOU (HEAD) WORKING NOW, UNEMPLOYED OR LAID OFF, OR WHAT?

Working	97
Unemployed, sick, or laid off	3
Total	100

	Percent of Nonretired Family Heads (35-59)

B2. WHAT IS YOUR MAIN OCCUPATION? WHAT SORT OF WORK DO YOU DO?

	Percent of Nonretired Family Heads (35-59)
Professional and technical workers	14
Managers, and nonself-employed officials	8
Self-employed businessmen and artisans	10
Clerical and sales workers	12
Craftsmen and foremen	20
Operatives and kindred	16
Unskilled workers and service workers	12
Farmers and farm managers	6
Miscellaneous; not ascertained	2
Total	100

B3. WHAT KIND OF BUSINESS IS THAT IN?

Agriculture, forestry, and fishing	8
Mining and extracting	1
Manufacturing	26
Construction	11
Transportation, communications, and utilities	8
Retail and wholesale trade	13
Finance, insurance, and real estate	4
Services (including professional services)	12
Government medical, health, and educational services (including all federal employees)	14
Not ascertained	3
Total	100

B4. DO YOU SUPERVISE OTHER PEOPLE?

Yes	40
No	59
Not ascertained	1
Total	100

B5. DO YOU WORK FOR SOMEONE ELSE, OR YOURSELF, OR WHAT?

Someone else	81
Self	18
Both self and someone else	1
Total	100

B6. IS THERE A COMPULSORY RETIREMENT AGE WHERE YOU WORK, THAT IS, A TIME WHEN YOU MUST RETIRE?

Yes	37
No	42
Not ascertained	3
Self-employed (not asked of this group)	18
Total	100

	Percent of Nonretired Family Heads (35-59)
B6a. WHAT IS THE AGE?	
Under 65	1.5
65	25.9
Over 65	8.3
Not ascertained	3.8
No compulsory retirement age	60.5
Total	100.0

B7a. DO YOU BELONG TO A LABOR UNION?

Yes	28
No	53
Not ascertained	1
Self-employed (not asked of this group)	18
Total	100

B8. WE'RE INTERESTED IN HOW PEOPLE RATE DIFFERENT
OCCUPATIONS. WOULD YOU PLEASE LOOK AT THIS CARD AND TELL ME
WHICH THING ON THIS LIST ABOUT A JOB (OCCUPATION) YOU WOULD
MOST PREFER, WHICH COMES NEXT, AND SO FORTH?

The card showed to the respondents had the following characteristics
of an occupation to rank from first preference to last preference:

The work is important, gives a feeling of accomplishment
Income is steady
Working hours are short, lots of free time
There's no danger of being fired or unemployed
Chances for advancement are good
Income is high

RANK OF A. THE WORK IS IMPORTANT, GIVES A FEELING OF
ACCOMPLISHMENT

Highest preference among the characteristics	36
Second	15
Third	15
Fourth	12
Fifth	12
Lowest preference	7
Not ascertained	3
Total	100

RANK OF B. INCOME IS STEADY	Percent of Nonretired Family Heads (35-59)
Highest	34
Second	26
Third	18
Fourth	13
Fifth	4
Lowest	2
Not ascertained	3
Total	100

RANK OF C.   WORKING HOURS ARE SHORT, LOTS OF FREE TIME

Highest	2
Second	5
Third	8
Fourth	11
Fifth	21
Lowest	48
Not ascertained	5
Total	100

RANK OF D.   THERE'S NO DANGER OF BEING FIRED, OR UNEMPLOYED

Highest	8
Second	15
Third	17
Fourth	17
Fifth	23
Lowest	16
Not ascertained	4
Total	100

RANK OF E.   CHANCES FOR ADVANCEMENT ARE GOOD

Highest	9
Second	20
Third	20
Fourth	22
Fifth	15
Lowest	9
Not ascertained	5
Total	100

B9. FOR SOME PEOPLE THE WORK THEY DO IS DRUDGERY;
WITH OTHERS IT IS ALL RIGHT; WHILE SOME OTHERS MAY
GREATLY ENJOY THE WORK THEY DO. HOW DO YOU FEEL ABOUT
YOUR WORK?

Strongly enjoys work	24
Enjoys work	54
Pro-con response	14
Dislikes work	3
Strongly dislikes work	3
Not ascertained	2
Total	100

B10. HAVE YOU EVER THOUGHT OF LEAVING YOUR PRESENT JOB
IN ORDER TO GET INTO SOME MORE INTERESTING OR MORE
PROMISING WORK?

Yes	34
No	65
Not ascertained	1
Total	100

B11. SOME FOLKS WOULD MISS THE PEOPLE THEY WORK WITH IF
THEY CHANGED JOBS: OTHERS WOULDN'T REALLY CARE. HOW IS
IT WITH YOU?

Would miss co-workers	53
Would miss some but not others	5
Would not miss co-workers	36
Not ascertained	6
Total	100

B12. WAS THERE A TIME WHEN YOU EARNED MORE ON YOUR JOB
THAN YOU DID IN 1965? WHEN WAS THAT?

Before 1960	13.5
1960	2.1
1961	1.9
1962	1.8
1963	3.9
1964	8.1
Not ascertained	2.5
Did not earn more in a previous year	66.2
Total	100.0

B13. ARE YOU NOW EARNING MORE THAN YOU DID FIVE YEARS AGO?	Percent of Nonretired Family Heads (35-59)
Yes	77
No	22
Not ascertained	1
Total	100

B13a. WHAT ARE THE MAIN REASONS YOU MAKE MORE?

Achievement (deserved better pay; did a good job)	5
Advancement (more years on job; moved to better job)	16
Job mobility	8
Inflation; "everybody got a raise"	8
Non-inflation external forces (better economic conditions, union negotiations)	6
Superficial reasons	40
Other reasons	3
Not ascertained	1
Not earning more now; N.A. whether earning more now	23
Total	*

B14. COMPARING YOURSELF WITH OTHER PEOPLE WHO ARE IN A SIMILAR LINE OF WORK, WOULD YOU SAY THAT DURING THE LAST FEW YEARS YOUR INCOME HAS INCREASED IN THE SAME WAY AS THEIRS, OR DID IT INCREASE LESS OR MORE THAN THEIRS?

Increased much more than others'	1
Increased (somewhat) more than others'	16
Increased about the same	56
Increased (somewhat) less than others'	12
Increased much less than others'	1
Decreased	1
Doesn't know relative change in income	7
Not ascertained	6
Total	100

B15. WHAT IS THE HIGHEST AMOUNT YOU ARE EVER LIKELY TO EARN IN YOUR LINE OF WORK?

Less than $3500	7
$3501 - 5500	11
$5501 - 7500	15
$7501 - 10,500	19
$10,501 - 15,500	16
$15,501 - 25,500	10
$25,501 and over	5
Doesn't know	12
Not ascertained	5
Total	100

Adds to more than 100 percent because some respondents mentioned more than one thing.

B16. HOW MANY WEEKS WERE YOU UNEMPLOYED
LAST YEAR?

Percent of Nonretired
Family Heads (35-59)

One	1.2
Two	0.8
Three	1.3
Four	1.6
Five to seven	1.6
Eight	1.2
Nine or more	6.1
Not ascertained	1.0
Not unemployed in 1965	85.2
Total	100.0

B17. HOW MANY WEEKS WERE YOU ILL OR NOT WORKING FOR
ANY OTHER REASON LAST YEAR?

One	8.4
Two	3.6
Three	2.8
Four	2.4
Five to seven	2.3
Eight	1.1
Nine or more	4.3
Not ascertained	2.8
Did not lose work because of illness, etc., in 1965	74.3
Total	100.0

B18. SOME PEOPLE WOULD LIKE TO WORK MORE HOURS A WEEK
IF THEY COULD BE PAID FOR IT; OTHERS WOULD NOT. HOW
IS IT WITH YOU?

Strongly would prefer more work/pay	25
Would prefer more work/pay	4
Pro-con response	1
Would not prefer more work/pay	1
Strongly would not prefer more work/pay	62
Not ascertained	6
Total	100

B19. SOME PEOPLE WOULD LIKE TO WORK FEWER HOURS A WEEK
EVEN IF THEY EARNED LESS. HOW DO YOU FEEL ABOUT THIS?

Strongly would prefer less work/pay	8
Would prefer less work/pay	3
Pro-con response	1
Would not prefer less work/pay	1
Strongly would not prefer less work/pay	82
Not ascertained	5
Total	100

	Percent of Nonretired Family Heads (35-59)
B20. SOME PEOPLE FEEL AS HEALTHY AND YOUNG AS THEY DID SEVERAL YEARS AGO, WHILE OTHERS FEEL THAT THEIR HEALTH IS NOT QUITE AS GOOD AS IT WAS THEN. HOW IS IT WITH YOU?	
Health much better now	1
Health better now	6
Health same, as good	43
Health worse now	30
Health much worse now	1
Not ascertained (including responses where no comparison was given)	19
Total	100
B21. HAVE YOU LOST MANY WORKDAYS BECAUSE OF ILLNESS DURING THE LAST FIVE YEARS?	
Many days lost	13
Some days lost	5
Only a few days lost; none lost	80
Not ascertained	2
Total	100
B22. HAVE YOU HAD AN ILLNESS, PHYSICAL CONDITION OR NERVOUS CONDITION WHICH LIMITS THE TYPE OF WORK OR THE AMOUNT OF WORK YOU CAN DO? HOW MUCH DOES IT LIMIT YOUR WORK?	
Complete limitation on work	0.2
Severe limitation on work	1.3
Some limitation on work	8.7
Limitation on work not ascertained	1.0
Whether disability not ascertained	0.7
No work-limiting disability	88.1
Total	100.0
B23. HOW LONG DOES IT TAKE YOU TO GET FROM YOUR HOME TO WHERE YOU WORK?	
Less than 15 minutes	14.8
15 to 30 minutes	12.3
More than 30 minutes	5.8
Not ascertained	1.6
Not asked this question	65.5
Total	100.0

	Percent of Nonretired Family Heads (35-59)

B24.   DO YOU ORGANIZE YOUR OWN WORK OR VARY ITS PACE, OR IS IT ALL DETERMINED BY A PRODUCTION LINE OR A CREW THAT HAS TO KEEP TOGETHER?

Has substantial control over work pace	21.4
Has some control, but does not consider it substantial	2.9
Does not have control over work pace	8.8
Not ascertained	1.4
Not asked this question	65.5
Total	100.0

SECTION C.   RETIREMENT AND THE FUTURE

C2.   WE'RE INTERESTED IN WHAT PEOPLE SEE FOR THEMSELVES IN THE FUTURE.   WHAT WILL THINGS BE LIKE FOR YOU WHEN YOU ARE SIXTY;   WHAT WILL YOU BE DOING THEN?

The question was coded in terms of these frames of reference: (1)   job vs. recreational activities, (2)   good vs. bad, and (3)   change vs. no change.

Job reference (e.g., "I'll be working then")	65
Recreational reference	5
Neither of these references occurred	22
Not ascertained	8
Total	100

"Good" reference (e.g., "Things will be good for me then")	3
"Bad" reference	1
Neither reference occurred	88
Not ascertained	8
Total	100

"Change" reference (e.g., "I'll be retired instead of working")	19
"No change" reference	41
Neither reference occurred	32
Not ascertained	8
Total	100

C3.   DO YOU THINK YOU'LL BE LIVING HERE IN THIS COMMUNITY THEN, OR IN ANOTHER CITY, OR WHERE?

Will live in same community	68
Will live in another community	14
Doesn't know	10
Not ascertained	8
Total	100

C4. WHO WILL BE LIVING WITH YOU THEN?

No one	10
Wife only	59
One person other than wife	4
Two people	8
Three people	5
Four or more people	3
Doesn't know	7
Not ascertained	4
Total	100

C5. NOW THINKING ABOUT THE PEOPLE YOU KNOW WHO ARE AROUND
SEVENTY YEARS OLD -- WOULD YOU SAY THEY ARE MOSTLY SATISFIED
OR DISSATISFIED WITH THEIR FINANCIAL SITUATION?

Satisfied	49
Pro-con response	7
Dissatisfied	32
Doesn't know	9
Not ascertained	3
Total	100

C6. DO YOU THINK YOU WILL FEEL THIS WAY WHEN YOU ARE SEVENTY?

Yes	50
No	24
Doesn't know whether will be like them	14
Doesn't know financial situation of 70-year-olds	12
Total	100

C7. DO YOU THINK YOU WILL BE BETTER OFF OR
WORSE OFF THAN THEY ARE?

Better off	20.5
Worse off	2.1
Not ascertained	1.6
Respondent feels that his financial situation will be similar to that of current 70-year-olds	75.8
Total	100.0

	Percent of Nonretired Family Heads (35-59)
C7a. WHY IS THAT?	

The question was coded in terms of the following
  frames of reference:

Health	1.3
Financial considerations	19.6
Job	2.0
Family	0.7
Recreational activities	0.7
Planning for retirement	0.9
Other frame of reference	1.2
Not ascertained	1.6
Respondent feels that his financial situation will be similar to that of current 70-year-olds	75.9
Total	*

C8. WE ARE INTERESTED IN YOUR THOUGHTS ABOUT
THE QUESTION OF WHEN IT'S A GOOD TIME TO RETIRE.
FIRST OF ALL, HAVE YOUR IDEAS ABOUT RETIREMENT
CHANGED IN RECENT YEARS? IN WHAT WAY HAVE THEY CHANGED?

Ideas have changed in a direction favorable to (early) retirement	8.2
Ideas have changed in a direction unfavorable to (early) retirement	2.7
Ideas about retirement have changed, but direction not ascertained	1.1
Ideas have not changed	21.7
Not ascertained whether ideas have changed	0.8
Not asked this question	65.5
Total	100.0

C9. HAVE YOU DISCUSSED THIS QUESTION WITH YOUR WIFE?

Yes	39
No	44
Head is not married	17
Total	100

C10. WHEN DOES YOUR WIFE THINK YOU SHOULD RETIRE --
I MEAN AT WHAT AGE?

Before 60	5.1
60 - 64	9.3
65 - 69	9.9
70 or older	0.9
Never	2.0
Wife leaves decision to head	3.1
Doesn't know what wife thinks about retirement age	3.0
Not ascertained	0.9
Not married or hasn't talked about retirement with wife	60.8
Total	100.0

---

* Adds to more than 100 percent because some respondents mentioned
more than one reason

C10a.   WHY DOES SHE THINK THAT?

Percent of Nonretired
Family Heads (35-59)

The question was coded in terms of the following
frames of reference:*

Health	6.4
Finances	5.9
Job	2.8
Family	3.3
Recreational activities	7.7
Deserves retirement, has worked long enough	1.1
Compulsory retirement age mentioned	3.0
Other frames of reference	1.8
Not ascertained	9.5
Not married or hasn't talked with wife about retirement	60.8
Total	**

---

* Some illustrations of the frames of reference used in this
and subsequent questions follow:

Health	association of work activity with good health and/or retirement with poor health; association of continued work with poor health and of retirement with good health
Finances	need for job income and/or fear of inadequate retirement income; anticipation of adequate retirement income
Job	enjoyment of job and/or co-workers; dislike of job
Family	need for income from work to support family members, feeling that family members do not want one to retire; desire for more leisure time to be spent with family
Recreational activities	fear of boredom after retirement; anticipation of leisure time activities after retirement
Pressure to leave work	feeling that co-workers, union, or employer is encouraging respondent to leave work
Deserves retirement	feeling that one has worked long enough, has contributed his share to society

** Adds to more than 100 percent because some respondents mentioned more
than one reason.

	Percent of Nonretired Family Heads (35-59)
C11. HAVE YOU TALKED ABOUT THE QUESTION OF WHEN TO RETIRE WITH OTHER PEOPLE?	
Yes	32
No	66
Not ascertained	2
Total	100

C12. WHEN DO YOU THINK YOU WILL RETIRE FROM THE MAIN WORK YOU ARE NOW DOING -- I MEAN AT WHAT AGE?

Before 60	10
60 - 64	26
65 - 69	35
70 or older (definite age given)	3
Head plans to work as long as able	7
Head "never" plans to retire	5
Doesn't know	10
Not ascertained	4
Total	100

C12a. WHY DO YOU THINK SO?

The question was coded in terms of the following frames of reference:

Health	16
Finances	24
Job	13
Family	3
Recreational activities	8
Pressure to leave work	2
Deserves retirement, has worked long enough	2
Other frames of reference	5
Mentions only compulsory retirement age	21
Not ascertained	16
Total	*

C13. MANY PEOPLE NOW RETIRE BEFORE THEY ARE SIXTY-FIVE. WHY DO YOU THINK THEY DO THIS?

The question was coded in terms of the following frames of reference:

Health	37
Finances	48
Job	20
Family	1
Recreational activities	19
Pressure to leave work	3
Other frames of reference	2
Mentions only compulsory retirement age	1
Not ascertained	7
Total	*

---

* Adds to more than 100 percent because some respondents mentioned more than one reason.

	Percent of Nonretired Family Heads (35-59)
C14. DO YOU KNOW ANYONE WHO HAS RETIRED EARLY?	
Yes	47
No	51
Not ascertained	2
Total	100
C15. DO YOU THINK EMPLOYERS ARE PUTTING PRESSURE ON PEOPLE TO RETIRE EARLY THESE DAYS?	
Yes	27
Some are; some are not	12
No	45
Doesn't know	14
Not ascertained	2
Total	100
C16. HOW ABOUT THE UNIONS? (ARE THEY URGING EARLY RETIREMENT?)	
Yes	31
Some are, some are not	2
No	23
Doesn't know	41
Not ascertained	3
Total	100
C17. NOW ABOUT YOUR INCOME AND FINANCIAL SITUATION AFTER RETIREMENT, SOME PEOPLE FEEL SURE THAT THEY WILL BE FAIRLY COMFORTABLE AT THAT TIME, WHILE OTHERS THINK THAT RETIREMENT WILL CAUSE FINANCIAL PROBLEMS FOR THEM. HOW IS IT WITH YOU?	
Expects favorable situation	30
Expects somewhat favorable situation	32
Pro-con response	2
Expects somewhat unfavorable situation	14
Expects unfavorable situation	5
Doesn't know; "depends"	10
Not ascertained	7
Total	100
C18. WILL YOU GET SOCIAL SECURITY WHEN YOU RETIRE?	
Yes	93
No	6
Not ascertained	1
Total	100

	Percent of Nonretired Family Heads (35-59)

C19. WILL YOU GET OTHER GOVERNMENT PENSIONS OR
RAILROAD RETIREMENT?

Yes	9.7
No	28.3
Not ascertained*	62.0
Total	100.0

C20. WILL YOUR WIFE BE ELIGIBLE FOR SOCIAL SECURITY
BENEFITS BECAUSE OF HER OWN WORK?

Yes	50
No	31
Not ascertained	2
Not married	17
Total	100

C21. HOW MUCH INCOME PER MONTH CAN YOU (AND YOUR WIFE)
EXPECT FROM SOCIAL SECURITY OR OTHER GOVERNMENT
OR RAILROAD PENSIONS?

Less than $50	2
$50 - 99	2
$100-149	7
$150-199	8
$200-249	7
$250 and over	11
"The maximum"	10
Doesn't know	50
Not ascertained	3
Total	100

C22. WHAT ABOUT OTHER PENSIONS -- WILL YOU (OR YOUR WIFE)
RECEIVE ANY PRIVATE PENSIONS WHEN YOU RETIRE?

Yes	40
No	58
Not ascertained	2
Total	100

---

* The question was restructured for the second wave of the survey;
  this produced the large "not ascertained" category.

	Percent of Nonretired Family Heads (35-59)
C23. HOW MUCH INCOME DO YOU EXPECT UNDER THE PENSION PLAN IF YOU RETIRE AT THE REGULAR RETIREMENT AGE?	
$1 - 49 (per month)	1.3
$50 - 99	3.3
$100 - 149	5.0
$150 - 199	2.6
$200 - 299	5.3
$300 - 499	5.2
$500 and over	3.3
Doesn't know amount, but will receive	13.9
Will not receive private pension; N.A. whether will receive	60.1
Total	100.0

	Percent of Nonretired Family Heads (35-59)
C24. IS THERE AN EARLIER TIME AT WHICH YOU MAY RETIRE AND STILL RECEIVE PENSIONS?	
Yes	24.7
No	12.9
Not ascertained	2.3
Will not receive private pension; N.A. whether will receive	60.1
Total	100.0

C24a. WHAT IS THE EARLIEST TIME?	
Before age 50	0.9
50 - 54	1.5
55 - 59	6.4
60 - 64	8.9
Not ascertained	7.0
Will not receive private pension before regular retirement age	75.3
Total	100.0

C25. HOW MUCH WOULD YOU RECEIVE SHOULD YOU RETIRE AT THAT TIME?	
$1 - 49 (per month)	0.6
$50 - 99	2.0
$100 - 149	2.0
$150 - 199	1.5
$200 - 299	2.7
$300 - 499	2.2
$500 and over	0.9
Doesn't know amount, but can receive early pension	12.6
Not ascertained	0.2
Will not receive private pension before regular retirement age	75.3
Total	100.0

	Percent of Nonretired Family Heads (35-59)

C26. SUPPOSE YOU WANTED TO CHANGE JOBS, WOULD YOU LOSE THE PENSION RIGHTS OR SOME PART OF THEM BY QUITTING YOUR PRESENT JOB?

Would lose all pension rights	14.3
Would lose some pension rights	6.2
Would lose pension rights, N.A. whether some or all	3.4
Would retain all pension rights	9.7
Doesn't know	2.4
Not ascertained	3.9
Will not receive private pension	60.1
Total	100.0

C27. DO YOU HAVE SOME ANNUITY POLICIES OR SOME INSURANCE THAT TURNS INTO CASH OR INTO A PENSION WHILE YOU ARE STILL LIVING?

Yes	27
No	72
Not ascertained	1
Total	100

C27a. HOW MUCH DO YOU EXPECT FROM THEM?

Per-month Amount:

$1 - 49	1.3
$50 - 99	2.7
$100 - 149	2.5
$150 - 199	1.0
$200 - 299	1.9
$300 - 499	0.7
$500 and over	0.2
Doesn't know amount, but will receive	1.3
Not ascertained	5.7
Will not receive monthly annuity	82.7
Total	100.0

C27a. (continued)

Lump-sum Amount:

$1 - 499	0.1
$500 - 999	0.2
$1000 - 1999	1.2
$2000 - 2999	1.3
$3000 - 4999	1.1
$5000 - 7499	3.1
$7500 - 9996	1.0
$9997 - and over	5.0
Amount not ascertained	6.0
Will not receive lump-sum annuity	81.0
Total	100.0

	Percent of Nonretired Family Heads (35-59)

C28. WILL YOU HAVE SOME LIFE INSURANCE
THAT IS ALL PAID UP BY THE TIME YOU RETIRE?

Yes	61
No	37
Not ascertained	2
Total	100

C29. SOME PEOPLE EXPECT TO DO SOME WORK OR GO INTO
BUSINESS FOR THEMSELVES AFTER THEY RETIRE.
DO YOU THINK YOU MIGHT DO SOMETHING LIKE THIS?

Yes	43
No	54
Not ascertained	3
Total	100

C30. WILL YOU WORK FOR SOMEONE ELSE, OR YOURSELF,
OR WHAT?

Self	10.8
Someone else	4.5
Not ascertained	0.7
Will not work after retirement	18.5
Not asked this question	65.5
Total	100.0

C31. WILL THE WORK BE PART-TIME OR FULL-TIME?

Part-time	12.4
Full-time	2.8
Not ascertained	0.8
Will not work after retirement	18.5
Not asked this question	65.5
Total	100.0

C32. HOW MUCH DO YOU THINK YOU MIGHT EARN?

$1 - 499	0.8
$500 - 999	1.8
$1000 - 1999	7.6
$2000 - 2999	3.1
$3000 - 4999	2.5
$5000 - 7499	2.5
$7500 - 9996	0.8
$9997 and over	1.6
Will receive earnings, but amount not ascertained	21.9
Will not work after retirement	57.4
Total	100.0

Percent of Nonretired
Family Heads (35-59)

C34. HOW ABOUT YOUR WIFE. DO YOU THINK
SHE WILL WORK AFTER YOU RETIRE?

Yes	7
Perhaps	6
No	65
Doesn't know	3
Not ascertained	2
Not married	17
Total	100

C35. DO YOU EXPECT TO GIVE ANY FINANCIAL HELP TO
YOUR CHILDREN AFTER YOU RETIRE?

Yes	14
Perhaps	17
No	62
Doesn't know	3
Not ascertained	4
Total	100

C36. DO YOU EXPECT TO RECEIVE ANY FINANCIAL SUPPORT
FROM YOUR CHILDREN, FROM RELATIVES, OR FROM ANYONE ELSE
AFTER YOU RETIRE?

Yes	2
Perhaps	3
No	91
Doesn't know	1
Not ascertained	3
Total	100

C37. SOME PEOPLE LOOK FORWARD TO RETIREMENT BECAUSE THEY
WISH TO HAVE MORE TIME TO DO THINGS; OTHERS THINK THEY
MIGHT BE BORED AFTER THEY RETIRE, HOW IS IT WITH YOU?

Looks forward strongly to retirement	6
Looks forward to retirement	49
Pro-con response	6
Does not look forward to retirement; dreads it	23
Does not look forward to retirement at all; strongly dreads it	6
Not ascertained	10
Total	100

C38. DO YOU THINK YOU WILL MOVE INTO A DIFFERENT HOUSE OR APARTMENT AFTER YOU RETIRE?	Percent of Nonretired Family Heads (35-59)
Yes	13.3
No	14.7
Doesn't know	6.4
Not ascertained	0.1
Not asked this question	65.5
Total	100.0

C39. DO YOU HAVE ANY HOBBIES YOU HOPE TO SPEND MORE TIME ON WHEN YOU RETIRE?

Yes	64
No	35
Not ascertained	1
Total	100

C39a. WHAT ARE THEY?

Active hobbies (e.g., carpentry, gardening)	22
Inactive hobbies (e.g., writing, collecting)	16
Sports and games	46
Travel and vacationing	7
Relaxing, loafing, sitting around	2
Other activities	2
Does not have hobbies to pursue later (or N.A. whether hobbies)	36
Total	*

C40. HOW ABOUT WORK WITHOUT PAY FOR CHURCH, CHARITY, OR YOUR CHILDREN: WILL YOU BE DOING MORE OF THAT WHEN YOU RETIRE, OR LESS THAN YOU DO NOW?

Expects to do more such work	45
Expects to do about the same amount	19
Expects to do less	8
Not ascertained; might do more or less	28
Total	100

---

* Adds to more than 100 percent because some respondents mentioned more than one activity.

	Percent of Nonretired Family Heads (35-59)

C41. WHAT OTHER THINGS DO YOU THINK YOU
WILL DO AFTER YOU RETIRE?

Active hobbies	10
Inactive hobbies	5
Sports and games	10
Travel and vacationing	35
Relaxing, loafing, sitting around	8
Other activities	9
Doesn't know	10
Not ascertained	10
Does not plan to do anything after retirement other than that mentioned in C39-C40	19
Total	*

C42. IN YOUR OPINION, DO YOUNGER PEOPLE FEEL THAT
OLDER WORKERS SHOULD RETIRE EARLY AND MAKE ROOM FOR OTHERS?

Most younger people feel this way	58
Some feel this way	5
None feel this way; only a few do	22
Doesn't know	11
Not ascertained	4
Total	100

C42a. HOW DO YOU FEEL ABOUT IT?

Agrees strongly that older people should retire to make jobs available	5
Agrees that older people should retire	33
Pro-con response	6
Disagrees that older people should retire	41
Disagrees strongly that older people should retire	8
Not ascertained	7
Total	100

C43. SOME PEOPLE SAVE FOR THEIR OLD AGE TO ADD TO
THEIR PENSIONS AND SOCIAL SECURITY. WHAT ABOUT SAVINGS
ACCOUNTS, GOVERNMENT BONDS, AND DEPOSITS IN SAVINGS AND
LOAN ASSOCIATIONS AND CREDIT UNIONS -- DO YOU EXPECT TO
HAVE ANY OF THESE WHEN YOU RETIRE?

Yes	69
No	28
Not ascertained	3
Total	100

---

* Adds to more than 100 percent because some respondents
mentioned more than one activity.

	Percent of Nonretired Family Heads (35-59)

C44. DO YOU EXPECT TO HAVE ANY COMMON STOCK
OR FARMS OR OTHER REAL ESTATE, NOT COUNTING
YOUR HOME?

Yes	42
No	55
Not ascertained	3
Total	100

C45. WHAT ABOUT INVESTMENTS IN BUSINESS, DO YOU
EXPECT TO HAVE ANY OF THESE?

Yes	18
No	78
Not ascertained	4
Total	100

C46. HOW MUCH DO YOU PEOPLE EXPECT TO HAVE ALTOGETHER
IN THESE SAVINGS AND INVESTMENTS (THE ONES I JUST MENTIONED
IN THE PRECEDING QUESTIONS) BY THE TIME YOU RETIRE?

Less than $100	9
$100 - 499	1
$500 - 1999	4
$2000 - 4999	8
$5000 - 9999	17
$10,000 - 24,999	21
$25,000 - 49,999	15
$50,000 - 99,999	9
$100,000 or more	8
Not ascertained	8
Total	100

C47. HOW MUCH DO YOU HAVE RIGHT NOW ALTOGETHER IN
SAVINGS AND INVESTMENTS LIKE THESE?

Less than $100	23
$100 - 499	7
$500 - 1999	12
$2000 - 4999	14
$5000 - 9999	11
$10,000 - 24,999	13
$25,000 - 49,999	7
$50,000 - 99,999	4
$100,000 or more	3
Not ascertained	6
Total	100

SECTION D: INCOME; WIFE'S OCCUPATION

D1. TO GET AN ACCURATE PICTURE OF PEOPLE'S
FINANCIAL SITUATION, WE NEED TO KNOW THE INCOME
OF ALL THE FAMILIES THAT WE INTERVIEW. WOULD YOU
PLEASE TELL ME THE LETTER OF THE GROUP ON THIS CARD THAT
INDICATES HOW MUCH INCOME YOU RECEIVED FROM WAGES AND
SALARIES IN 1965, INCLUDING ANY INCOME FROM OVERTIME,
BONUSES, OR COMMISSIONS, I MEAN BEFORE DEDUCTIONS FOR TAXES
OR ANYTHING ELSE.

Less than $1000	11
$1000 - 1999	3
$2000 - 2999	6
$3000 - 4999	14
$5000 - 7499	25
$7500 - 9999	18
$10,000 and over	22
Not ascertained	1
Total	100

D5. TAKING EVERYTHING TOGETHER, WOULD YOU PLEASE TELL ME
THE LETTER OF THE GROUP ON THIS CARD THAT INDICATES HOW
MUCH INCOME YOU AND YOUR FAMILY RECEIVED FROM ALL SOURCES
DURING THE YEAR 1965, I MEAN BEFORE TAXES OR ANY DEDUCTIONS

Less than $1000	1
$1000 - 1999	2
$2000 - 2999	4
$3000 - 3999	5
$4000 - 4999	7
$5000 - 7499	21
$7500 - 9999	31
$10,000 - 14,999	23
$15,000 and over	15
Not ascertained	1
Total	100

D6. SINCE THE FIRST OF THIS YEAR, 1966, HAS YOUR TOTAL
FAMILY INCOME GONE UP, REMAINED THE SAME, OR GONE DOWN?

Gone up	57
Remained the same	28
Gone down	14
Not ascertained	1
Total	100

	Percent of Nonretired Family Heads (35-59)
D6a. WHY IS THIS?	

If went up:

Increase in pay rate	33
Increase in number of hours worked by family members	19
Increase in profits or self-employment income	2
Other reasons for income increase; reason not ascertained	3

If went down:

Decrease in pay rate	2
Decrease in number of hours worked by family members	10
Decrease in profits or self-employment income	1
Other reasons for income decline; reason not ascertained	1
Income did not change; N.A. whether income changes	29
Total	100

B53. DID YOUR WIFE DO ANY WORK FOR MONEY LAST YEAR?

Yes	38
No	45
Not married	17
Total	100

B54. WHAT KIND OF WORK DID SHE DO?

Professional and technical workers	4.5
Managers and nonself-employed officials	1.1
Self-employed businesswomen	1.5
Clerical and sales workers	14.0
Craftsmen and foremen	0.2
Operatives and kindred	6.7
Unskilled laborers and service workers	8.4
Farmers and farm managers	0.2
Miscellaneous; not ascertained	1.2
Wife did not work for money in 1965; not married	62.2
Total	100.0

B55. WHAT KIND OF BUSINESS IS THAT IN?	Percent of Nonretired Family heads (35-59)
Agriculture, forestry, and fishing	0.5
Mining and extracting	7.0
Construction	0.4
Transportation, communications, and utilities	1.0
Retail and wholesale trade	7.9
Finances, insurance, and real estate	2.1
Services (including professional services)	7.9
Government medical, health, and educational services (including all federal employees)	9.1
Not ascertained	1.8
Wife did not work for money in 1965; not married	62.2
Total	100.0

B56. WAS SHE WORKING FOR SOMEONE ELSE, HERSELF, OR WHAT?	
Someone else	34.4
Self	2.7
Not ascertained	0.7
Wife did not work for money in 1965; not married	62.2
	100.0

B57. DID SHE WORK FULL TIME OR PART TIME?	
Full time	17.9
Part time	18.2
Not ascertained	1.7
Wife did not work for money in 1965; not married	62.2
Total	100.0

SECTION E: HOUSING

E1. DO YOU OWN THIS HOME OR PAY RENT OR WHAT?	
Owns house or apartment	73
Owns trailer	1
Rents	24
Neither owns nor rents	2
Total	100

CURRENT INCOME--EXPECTED RETIREMENT INCOME DIFFERENCE	Percent of nonretired family heads (35-59)
Current family income is 6 or more brackets greater than expected pension income	6
Current income is 5 brackets greater than expected pension income	8
Current income is 4 brackets greater than expected pension income	15
Current income is 3 brackets greater than expected pension income	24
Current income is 2 brackets greater than expected pension income	23
Current income is 1 bracket greater than expected pension income	14
Current income is less than or equal to expected pension income	9
Current income not ascertained	1
Total	100

OCCUPATIONAL CRITERIA COMBINATION CODE*	
Achievement/accomplishment is ranked first	36
Steady income or job security is ranked first	42
High income is ranked first or second (if neither of above)	11
Other combinations of rankings (including not ascertained cases)	11
Total	100

---

*For an elaboration of these codes, see pages 187-188.

SECTION F: INFORMATION ABOUT THE FAMILY

F1.   ARE YOU MARRIED, SINGLE, WIDOWED, DIVORCED,
      OR SEPARATED?

Married	83
Single	4
Widowed	6
Divorced	5
Separated	2
Total	100

F2.   HOW LONG HAVE YOU BEEN MARRIED?

Less than 5 years	4
5-9 years	5
10-19 years	31
20 years and over	43
Not married	17
Total	100

F3-F7.   HOW MANY GRADES OF SCHOOL DID YOU FINISH?
         HAVE YOU HAD ANY OTHER SCHOOLING?
         WHAT OTHER SCHOOLING DID YOU HAVE?
         DO YOU HAVE A COLLEGE DEGREE?
         WHAT DEGREE(S) DO YOU HAVE?

0-5 grades	5
6-8 grades	20
9-11 grades	20
12 grades	16
12 grades plus nonacademic training	12
College, no degree	13
College, Bachelor's degree	7
College, advanced or professional degree	6
Not ascertained	1
Total	100

F8-F9.   IS YOUR CHURCH PREFERENCE PROTESTANT, CATHOLIC,
         OR JEWISH?   (IF PROTESTANT) WHAT DENOMINATION
         IS THAT?

Baptists	6.7
Methodists	4.9
Episcopalians	1.0
Presbyterians	1.6
Lutherans	3.0
Congregationalists; Christian Scientists; Dutch Reformed; Quakers; Latter Day Saints; Unitarians; Bahai; Evangelical and Reformed	3.6
Other Protestants	3.5
Catholic	7.6
Jewish	1.3
Other; none	1.3
Not asked this question	65.5
Total	100.0

F10.   ABOUT HOW OFTEN DO YOU USUALLY ATTEND   Percent of nonretired
       RELIGIOUS SERVICES?   family heads (35-59)

More than once a week	3.2
Once a week	9.0
Two to three times a month	4.5
Once a month	2.5
A few times a year	10.3
Never	4.7
Not ascertained	0.3
Not asked this question	65.5
Total	100.0

F11.   ARE THERE ANY PEOPLE THAT DO NOT LIVE WITH YOU
       WHO ARE DEPENDENT ON YOU FOR MORE THAN HALF OF
       THEIR SUPPORT?

The number of such dependents was coded:

One	4.9
Two	1.3
Three	0.5
Four or more	0.3
Number of dependents not ascertained	0.4
No nonresident dependents	92.6
Total	100.0

F11a.   (IF NONRESIDENT DEPENDENTS)   HOW OLD ARE THEY?

One or more under 25	5.1
One or more 25-64	0.4
One or more under 25 and one or more 25-64	0.1
One or more 65 and over	1.0
One or more under 25 and one or more 65 and over	0.1
One or more 25-64 and one or more 65 and over	0.1
One or more under 25 and one or more 25-64 and one or more 65 and over	0.1
Not ascertained	0.4
No nonresident dependents; N.A. whether nonresident dependents	93.0
Total	100.0

SECTION G: BY OBSERVATION ONLY (FILLED OUT BY INTERVIEWER)

G1.   SEX OF FAMILY UNIT HEAD

Male	90
Female	10
Total	100

G2.   IS THE RESPONDENT THE HEAD OF THE FAMILY UNIT?

Yes	95
No	5
Total	100

G3. RACE	Percent of nonretired family heads (35-59)
White	91
Negro	8
Other	1
Total	100

G6. TYPE OF STRUCTURE IN WHICH FAMILY LIVES

Detached single-family house	80
2-4 family house, duplex, or row house	11
Apartment house (5 or more units, 3 stories or less)	6
Apartment house (5 or more units, 4 stories or more)	2
Other	1
Total	100

DEMOGRAPHIC ITEMS CODED FOR EACH INTERVIEW

SIZE OF PLACE WHERE RESPONDENT LIVES

In central cities of the 12 largest Standard Metropolitan Areas	12
In cities of 50,000 and over population (exclusive of the central cities of the 12 largest SMA's)	17
Urban places with 10,000-49,999 population	18
Urban places with 2500-9999 population	22
Rural areas near a metropolitan area	7
Rural areas not near a metropolitan area	24
Total	100

REGION OF COUNTY WHERE INTERVIEW TAKEN*

Northeast	25
North Central states	31
South	27
West	17
Total	100

---

*The above definition is that used by the U.S. Bureau of the Census. Northeast includes Conn., Maine, Mass., N.H., N.J., N.Y., Penna., R. I., and Vt. The North Central states include Ill., Ind., Iowa, Kan., Mich., Minn., Mo., Neb., N.D., Ohio, S.D., and Wisc. The South includes Ala., Ark., Del., Fla., Ga., Ky., La., Md., Miss., N.C., Okla., S.C., Tenna., Texas, Va., Wash. D.C., and W. Va. The West includes Ariz., Calif., Colo., Id., Mont., N.M., Nev., Oreg., Utah., Wash., and Wyo.

VARIABLES CONSTRUCTED FOR NONRETIRED RESPONDENTS	Percent of nonretired family heads (35-59)
EXPECTED RETIREMENT PENSION AND ANNUITY INCOME	
Less than $1000	2
$1000-1999	18
$2000-2999	28
$3000-3999	17
$4000-4999	12
$5000-5999	8
$6000-7499	7
$7500-9999	5
$10,000-14,999	2
$15,000 and over	1
Total	100
POTENTIAL RETIREMENT INCOME FROM ASSETS	
Less than $1000	32
$1000-1999	26
$2000-2999	14
$3000-3999	9
$4000-4999	4
$5000-5999	5
$6000-7499	3
$7500-9999	3
$10,000 and over	4
Total	100
POTENTIAL TOTAL RETIREMENT INCOME (SUM OF PENSION INCOME AND ASSET INCOME)	
Less than $1000	1
$1000-1999	8
$2000-2999	13
$3000-3999	12
$4000-4999	13
$5000-5999	11
$6000-7499	12
$7500-9999	13
$10,000-14,999	12
$15,000 and over	5
Total	100
FAMILY HEAD'S AGE WHEN HOME IS OWNED MORTGAGE-FREE	
Before 51	28
51-55	12
56-60	12
61-64	9
65-70	8
71 and over	4
Does not own home	27
Total	100

PART II: THE RETIRED

INFORMATION CODED FROM FIRST PAGE OF QUESTIONNAIRE	Percent of Retired Family Heads

(Questions 1 - 4 not coded)

5. LIST ALL PERSONS, INCLUDING CHILDREN, LIVING IN THE DWELLING UNIT, BY THEIR RELATION TO THE HEAD

FROM QUESTION 5. AGE OF FAMILY HEAD

Less than 35	1
35 - 44	3
45 - 49	3
50 - 54	3
55 - 59	6
60 - 64	11
65 - 69	22
70 - 74	23
75 and over	28
Total	100

FROM QUESTION 5. AGE OF WIFE OF FAMILY HEAD

Less than 35	1
35 - 44	3
45 - 54	8
55 - 64	17
65 and over	29
Not married	42
Total	100

FROM QUESTION 5. NUMBER OF ADULTS IN FAMILY UNIT

One	33
Two	55
Three	9
Four or more	3
Total	100

FROM QUESTION 5. NUMBER OF CHILDREN (UNDER 18) IN FAMILY UNIT

One	5
Two	4
Three	2
Four or more	2
No children	87
Total	100

A1. WE ARE INTERESTED IN HOW PEOPLE ARE GETTING ALONG
FINANCIALLY THESE DAYS. WOULD YOU SAY THAT YOU AND YOUR
FAMILY ARE BETTER OFF OR WORSE OFF FINANCIALLY THAN YOU
WERE A YEAR AGO?

Better now	13
Same	59
Worse now	27
Not ascertained (including "uncertain")	1
Total	100

A2. ARE YOU PEOPLE MAKING AS MUCH MONEY NOW AS YOU WERE
A YEAR AGO, OR MORE, OR LESS?

More now	4.7
About the same	21.3
Less	7.6
Not ascertained	1.5
Not asked this question	64.9
Total	100.0

A3. NOW LOOKING AHEAD -- DO YOU THINK THAT A YEAR FROM NOW
YOU PEOPLE WILL BE BETTER OFF FINANCIALLY, OR WORSE OFF, OR
JUST ABOUT THE SAME AS NOW?

Better then	8
About the same	64
Worse then	15
Uncertain; doesn't know	12
Not ascertained	1
Total	100

SECTION B: FORMER OCCUPATION/CURRENT RETIREMENT SITUATION

B25. WHAT KIND OF WORK DID YOU DO WHEN YOU WORKED?

Professional and technical workers	9
Managers and nonself-employed officials	6
Self-employed businessmen and artisans	10
Clerical and sales workers	12
Craftsmen and foremen	13
Operatives and kindred	13
Unskilled laborers and service workers	19
Farmers and farm managers	10
Miscellaneous	8
Total	100

	Percent of Retired Family Heads
B26. WHAT KIND OF BUSINESS WAS THAT IN?	
Agriculture, forestry, and fishing	13
Mining and extracting	3
Manufacturing	20
Construction	8
Transportation, communications, and utilities	7
Retail and wholesale trade	15
Finance, insurance, and real estate	4
Services (including professional services)	13
Government medical, health, and educational services; all federal employees	14
Not ascertained	3
Total	100

B27. DID YOU WORK FOR SOMEONE ELSE, YOURSELF, OR WHAT?

Someone else	75
Self	20
Both self and someone else	3
Not ascertained	2
Total	100

B28. DID YOU SUPERVISE OTHER PEOPLE?

Yes	38
No	59
Not ascertained	3
Total	100

B29. WHEN DID YOU RETIRE?

The respondent's age at retirement was coded:

Less than 51	16
51 - 55	7
56 - 60	10
61 - 62	8
63 - 64	8
65	18
66 - 70	17
71 and over	11
Not ascertained	5
Total	100

B30. HOW DID YOU HAPPEN TO RETIRE WHEN YOU DID?	Percent of Retired Family Heads

The question was coded in terms of the following frames
of reference:*

Health	42
Finances	9
Job	9
Family	12
Recreational Activities	2
Pressure to leave work	8
Deserves retirement; worked long enough	1
Other frames of reference	4
Mentions only compulsory retirement age	12
Not ascertained	8
Total	**

B31.   THINKING BACK TO THE LAST FEW YEARS BEFORE YOU RETIRED,
WERE YOU BOTHERED BY ILLNESS OR HEALTH PROBLEMS THAT AFFECTED
YOUR WORK?   (IF YES) ABOUT HOW MANY WEEKS OF WORK DID YOU LOSE
BECAUSE OF YOUR HEALTH DURING THE TWO YEARS BEFORE YOU RETIRED?

1 - 2	0.3
3 - 4	0.6
5 - 8	1.5
9 - 12	1.3
More than 12	2.8
None lost because of illness	25.0
Not ascertained	3.6
Not asked this question	64.9
Total	100.0

B32.   HOW ABOUT UNEMPLOYMENT OR LACK OF WORK -- WERE YOU ABLE
TO WORK AS MUCH AS YOU WANTED BEFORE RETIREMENT?   (IF NO)
ABOUT HOW MANY WEEKS OF WORK DID YOU LOSE BECAUSE OF UNEMPLOY-
MENT DURING THE TWO YEARS BEFORE YOU RETIRED?

1 - 2	0.4
3 - 4	0.4
5 - 8	0.2
9 - 12	0.2
More than 12	1.3
None lost because of illness	29.0
Not ascertained	3.6
Not asked this question	64.9
Total	100.0

*For an elaboration of this code, see page 196 of this Appendix.

**Adds to more than 100 percent because some respondents mentioned more
than one thing.

B33. HOW DID YOU FEEL ABOUT RETIRING WHEN YOU DID?

Very good; very satisfied	9
Good; satisfied	29
Pro-con response	8
Bad; dissatisfied	30
Very bad; very dissatisfied	10
Not ascertained	14
Total	100

B34. HAD YOU PLANNED TO RETIRE THEN, OR DID YOU HAVE TO
RETIRE UNEXPECTEDLY, OR WHAT?

Retired as planned	41
Retired unexpectedly (including those who made plans but had to change them)	48
Not ascertained	11
Total	100

B34a. WHY DID YOU HAVE TO CHANGE YOUR PLANS?

Problems with job	8.9
Problems with health	28.7
Problems in family	6.2
Windfall gain enabled retirement	0.3
Combination of above reasons	0.4
Did not change retirement plans	51.4
Not ascertained	4.1
Total	100.0

B35. DID YOUR EMPLOYER URGE YOU TO RETIRE WHEN YOU DID?

Yes	13
No	55
Not ascertained	12
Respondent was self-employed	20
Total	100

B36. HOW DID YOUR WIFE FEEL ABOUT YOUR RETIRING WHEN YOU DID?

Very pleased; very satisfied	5
Pleased; satisfied	25
Pro-con response	9
Displeased; dissatisfied	10
Very displeased; very dissatisfied	3
Not ascertained	13
Not married at time of retirement	35
Total	100

	Percent of Retired Family Heads
B37. DID YOU HAVE ANY SAVINGS PUT AWAY WHEN YOU RETIRED?	
Yes	66
No	28
Not ascertained	6
Total	100
B38. WHAT ABOUT NOW; WOULD YOU SAY YOU HAVE MORE OR LESS IN SAVINGS THAN WHEN YOU RETIRED?	
More now	23
Same	41
Less now	29
Not ascertained	7
Total	100
B39. (IF SAVINGS HAVE DECREASED) WAS THIS AN UNEXPECTED DECREASE?	
Yes	9.6
Yes and no: some things expected, some unexpected	0.6
No	15.3
Not ascertained	4.0
Savings have not decreased	70.5
Total	100.0
B40. HAVE YOU HAD A CHANCE TO WORK FOR MONEY SINCE YOUR RETIREMENT?	
Yes	36
No	58
Not ascertained	6
Total	100
B41. HAVE YOU WORKED AT ALL SINCE YOU RETIRED?	
Yes	24.1
No	10.2
Not ascertained	1.6
Has not had chance to work for money	64.1
Total	100.0
B42. DID YOU WORK FOR SOMEONE ELSE, OR YOURSELF, OR WHAT?	
Someone else	8.0
Self	1.0
Both self and someone else	0.2
Not ascertained	0.7
Has not worked since retirement	25.2
Not asked this question	64.9
Total	100.0

Percent of Retired
Family Heads

B43. DID YOU WORK FOR MONEY AT ANY TIME DURING
1965? (IF NO) WHEN WAS THE LAST TIME YOU WORKED
FOR MONEY?

Before 1956	1.2
1956 - 1960	3.0
1961 - 1962	1.8
1963	1.2
1964	1.5
1965 - 1966	15.5
Has not worked since retirement	75.8
Total	100.0

B44. DO YOU DO ANY WORK WITHOUT PAY FOR CHURCH OR CHARITY
OR YOUR CHILDREN?

Yes	35
No	60
Not ascertained	5
Total	100

B44a. (IF DOES CHARITABLE WORK) ARE YOU DOING MORE OR
LESS OF THIS THAN BEFORE YOU RETIRED?

More	17.9
Same	9.8
Less	7.1
Not doing charitable work	65.2
Total	100.0

B45. HOW ABOUT YOUR CURRENT LIVING EXPENSES -- ARE YOU
SPENDING LESS THAN BEFORE YOU RETIRED, OR MORE, OR THE
SAME? IF LESS, IS IT A LOT LESS?

Spending more	47
Spending same	25
Spending less	15
Spending "a lot" less	8
Not ascertained	5
Total	100

	Percent of Retired Family Heads
B46. (IF LIVING EXPENSES HAVE CHANGED) WHAT ARE THE THINGS THAT MAKE A DIFFERENCE IN YOUR EXPENSES? ANYTHING ELSE?	
Medical and dental expenses	9
Change in debt position	1
Change in financial responsibility for family	6
Change in specific, ordinary living expenses	41
Changes associated with expenses for recreation and travel	5
Required downward change or desired upward shift in living standard	6
General reference to prices or cost of living	22
Other references	2
Not ascertained	1
No change in living expenses since retirement	30
Total	*

B47. ARE YOU GIVING ANY FINANCIAL HELP TO YOUR CHILDREN OR OTHER RELATIVES?	
Yes	13
No	80
Not ascertained	7
Total	100

B48. ARE YOU RECEIVING FINANCIAL SUPPORT FROM YOUR CHILDREN, FROM RELATIVES, OR ANYONE LIKE THAT?	
Yes	9
No	84
Not ascertained	7
Total	100

B49. HOW DOES YOUR INCOME NOW COMPARE WITH YOUR INCOME THE YEAR BEFORE YOU RETIRED -- IS IT CLOSER TO ONE-QUARTER AS LARGE, ONE-HALF AS LARGE, OR ALMOST AS LARGE AS BEFORE YOU RETIRED?	
Less than 1/4; less than 20%	8
About 1/4; 20-29%	26
Smaller, but NA how much; 30-39%	4
About 1/2; 40-59%	26
About 3/4; 60-79%	4
Almost as large or the same; 80-100%	13
Larger (than pre-retirement income)	5
Not ascertained	14
Total	100

---

*Adds to more than 100 percent because some respondents mentioned more than one thing.

Percent of Retired
Family Heads

B50. CONSIDERING INCOME AND EXPENSES, ARE YOU LIVING
ABOUT AS WELL AS BEFORE YOU RETIRED, NOT QUITE AS
WELL, OR WHAT?

Much better	1
Better	5
Same	53
Worse	29
Much worse	3
Not ascertained	9
Total	100

B50a. (IF NOT LIVING AS WELL) DO YOU FEEL THAT YOU
HAVE ENOUGH TO LIVE COMFORTABLY?

Yes	9.0
Yes, qualified	8.3
No, qualified	2.2
No	11.7
Not ascertained	0.8
Living as well as or better than before retirement	68.0
Total	100.0

B51. WHAT ABOUT YOUR HEALTH? SOME PEOPLE FEEL AS HEALTHY
AND YOUNG AS THEY DID SEVERAL YEARS AGO, WHILE OTHERS FEEL
THAT THEIR HEALTH IS NOT QUITE AS GOOD AS IT WAS THEN. HOW
IS IT WITH YOU?

Much better now	1
Better now	5
Same	18
Worse now	42
Much worse now	8
Not ascertained (including responses which did not compare current with previous health)	26
Total	100

SECTION D: INCOME; WIFE'S OCCUPATION

D1. TO GET AN ACCURATE PICTURE OF PEOPLE'S FINANCIAL SITUA-
TION, WE NEED TO KNOW THE INCOME OF ALL THE FAMILIES THAT WE
INTERVIEW. WOULD YOU PLEASE TELL ME THE LETTER OF THE GROUP
ON THIS CARD THAT INDICATES HOW MUCH INCOME YOU RECEIVED FROM
WAGES AND SALARIES IN 1965, INCLUDING ANY INCOME FROM OVER-
TIME, BONUSES, OR COMMISSIONS; I MEAN BEFORE DEDUCTIONS FOR
TAXES OR ANYTHING ELSE.

Less than $1000	84
$1000 - 1999	5
$2000 - 2999	2
$3000 - 4999	3
$5000 - 7499	3
$7500 - 9999	1
$10,000 and over	1
Not ascertained	1
Total	100

	Percent of Retired Family Heads
D5. TAKING EVERYTHING TOGETHER, WOULD YOU PLEASE TELL ME THE LETTER OF THE GROUP ON THIS CARD THAT INDICATES HOW MUCH INCOME YOU AND YOUR FAMILY RECEIVED FROM ALL SOURCES DURING THE YEAR 1965; I MEAN BEFORE TAXES OR ANY DEDUCTIONS.	

Less than $1000	8
$1000 - 1999	22
$2000 - 2999	18
$3000 - 3999	14
$4000 - 4999	7
$5000 - 7499	13
$7500 - 9999	7
$10,000 - 14,999	5
$15,000 and over	4
Not ascertained	2
Total	100

D6.   SINCE THE FIRST OF THIS YEAR, 1966, HAS YOUR TOTAL FAMILY INCOME GONE UP, REMAINED THE SAME, OR GONE DOWN?

Gone up	23
Remained the same	60
Gone down	16
Not ascertained	1
Total	100

D6a.   WHY IS THIS?

If went up:

Increase in pay rate	2.4
Increase in number of hours worked by family members	3.4
Increase in profits or self-employment income	2.2
Other reasons for income increase; reason not ascertained	15.7

If went down:

Decrease in pay rate	0.3
Decrease in number of hours worked by family members	9.9
Decrease in profits or self-employment income	1.3
Other reasons for income decline; reason not ascertained	4.4
Income did not change	60.4
Total	100.0

B53.   DID YOUR WIFE DO ANY WORK FOR MONEY LAST YEAR?

Yes	14
No	44
Not married	42
Total	100

	Percent of Retired Family Heads

B54. WHAT KIND OF WORK DID SHE DO?

Professional and technical workers	1.6
Managers and nonself-employed officials	0.6
Self-employed businesswomen	0.6
Clerical and sales workers	3.4
Operatives and kindred	3.4
Unskilled laborers and service workers	3.9
Miscellaneous; not ascertained	0.3
Wife did not work; not married	86.2
Total	100.0

B55. WHAT KIND OF BUSINESS WAS THAT IN?

Manufacturing	2.5
Transportation, communications, and utilities	0.2
Retail and wholesale trade	3.1
Finance, insurance, and real estate	0.3
Services, (including professional services)	4.9
Government medical, health, and educational services; all federal employees	2.8
Wife did not work; not married	86.2
Total	100.0

B56. WAS SHE WORKING FOR SOMEONE ELSE, HERSELF, OR WHAT?

Someone else	11.6
Self	2.2
Wife did not work; not married	86.2
Total	100.0

B57. DID SHE WORK FULL TIME OR PART TIME?

Full time	7.7
Part time	5.5
Not ascertained	0.6
Wife did not work; not married	86.2
Total	100.0

SECTION E: HOUSING

E1. DO YOU OWN THIS HOME OR PAY RENT OR WHAT?

Owns house or apartment	65
Owns trailer	3
Rents	28
Neither owns nor rents	4
Total	100

SECTION F: INFORMATION ABOUT THE FAMILY

Percent of Retired
Family Heads

F1.   ARE YOU MARRIED, SINGLE, WIDOWED, DIVORCED, OR
SEPARATED?

Married	58
Single	7
Widowed	28
Divorced	4
Separated	3
Total	100

F2.   HOW LONG HAVE YOU BEEN MARRIED?

Less than 10 years	4
10 - 19 years	6
20 years and over	48
Not married	42
Total	100

F3-F7.   HOW MANY GRADES OF SCHOOL DID YOU FINISH?   HAVE YOU
HAD ANY OTHER SCHOOLING?   WHAT OTHER SCHOOLING DID YOU HAVE?
DO YOU HAVE A COLLEGE DEGREE?   WHAT DEGREE(S) DO YOU HAVE?

0 - 5 grades	19
6 - 8 grades	35
9 - 11 grades	14
12 grades	10
12 grades and nonacademic training	7
College, no degree	7
College, Bachelor's degree	4
College, advanced or professional degree	3
Not ascertained	1
Total	100

F8-F9.   IS YOUR CHURCH PREFERENCE PROTESTANT, CATHOLIC, OR JEWISH?
(IF PROTESTANT) WHAT DENOMINATION IS THAT?

Baptists	7.3
Methodists	5.5
Episcopalians	1.0
Presbyterians	2.4
Lutherans	3.6
Congregationalists; Christian Scientists; Dutch Reformed; Quakers; Latter Day Saints; Unitarians; Bahai; Evangelical and Reformed	2.2
Other Protestants	3.6
Catholic	5.9
Jewish	1.6
Other; none	2.0
Not asked this question	64.9
Total	100.0

	Percent of Retired Family Heads
F10. ABOUT HOW OFTEN DO YOU USUALLY ATTEND RELIGIOUS SERVICES?	
More than once a week	3.4
Once a week	9.6
Two to three times a month	3.6
Once a month	1.6
A few times a year	8.9
Never	6.7
Not ascertained	1.3
Not asked this question	64.9
Total	100.0

F11. ARE THERE ANY PEOPLE THAT DO NOT LIVE WITH YOU WHO ARE DEPENDENT ON YOU FOR MORE THAN HALF OF THEIR SUPPORT?	
Yes	2
No	97
Not ascertained	1
Total	100

SECTION G: BY OBSERVATION ONLY (FILLED OUT BY INTERVIEWER)

G1. SEX OF FAMILY UNIT HEAD	
Male	69
Female	31
Total	100

G2. IS THE RESPONDENT THE HEAD OF THE FAMILY UNIT?	
Yes	97
No	3
Total	100

G3. RACE	
White	91
Negro	8
Other	1
Total	100

G6. TYPE OF STRUCTURE IN WHICH FAMILY LIVES	
Detached single-family house	68
2 - 4 family house, duplex, or row house	16
Apartment house (5 or more units, 3 stories or less)	7
Apartment house (5 or more units, 4 stories or more)	3
Other	6
Total	100

DEMOGRAPHIC ITEMS CODED FOR EACH INTERVIEW	Percent of Retired Family Heads
SIZE OF PLACE WHERE RESPONDENT LIVES	
In central cities of the 12 largest Standard Metro- politan Areas	12
In cities of 50,000 and over population, exclusive of the central cities of the 12 largest SMA's	24
Urban places with 10,000 - 49,999 population	14
Urban places with 2500 - 9999 population	17
Rural areas near a metropolitan area	6
Rural areas not near a metropolitan area	27
Total	100
REGION OF COUNTRY WHERE INTERVIEW TAKEN*	
Northeast	23
North Central states	27
South	35
West	15
Total	100

---

*For definition of these regions, see page 213.

Appendix F

SUMMARY OF REPLIES TO QUESTIONS: THE AUTOMOBILE WORKER SAMPLE

The distributions of answers to all questions asked of automobile worker sample respondents is given in this appendix, in the order in which the questions were coded. (Generally, this is also the order in which questions were asked, though some reordering was allowed to facilitate coding operations.) The distributions are presented in three parts: Part I contains those questions asked of both retired and nonretired auto workers, Part II contains questions asked of nonretired workers, and Part III contains questions asked of retired workers.

As in Appendix E, some questions were asked only of an appropriate subgroup, but the percentages given are always of the total relevant (sub-) sample (all workers, the nonretired, or the retired). Where the appropriate subgroup is less than one-half the relevant sample, percentages are carried to one-tenth of a percent. Where the subgroup is more than one-half the relevant sample, however, percentages are rounded to the nearest whole percent.

PART I: QUESTIONS ASKED OF RETIRED AND NONRETIRED AUTO WORKERS

	Percent of
INFORMATION CODED FROM FIRST PAGE OF QUESTIONNAIRE	entire sample

Questions 1-4 not coded

5.   LIST ALL PERSONS, INCLUDING CHILDREN, LIVING IN THE FAMILY
UNIT BY THEIR RELATION TO THE AUTO WORKER.

FROM QUESTION 5.   SEX OF RESPONDENT

Male	92
Female	8
Total	100

FROM QUESTION 5.   AGE OF RESPONDENT

Less than 59 years	1
59	16
60	25
61	25
62	22
63	11
64 or older	0
Not ascertained	0
Total	100

FROM QUESTION 5.   AGE OF RESPONDENT'S SPOUSE

Less than 45 years	16
45-49	5
50-54	20
55-59	34
60-64	20
65-69	3
70 or older	1
Not ascertained	1
Total	100

FROM QUESTION 5.   NUMBER OF ADULTS IN FAMILY UNIT

One	9
Two	67
Three	18
Four	6
Five	0
Six	0
Total	100

| | Percent of entire sample |
FROM QUESTION 5. NUMBER OF CHLILDREN UNDER 18 IN FAMILY UNIT	
One	8.1
Two	3.7
Three	0.8
Four	0.7
Five	0.4
Six	0.3
No children under 18; not ascertained whether any children	86.0
Total	100.0

FROM QUESTION 5. INCLUDING SPOUSE, NUMBER OF DEPENDENTS
OF RESPONDENT

One	65
Two	15
Three	4
Four	2
Five	1
Six	1
Seven	0
Eight or more	0
Number of dependents not ascertained	0
None; no ascertained whether any dependents	12
Total	100

FROM QUESTION 5. EXCLUDING SPOUSE, NUMBER OF DEPENDENTS
OF RESPONDENT

One	15.1
Two	3.8
Three	2.2
Four	0.7
Five	0.5
Six	0.2
Seven	0.2
Eight or more	0.0
Number of dependents not ascertained	0.3
None; not ascertained whether any dependents	77.0
Total	100.0

10. MARITAL STATUS OF RESPONDENT

Married	86
Single	4
Widowed (widower)	5
Divorced, separated	5
Total	100

11. HOW MANY YEARS HAVE YOU BEEN MARRIED?

Less than 10 years	6
10-19	7
20-29	14
30-39	44
40 or more	14
Not ascertained	1
Not asked this question: not married	14
Total	100

12-13. DO YOU HAVE ANY OTHER CHILDREN WHO DO NOT
LIVE HERE? WHAT STATES DO THEY LIVE IN?

Children all live in same state as respondent.	47
Children all live in the midwest states of MICHIGAN, OHIO, INDIANA, ILLINOIS, WISCONSIN, MINNESOTA, and/or IOWA - but do not all live in respondent's state of residence.	7
Some children live outside the midwest states region.	18
All children live outside the midwest states region.	5
Not ascertained, don't know.	1
No children	22
Total	100

14-15. DO YOU HAVE ANY GRANDCHILDREN OR GREAT-GRANDCHILDREN
UNDER 12 YEARS OF AGE? WHAT STATES DO THEY LIVE IN?

(Great)grandchildren all live in same state as respondent.	47
(Great)grandchildren all live in the midwest states of MICHIGAN, OHIO, INDIANA, ILLINOIS, WISCONSIN, MINNESOTA, and/or IOWA - but do not all live in respondent's state of residence.	6
Some (great)grandchildren live outside the midwest states region.	11
All (great)grandchildren live outside the midwest states region.	5
Not ascertained, don't know.	2
No (great)grandchildren under 12.	29
Total	100

SECTION F: FAMILY INFORMATION

F1. WHERE DID YOU GROW UP?

In state of current residence.	42
In midwest states of MICHIGAN, OHIO, INDIANA, ILLINOIS, WISCONSIN, MINNESOTA, or IOWA.	13
In south, ALABAMA, ARKANSAS, FLORIDA, GEORGIA, LOUISIANA, MISSISSIPPI, N. CAROLINA, S. CAROLINA, TEXAS, VIRGINIA.	14
In some other region of U.S., or in Canada.	22
Rest of world.	9
Total	100

	Percent of entire sample
F2. WAS THAT ON A FARM, OR IN A CITY, OR WHAT?	
Farm only	41
Nonfarm; not ascertained	59
Total	100

F3-F7. EDUCATION OF RESPONDENT

0-5 grades	10
6-8 grades	39
9-11 grades; 0-11 grades plus noncollege training	30
12 grades; completed high school	10
Completed high school plus noncollege training	5
College, no degree (including junior college degrees)	5
Completed college (any degree)	1
Not ascertained, don't know	0
Total	100

F8. IN THE LAST FEW YEARS HAVE YOU HELD AN OFFICE OR BEEN ON A COMMITTEE IN THE UNION?

Yes	5
No	94
Not ascertained, don't know	1
Total	100

F9. (BEFORE YOU RETIRED) ABOUT HOW MANY TIMES A YEAR DO (DID) YOU GO TO UNION MEETINGS?

None, did not attend any meetings	19
1-2 meetings	22
3-4 meetings	24
5-6 meetings	13
7-8 meetings	3
9-11 meetings	2
12 meetings or more	8
Not ascertained, don't know	9
Total	100

F10-F11. IS YOUR RELIGIOUS PREFERENCE PROTESTANT, CATHOLIC, OR JEWISH? (IF PROTESTANT) WHAT DENOMINATION IS THAT?

Baptist	23
Other Fundamentalist Protestant	9
Roman Catholic; Eastern Churches	28
Lutheran	9
Atheist, agnostic; non-Judeo-Christian; no preference; preference not ascertained	4
Methodist; Methodist Episcopal	13
Other liberal Protestant	8
Presbyterian	5
Jewish	0
Episcopal	1
Total	100

F12. ABOUT HOW OFTEN DO YOU USUALLY ATTEND RELIGIOUS SERVICES?	Percent of entire sample
More than once a week	9
Once a week	35
2-3 times a month	10
Once a month	6
A few times a year, or so	25
Never	14
Not ascertained, don't know	1
Total	100

SECTION G: OBSERVATION SHEET

G2. RACE

White	84
Nonwhite	16
Total	100

G3. NUMBER OF CALLS

1	38
2	29
3	18
4	8
5	3
6	2
7 or more	2
Total	100

G4. WHO WAS PRESENT DURING INTERVIEW?

Auto worker only	35
Auto worker and spouse only	51
Auto worker and someone other than spouse	5
Auto worker, spouse, and someone else	8
Not ascertained	1
Total	100

Question G5 not coded

G6. TYPE OF STRUCTURE IN WHICH FAMILY LIVES:

Trailer	3
Detached single family house	80
2-Family house, 2 units side by side	1
2-Family house, 2 units one above the other	8
Detached 3-4 family house	1
Row house (3 or more units in an attached row).	1
Apartment house (5 or more units, 3 stories or less)	3
Apartment house (5 or more units, 4 stories or more)	0
Apartment in a partly commercial structure	1
Other; not ascertained	2
Total	100

<ins>G7. NEIGHBORHOOD</ins>	
Vacant land only	7
Trailer	2
Detached, single family house	65
2-Family house, 2 units side by side	1
2-Family house, 2 units one above the other	9
Detached 3-4 family house	4
Row house (3 or more units in an attached row)	1
Apartment house (5 or more units, 3 stories or less)	3
Apartment house (5 or more units, 4 stories or more)	1
Apartment in a partly commercial structure	1
Wholly commercial or industrial structure	4
Other	1
Not ascertained	1
Total	100

<ins>G8. DID THE RESPONDENT UNDERSTAND THE QUESTIONS AND
ANSWER READILY, OR DID HE HAVE SOME DIFFICULTY
UNDERSTANDING AND ANSWERING?</ins>

Respondent was alert and quick to answer	47
Respondent could understand and answer questions satisfactorily.	42
Respondent was slow to understand and had difficulty answering questions.	10
Not ascertained	1
Total	100

<ins>SECTION D: INCOME</ins>

<ins>D8. TYPES OF INCOME RECEIVED BY RESPONDENT AND HIS FAMILY
(CURRENT OR PAST)</ins>

A professional practice or a trade	1.5
A business in which respondent's family had a financial interest	1.3
Farming or market gardening	2.6
Dividends, rent, interest, trust funds, annuities, or royalties	47.8
Government pensions other than social security	2.5
Non-government pensions other than negotiated pension	1.3
Unemployment compensation (including Supplemental Unemployment Benefits), sick or accident benefits.	20.4
Anything else (alimony, welfare, help from relatives, etc.)	0.8
Total	*

---

*Does not add to 100 since all workers did not receive non-wage
(or non-pension) income.

TRANSFER RETIREMENT INCOME	Percent of entire sample
Less than $1,000	23
$1,000-1,999	5
$2,000-2,999	9
$3,000-3,999	14
$4,000-4,999	33
$5,000-7,499	15
$7,500-9,999	1
$10,000-14,999	0
$15,000 or more	0
Total	100

EARNED RETIREMENT INCOME	
$1-499	16.0
$500-999	1.8
$1,000-1,999	7.3
$2,000-2,999	2.0
$3,000-4,999	4.6
$5,000-7,499	2.9
$7,500-9,999	1.2
$10,000 or more	0.4
No such income	63.8
Total	100.0

RETURN ON ASSETS	
$1-499	20
$500-999	28
$1,000-1,999	32
$2,000-2,999	7
$3,000-4,999	2
$5,000-7,499	1
$7,500-9,999	0
$10,000 or more	-
No such income	10
Total	100

RESPONDENT'S WAGES AND SALARIES	
Less than $2,000	0
$2,000-3,999	1
$4,000-4,999	2
$5,000-5,999	7
$6,000-6,999	22
$7,000-7,999	20
$8,000-9,999	26
$10,000-14,999	18
$15,000 or more	1
Not ascertained	3
Total	100

SPOUSE'S WAGES AND SALARIES INCOME	Percent of entire sample
Less than $1,000	75.2
$1,000-1,999	2.9
$2,000-2,999	3.8
$3,000-3,999	3.0
$4,000-4,999	3.0
$5,000-7,499	6.9
$7,500-9,999	1.5
$10,000-14,999	0.1
$15,000 or more	0.0
Not ascertained	3.6
Total	100.0

FAMILY UNIT WAGES AND SALARIES INCOME	
Less than $2,000	0
$2,000-3,999	1
$4,000-4,999	1
$5,000-5,999	4
$6,000-6,999	13
$7,000-7,999	13
$8,000-9,999	22
$10,000-14,999	28
$15,000 or more	6
Not ascertained	12
Total	100

TOTAL FAMILY UNIT INCOME	
Less than $2,000	0
$2,000-3,999	0
$4,000-4,999	1
$5,000-5,999	3
$6,000-6,999	11
$7,000-7,999	11
$8,000-9,999	22
$10,000-14,999	28
$15,000 or more	7
Not ascertained	17
Total	100

RATIO OF RETIREMENT PENSION, ANNUITY, AND EARNED INCOME TO RESPONDENT'S WAGES AND SALARIES INCOME EARNED BEFORE REITREMENT	
0 percent (no expected retirement income)	13
1-19 percent	10
20-29	5
30-39	9
40-49	12
50-59	11
60-69	12
70-79	5
80 percent or larger	20
Not ascertained	3
Total	100

RATIO OF RETIREMENT PENSION AND ANNUITY INCOME TO RESPONDENT'S WAGES AND SALARIES INCOME EARNED BEFORE RETIREMENT	Percent entire sample
0 percent (no expected retirement income)	20
1-19 percent	5
20-29	5
30-39	8
40-49	14
50-59	13
60-69	13
70-79	8
80 percent or larger	11
Not ascertained	3
Total	100

RATIO OF RETIREMENT PENSION, ANNUITY, AND EARNED INCOME TO TOTAL INCOME RECEIVED BY RESPONDENT'S FAMILY BEFORE RETIREMENT	
0 percent (no expected retirement income)	12
1-19	9
20-29	7
30-39	10
40-49	10
50-59	10
60-69	9
70-79	6
80 percent or larger	10
Not ascertained	17
Total	100

SECTION D: INCOME

D10, D12. WAS YOUR FAMILY'S TOTAL INCOME IN THE LAST FULL YEAR BEFORE RETIREMENT HIGHER OR LOWER THAN IT WAS THE YEAR BEFORE THAT--I MEAN TWO YEARS BEFORE YOU RETIRED?	
Higher, a lot	13
Higher, a little (or nor ascertained how much)	32
Same	25
Lower, a little (or not ascertained how much)	17
Lower, a lot	12
Don't know	0
Not ascertained	1
Total	100

D11. WHY WAS THAT? (REASONS WHY FAMILY UNIT INCOME HIGHER)	Percent of entire sample
Better pay rate for respondent: raise in wages or salary on present job, promotion, change to higher paying job	15.4
Higher earned income for respondent: worked more hours; more business or farm income; more from professional practice or trade; higher commissions	26.7
Other members in family unit started working more or earning more (wife, children, etc.)	1.3
Higher income from property (rent, interest, dividends)	0.3
Increased contributions from outside family unit (from private individuals, government, pension, relief or welfare)	0.1
Other	0.4
Don't know	0.0
Not ascertained	0.4
Not asked this question	55.4
Total	100.0

D11. WHY WAS THAT? (REASONS WHY FAMILY UNIT INCOME LOWER)	
Lower pay rate for respondent: decrease in wages or salary on present job, changed to lower paying job	0.5
Lower earned income for respondent: worked less hours; less business or farm income; less from professional practice or trade	25.2
Other members in family unit worked fewer hours or earned less: (wife, children, etc.)	1.0
Less income from property (lower rent, dividends, interest)	0.2
Decreased contributions from outside family unit	0.0
Other	0.6
Don't know	0.2
Not ascertained	0.7
Not asked this question	71.6
Total	100.0

D13. NOW, HOW WILL YOUR FAMILY INCOME FOR THIS YEAR (1967) COMPARE WITH THAT OF LAST YEAR (1966)-- WILL IT BE HIGHER OR LOWER?	
1967 Higher	10
Same	34
1967 Lower	53
Don't know	2
Not ascertained	1
Total	100

D14. WHY DO YOU THINK SO? (REASONS WHY FAMILY UNIT
INCOME WILL BE HIGHER IN 1967)

Percent of
entire sample

Better pay rate for respondent: raise in wages or salary on present job, promotion, change to higher paying job	3.5
Higher earned income for respondent: worked more hours; more business or farm income; more from professional practice or trade; higher commissions	4.4
Other members in family unit start working more or earning more (wife, children, etc.)	0.8
Higher income from property (rent, interest, dividends)	0.2
Increased contributions from outside family unit (from private individuals, government, pension, relief or welfare)	0.9
Other	0.3
Don't know	0.0
Not ascertained	0.3
Not asked this question	89.6
Total	100.0

D15. WHY DO YOU THINK SO? (REASONS WHY FAMILY UNIT
INCOME WILL BE LOWER IN 1967)

Lower pay rate for respondent: decrease in wages or salary on present job, change to lower paying job	1
Lower earned income for respondent: work less hours, less business or farm income; less from professional practice or trade; retired from former work	48
Other member in family unit work fewer hours or earn less: (wife, children, etc.)	1
Less income from property (lower rent, dividends, in interest)	0
Decreased contributions from outside family unit	1
Other	1
Don't know	0
Not ascertained	1
Not asked this question	47
Total	100

SECTION E: HOUSING AND DEBT

E1. HOUSING STATUS [DO YOU OWN THIS (HOME/APARTMENT),
OR PAY RENT, OR WHAT?]

Owns home, apartment building, farm, etc. - anything but a trailer	83
Owns trailer	2
Rents (or shares rent)	13
Neither owns nor rents	2
Not ascertained	0
Total	100

	Percent of entire sample
E2. (IF NEITHER OWNS NOR RENTS) HOW IS THAT?	

Servant	0.1
Farm laborer	0.0
Other person for whom housing is part of compensation (janitors, gardeners, nurses, etc.)	0.3

Persons for whom housing is a gift, paid for by someone
  outside of family unit, owned by relative, pays no rent
  or only taxes
	0.7

Sold own home, but still living there	0.2
Living in house which will inherit; estate in process	0.2
Living in temporary quarters (garage, shed, etc.) while home is under construction	0.1
Other	0.4
Not ascertained	-
Not asked this question	98.0
Total	100.0

E3. (IF RENTS) ABOUT HOW MUCH RENT DO YOU PAY A MONTH?

$1-24	0.2
$25-49	2.4
$50-74	4.7
$75-99	2.8
$100-124	0.6
$125-149	0.7
$150 or more	0.3
Not ascertained	0.6
Not asked this question, respondent does not rent	87.7
Total	100.0

E4. IN WHAT YEAR DID YOU MOVE INTO THIS (HOUSE?APARTMENT)?

1952 or earlier	45
1953-1957	17
1958-1962	11
1963	2
1964	3
1965	2
1966	3
1967	1
Not ascertained, don't know	1
Not asked this question	15
Total	100

E5-E6. PRESENT VALUE OR COST OF HOUSE

$1-2,499	0
$2,500-4,999	1
$5,000-7,499	7
$7,500-9,999	11
$10,000-12,499	18
$12,500-14,999	7
$15,000-19,999	18
$20,000 or more	14
Not ascertained	9
Not asked this question, respondent does not own house	15
Total	100

E7-E8. DO YOU HAVE A MORTGAGE ON THIS PROPERTY? DO YOU ALSO HAVE A SECOND MORTGAGE?	Percent of entire sample
Yes, first mortgage only	24
Yes, two mortgages	0
No mortgage	57
Don't know	0
Not ascertained	2
Not asked this question	17
Total	100

E10. HOW MUCH ARE YOUR PAYMENTS EVERY MONTH?

$1-24	0.3
$25-49	2.5
$50-74	8.5
$75-99	5.9
$100-124	3.2
$125-149	0.9
$150 or more	1.1
Not ascertained	1.4
Not asked this question, respondent does not have mortgage	76.2
Total	100.0

E11. HOW MANY YEARS WILL IT BE BEFORE THE MORTGAGE IS PAID OFF?

1-4	6.5
5-9	5.8
10-14	2.8
15-19	1.2
20-29	1.5
30 or more	0.5
Don't know	3.5
Not ascertained	2.0
Not asked this question, respondent does not have mortgage	76.2
Total	100.0

AGE MORTGAGE PAID

Age 60 or before	0.2
61-62	2.7
63-64	3.4
65-67	4.4
68-70	2.5
71 or older	5.4
Not ascertained	5.1
Not asked this question, respondent does not have mortgage	76.3
Total	100.0

CURRENT HOUSE EQUITY	Percent of entire sample
$1-2,499	2
$2,500-4,999	4
$5,000-7,499	10
$7,500-9,999	9
$10,000-12,499	15
$12,500-14,999	6
$15,000-19,999	15
$20,000 or more	12
Not ascertained	10
Not asked this question, respondent does not own home; respondent has negative equity in house	17
Total	100

PART II: QUESTIONS ASKED OF NONRETIRED AUTO WORKERS

SECTION A: RETIREMENT PLANS AND ATTITUDES

A1. HAVE YOU BEEN TO ANY MEETINGS OR CLASSES ABOUT THE NEGOTIATED EARLY RETIREMENT PROVISIONS?	Percent of nonretired respondents
Yes	11
No	89
Total	100

A2. DID YOU GO TO MORE THAN ONE MEETING?	
Yes	7.6
No	3.5
Not ascertained, don't know	0.4
Not asked this question	88.5
Total	100.0

A3. DID YOUR WIFE GO ALONG WITH YOU?	
Yes	3.0
No	4.1
Not ascertained, don't know	0.1
Not asked this question	92.8
Total	100.0

A4. DO YOU THINK THAT THE WRITTEN MATERIAL FROM THE UNION AND THE COMPANY HAS DESCRIBED THE PROGRAM CLEARLY ENOUGH?

Percent of nonretired respondents

Yes	65
No	21
Don't know	13
Not ascertained	1
Total	100

A5. WHAT PARTS NEED MORE EXPLANATION?

Parts covering eligibility	1.1
Parts covering benefits	4.9
Both eligibility and benefits	6.2
Other	2.6
Don't know (nothing specific mentioned)	11.7
Not ascertained	4.3
Not asked this question	69.2
Total	100.0

A6. WHAT DO YOU THINK ABOUT THE EARLY RETIREMENT PLAN IN GENERAL - IS IT A GOOD THING FOR UAW MEMBERS, OR NOT SO GOOD?

Plan is very good	18
Plan is good, not bad	52
Neutral response or mixed feelings ("plan is fair," etc.)	11
Plan is not so good, is bad	4
Plan is very bad	0
Depends (if can afford it, if wants to, etc.)	10
Don't know	3
Not ascertained	2
Total	100

A8. DID YOU CONSIDER RETIRING DURING THE LAST YEAR?

Yes	32
No	65
Not ascertained, don't know	3
Total	100

A9. WHAT WERE THE MAIN REASONS WHY YOU DIDN'T RETIRE?

Health reasons	6
Financial reasons	37
Job reasons	6
Family reasons	6
Boredom reasons (lack of other things besides work to do)	3
Reasons referring specifically to retirement age or eligibility	31
Other reasons	5
Respondent refers to having worked long enough, to being tired of working, etc.	0
Not ascertained, don't know	6
Total	100

A10. HOW HAS THE NEGOTIATED EARLY RETIREMENT PROVISION
AFFECTED YOUR PLANS FOR RETIREMENT?

Encouraged retirement	25
Had little or no effect on plans; both encouraged and discouraged retirement	61
Discouraged retirement	1
Don't know	5
Not ascertained	8
Total	100

A11. DO YOU KNOW ANYONE WHO HAS RETIRED BEFORE 65 UNDER
THE NEGOTIATED EARLY RETIREMENT PROVISION?

Yes	69
No	31
Don't know	0
Total	100

A12. HOW ARE THEY GETTING ALONG?   ARE THEY GENERALLY
SATISFIED WITH THINGS?

Very satisfied	11
Satisfied	33
Pro-con; neutral	8
Unsatisfied	2
Very unsatisfied	0
Don't know	12
Not ascertained	3
Not asked this question	31
Total	100

A13. SOME PEOPLE LOOK FORWARD TO RETIREMENT BECAUSE
THEY WISH TO HAVE MORE TIME TO DO THINGS, WHILE OTHERS
THINK THAT THEY MIGHT BE BORED AFTER THEY RETIRE.
HOW DO YOU FEEL ABOUT THIS?

Respondent looks forward strongly to retirement	10
Respondent looks forward to retirement	56
Respondent is pro-con, neutral	12
Respondent is skeptical about retirement; fears boredom; would rather continue work	13
Respondent does not look forward to retirement at all; strongly fears boredom	2
Don't know	4
Not ascertained	3
Total	100

	Percent of nonretired respondents
A14. HOW MUCH HAVE YOU TALKED WITH OTHER PEOPLE ABOUT THE QUESTION OF WHEN TO RETIRE?	
Very much, a lot, quite a bit; a lot of people	33
Some; "I've talked about it," amount unspecified; some people	14
A little, not very much; a few people	29
Not at all; nobody	23
Don't know	0
Not ascertained	1
Total	100

A15. WHEN DO YOU THINK YOU WILL RETIRE?	
Before 60 years of age	2
60-61	17
62	27
63-64	11
65	22
66-67	2
68 or older	3
Don't know	10
Not ascertained	6
Total	100

A16. WHY DO YOU SAY THAT IS WHEN YOU WILL RETIRE?	
Health reasons	8
Financial reasons	19
Job reasons	5
Family reasons	4
Recreational reasons, "to enjoy life"	5
Reasons referring specifically to retirement age or eligibility	33
Other reasons	7
Respondent refers to having worked long enough, to being tired of working	7
Not ascertained, don't know	12
Total	100

A17. HAS THE FACT THAT CONTRACT NEGOTIATIONS ARE COMING UP THIS YEAR INFLUENCED YOUR DECISION?	
Yes	38
No	61
Not ascertained, don't know	1
Total	100

	Percent of nonretired respondents
A18. MANY PEOPLE NOW RETIRE BEFORE THEY ARE 65. WHY DO YOU THINK THEY DO THIS?	
Health reasons	19
Financial reasons	21
Job reasons	10
Family reasons	1
Recreational reasons; "to enjoy life"	17
Reasons referring specifically to retirement age or eligibility	8
Other reasons	3
Respondent refers to having worked long enough, to being tired of working	16
Not ascertained, don't know	5
Total	100

A19. IN THE LAST FIVE OR TEN YEARS, HOW HAVE YOUR IDEAS CHANGED ABOUT WHEN YOU'D LIKE TO RETIRE?	
Ideas have changed in a direction favorable to (early) retirement; now thinks retirement is good, desirable (more desirable)	25.7
Ideas about retirement have changed, not ascertained in which direction	4.6
Ideas have changed in direction unfavorable to (early) retirement; now thinks retirement is bad, undesirable (less desirable)	1.4
Not ascertained, don't know	10.8
Ideas have not changed	57.5
Total	100.0

A20. NOW WE'D LIKE TO TALK A LITTLE ABOUT WHERE PEOPLE LIKE TO LIVE WHEN THEY RETIRE. IN GENERAL, WHAT MAKES A COMMUNITY A GOOD PLACE FOR RETIRED PEOPLE?	
Climate	12
Convenience and availability of recreational and cultural facilites	9
Housing and transportation (including ease of access to stores and shops)	8
Cost of living other than housing (e.g., references to generally low prices)	5
Neighborliness (friendly people)	14
Special advantages for older people not generally available to other, including any reference to subsidies for the elderly	2
Availability of medical facilities and personnel	1
Other mentions	29
Not ascertained, don't know	20
Total	100

A21, A22. ARE THERE SPECIAL THINGS THE COMMUNITY MIGHT PROVIDE FOR RETIRED PEOPLE? WHAT ARE THEY?	Percent of nonretired respondents
Climate	0
Convenience and availability of recreational and cultural facilities	33
Housing (except that included in 6) and transportation (including ease of access to stores and shops)	3
Cost of living other than housing (e.g., references to generally low prices)	1
Neighborliness (friendly people)	1
Special advantages for older people not generally available to others, including any reference to subsidies for the elderly	9
Availability of medical facilities and personnel	1
Other mentions	4
Not ascertained, don't know	14
No special things	34
Total	100

A23. DO YOU THINK YOU WILL BE LIVING HERE IN THIS COMMUNITY AFTER YOU RETIRE, OR IN ANOTHER AREA?	
Living elsewhere	25
Living here	62
Don't know	13
Total	100

A24. WILL YOU PERHAPS MOVE INTO A DIFFERENT HOUSE OR APARTMENT IN THIS COMMUNITY?	
Yes	7
No	49
Don't know	5
Not ascertained	1
Not asked this question	38
Total	100

A25. WHY WILL YOU MOVE?	
To go to a better climate	5.2
To get a smaller, easier-to-keep, and/or less expensive house or apartment	7.5
To be nearer relatives	1.5
To go to a community with certain desirable features, such as a retirement community	2.5
Other reasons	13.3
Not ascertained, don't know	2.0
Not asked this question	68.0
Total	100.0

A26. WHO WILL BE LIVING WITH YOU THEN (BESIDES YOUR SPOUSE)?

	Percent of nonretired respondents
No one, "I'll live alone"	7
One person - spouse only	64
One person who is not spouse	2
Two people (including spouse)	13
Three people (including spouse)	4
Four people (including spouse)	1
Five or more people (including spouse)	2
Don't know	6
Not ascertained	1
Total	100

A27. DO YOU HAVE ANY HOBBIES YOU HOPE TO SPEND MORE TIME ON WHEN YOU RETIRE?

Yes	79
No	21
Don't know	0
Not ascertained	0
Total	100

A28. WHAT ARE THEY?

Active hobbies: gardening, carpentry, woodworking, "working around the house", "handywork", etc.	27
Inactive hobbies: collecting, writing, photography, etc.	8
Sports, games, other recreational activities	35
Travel, vacationing, etc.	5
Relaxing, loafing, sitting around, "playing with grandchildren", etc.	1
Other	2
Not ascertained, don't know	0
Not asked this question	22
Total	100

A29. WHOW ABOUT WORK WITHOUT PAY FOR CHURCH OR CHARITY (OR YOUR CHILDREN) - WILL YOU BE DOING MORE OF THAT WHEN YOU RETIRE, OR LESS THAN YOU DO NOW?

Expect to do more work without pay	44
Expect to do about the same amount; (not doing any now, will not do any)	25
Expect to do less than now	6
Not ascertained, don't know; might do more or might do less	25
Total	100

A30. WHAT OTHER THINGS DO YOU THINK YOU WILL DO AFTER YOU RETIRE?	Percent of nonretired respondents
Active hobbies: gardening, carpentry, woodworking, "working around the house", "handywork", etc.	18
Inactive hobbies: collecting, writing, photography, etc.	3
Sports, games, other recreational activities	9
Travel, vacationing, etc.	29
Relaxing, loafing, sitting around, "playing with grandchildren", etc.	7
Other	8
Not ascertained, don't know	20
Not asked this question	6
Total	100

A31. IN YOUR OPINION, DO YOUNGER PEOPLE FEEL THAT OLDER WORKERS SHOULD RETIRE EARLY AND MAKE ROOM FOR OTHERS?

Yes, they feel this way; many feel this way; most do; almost all	74
Some; quite a few	6
Mixed response ("some do, some don't", etc.)	3
Only a few feel this way; not very many	1
No, none feel this way; hardly any feel this way	8
Don't know	6
Not ascertained	2
Total	100

A32. HOW DO YOU FEEL ABOUT IT?

Agree strongly that older workers should retire early and make room for others; respondent is emphatic	16
Agree that older workers should retire early; "I suppose so"	48
Pro-con; neutral; depends	20
Disagree with the idea that older workers should retire early; "I suppose not"	11
Disagree strongly with the idea that older workers should retire early and make room for others; respondent is emphatic	3
Don't know	1
Not ascertained	1
Total	100

A33. GENERALLY, HOW DO YOU FEEL ABOUT YOUR INCOME AND FINANCIAL OUTLOOK FOR RETIREMENT? DO YOU EXPECT TO BE FAIRLY COMFORTABLE, OR WILL YOU HAVE FINANCIAL PROBLEMS THEN?

No problems; (very) comfortable	21
Few problems; fairly comfortable; "I'll be OK"	41
Pro-con, no particular feelings	3
Some problems; not so comfortable	19
Many problems; (very) uncomfortable	1
Don't know; too far off to tell; depends ("might do OK")	12
Not ascertained	3
Total	100

A34. ARE YOU ELIGIBLE NOW FOR SUPPLEMENTARY EARLY RETIREMENT BENEFITS FROM THE NEGOTIATED PENSION PLAN?

	Percent of nonretired respondents
Yes	64
No	29
Don't know	7
Total	100

A35. WHY NOT?

Not old enough	9.0
Not enough seniority (haven't worked long enough for the company)	16.8
Other	0.3
Not ascertained, don't know	3.6
Not asked this question	70.3
Total	100.0

A36. HOW MUCH INCOME PER MONTH FROM THE NEGOTIATED PENSION PLAN WOULD YOU RECEIVE IF YOU RETIRED (NOW?AS SOON AS YOU WERE ELIGIBLE)?

Less than $100	8
$100-199	6
$200-249	6
$250-299	5
$300-349	9
$350-399	13
$400 or more	16
Don't know	35
Not ascertained	2
Total	100

A37. WOULD YOU CONTINUE TO RECEIVE THE SAME AMOUNT AS LONG AS YOU LIVE?

Yes	16
No	56
Don't know	26
Not ascertained	2
Total	100

A38. HOW MUCH PER MONTH WOULD YOU GET FROM THE PLAN IF YOU WAITED UNTIL YOU WERE 65 TO RETIRE?

Less than $100; "the minimum"	14
$100-149	10
$150-199	8
$200-249	3
$250 or more	14
"The maximum"	0
Don't know	47
Not ascertained	4
Total	100

	Percent of nonretired respondents
A39. HOW MUCH SOCIAL SECURITY WOULD YOU (AND YOUR SPOUSE) RECEIVE PER MONTH IF YOU STARTED GETTING IT AT AGE 62?	
Less than $100; "the minimum"	4
$100-149	24
$150-199	7
$200-249	2
$250 and over	1
"The maximum"	2
Don't know	60
Total	100

A40. IF YOU STARTED GETTING IT AT AGE 65 HOW MUCH WOULD YOU (AND YOUR SPOUSE) RECEIVE?

Less than $100; "the minimum"	1
$100-149	22
$150-199	7
$200-249	5
$250 and over	2
"The maximum"	5
Don't know	56
Not ascertained	2
Total	100

A41. WHEN DO YOU THINK YOU WILL BEGIN TO DRAW YOUR SECURITY BENEFITS?

Age 62 (or earlier)	32
63	5
64	2
65	34
After age 65	5
Don't know	17
Not ascertained	5
Total	100

A42. HAVE YOU DISCUSSED RETIREMENT WITH YOUR (WIFE/HUSBAND)?

Yes	67
No	20
Not ascertained, don't know	0
Not asked this question	13
Total	100

A43. WHEN DOES YOUR (WIFE/HUSBAND) THINK YOU SHOULD RETIRE - I MEAN AT WHAT AGE?	Percent of nonretired respondents
Age 60 or earlier	11
61	4
62	10
63	2
64	1
65	7
After age 65; never	3
She leaves it up to me; whenever I want; whenever I feel like it	22
Not ascertained, don't know	7
Not asked this question	33
Total	100

A44. WHY DOES (SHE/HE) THINK THAT?	
Health reasons	10
Financial reasons	8
Job reasons	1
Family reasons	6
Recreational reasons	8
Reasons referring specifically to retirement age or eligibility	2
Other reasons	8
R refers to haveing worked long enough; to being tired of working, etc.	9
Not ascertained, don't know	13
Not asked this question	35
Total	100

A45. WILL YOUR (WIFE/HUSBAND) BE ELIGIBLE FOR SOCIAL SECURITY RETIREMENT BENEFITS BECAUSE OF (HER/HIS) OWN WORK?	
Yes	41
No	45
Don't know	1
Not ascertained	-
Not asked this question	13
Total	100

A46. WHEN CAN (SHE/HE) FIRST GET SUCH BENEFITS?	
1967 (or earlier)	7.9
1968	1.8
1969	1.4
1970	1.9
1971	2.7
1972 or later	16.2
Don't know	7.7
Not ascertained	1.1
Not asked this question	59.3
Total	100.0

	Percent of nonretired respondents
A47. ABOUT HOW MUCH WOULD (SHE/HE) RECEIVE THEN?	
Less than $50; "the minimum"	2.4
$50-99	4.5
$100-149	3.5
$150-199	-
$200 and over	0.3
"The maximum"	1.2
Don't know	27.1
Not ascertained	1.8
Not asked this question	59.2
Total	100.0

A48. WILL (SHE/HE) BE ELIGIBLE FOR ANY OTHER (PRIVATE)
RETIREMENT BENEFITS FROM (HER/HIS) OWN WORK?

Yes	10
No	76
Don't know	0
Not ascertained	1
Not asked this question	13
Total	100

A49. WHEN CAN (SHE/HE) FIRST GET SUCH BENEFITS?

1967 (or earlier)	2.3
1968	0.4
1969	0.1
1970	0.2
1971	0.3
1972 or later	2.7
Don't know	2.6
Not ascertained	1.1
Not asked this question	90.3
Total	100.0

A50. ABOUT HOW MUCH WOULD (SHE/HE) RECEIVE THEN?

$1-49 per month	0.9
$50-99	0.3
$100-149	0.4
$150-199	0.5
$200-249	0.7
$250-299	0.3
$300 and over	0.0
Don't know	5.5
Not ascertained	0.9
Not asked this question	90.5
Total	100.0

A51.   UNDER THE NEGOTIATED PENSION PLAN, CAN YOU
ARRANGE TO PROVIDE SURVIVORS PROTECTION FOR YOUR
(WIFE/HUSBAND) AFTER YOU RETIRE?

	Percent of nonretired respondents
Yes	56
No	6
Don't know	25
Not ascertained	0
Not asked this question	13
Total	100

A52.   DO YOU THINK YOUR (WIFE/HUSBAND) WILL WORK AFTER
YOU RETIRE?

Yes	15
No	63
Don't know	9
Not ascertained	0
Not asked this question	13
Total	100

A53.   WILL YOU KEEP SOME LIFE INSURANCE AFTER YOU RETIRE?

Yes	74
Yes, but amount will change	8
No	4
Don't know	1
Not asked this question	13
Total	100

A54.   HOW MUCH WILL IT AMOUNT TO?

$1-1500	9
$1501-3500	16
$3501-5500	10
$5501-7500	11
$7501-9500	10
$9501-14,499	10
$14,500 and over	3
Don't know	12
Not ascertained	2
Not asked this question	17
Total	100

A55.   DO YOU HAVE SOME ANNUITY POLICIES OR ANYTHING ELSE
THAT AUTOMATICALLY TURNS INTO CASH OR INTO A PENSION WHILE
YOU ARE STILL LIVING?

Yes	8
No	91
Don't know	0
Not ascertained	1
Total	100

	Percent of nonretired respondents
A56. WHEN WILL YOU GET THE MONEY?	
1967 (or earlier)	1.3
1968	0.8
1969	0.4
1970	0.9
1971	1.0
1972 or later	1.7
Don't know	1.0
Not ascertained	0.9
Not asked this question	92.0
Total	100.0

A57. HOW MUCH DO YOU EXPECT FROM THEM? (PER-MONTH AMOUNT)	
$1-49	0.8
$50-99	0.9
$100-149	0.1
$150-199	0.1
$200-249	0.0
$250-299	0.0
$300 and over	0.0
Don't know	1.4
Not ascertained	2.0
Not asked this question	94.7
Total	100.0

A57. HOW MUCH DO YOU EXPECT FROM THEM? (LUMP SUM)	
$1-1500	2.2
$1501-3500	1.3
$3501-5500	0.8
$5501-7500	0.3
$7501-9500	0.1
$9501-14,499	0.1
$14,500 and over	0.2
Don't know	1.4
Not ascertained	1.0
Not asked this question	92.6
Total	100.0

A58. DO YOU THINK YOU MIGHT DO SOME WORK OR GO INTO BUSINESS FOR YOURSELF AFTER YOU RETIRE?	
Yes	35
No	54
Don't know	10
Not ascertained	1
Total	100

	Percent of nonretired respondents
A59. WILL YOU WORK FOR SOMEONE ELSE, OR YOURSELF, OR WHAT?	
Someone else	19.8
Self	13.2
Both self and someone else	0.5
Other	0.1
Don't know	1.2
Not ascertained	0.3
Not asked this question	64.9
Total	100.0

A60. WILL THE WORK BE FULL-TIME OR PART-TIME?

Full-time	0.9
Part-time	31.8
Don't know	2.3
Not ascertained	-
Not asked this question	65.0
Total	100.0

A61. HOW MUCH DO YOU THINK YOU MIGHT EARN?

$1-499	0.5
$500-999	1.9
$1000-1999	8.6
$2000-2999	1.2
$3000-4999	0.3
$5000-7499	0.1
$7500 and over	0.3
Don't know	18.0
Not ascertained	4.1
Not asked this question	65.0
Total	100.0

A62. WILL YOU DO THIS BECAUSE YOU NEED THE INCOME, OR MAINLY BECAUSE YOU WANT TO DO IT, OR WHAT?

Need income	8.1
Want to work	7.4
Need income and want to work	7.8
Want to keep busy	6.6
Need income and want to keep busy	3.2
Want to work and want to keep busy	0.1
Need income, want to work, and want to keep busy	0.1
Other, with or without any of above	1.4
Not ascertained, don't know	0.4
Not asked this question	64.9
Total	100.0

A63. WILL THIS WORK BE SOMETHING YOU'VE NEVER DONE
BEFORE, OR SOMETHING YOU'VE HAD SOME EXPERIENCE IN?

Percent of
nonretired
respondents

Something respondent has done before (is experienced in)	26.4
Something respondent has done before *and* something respondent has not done before	1.4
Something R has not done before	2.9
Don't know	2.5
Not ascertained	1.9
Not asked this question	64.9
Total	100.0

A64. DO YOU EXPECT TO GIVE ANY FINANCIAL HELP TO (YOUR
CHILDREN OR OTHER) RELATIVES AFTER YOU RETIRE?

Yes	20
Might, possibly	3
No	75
Don't know	2
Not ascertained	0
Total	100

A65. DO YOU EXPECT TO RECEIVE ANY FINANCIAL HELP FROM
(YOUR CHILDREN), RELATIVES, OR ANYONE ELSE AT THAT TIME?

Yes	2
Might, possibly	0
No, none	97
Don't know	1
Not ascertained	0
Total	100

A66. DURING THE PAST TWELVE MONTHS OR SO, DID YOU PEOPLE
SAVE ANY MONEY, OR DID YOU DECREASE YOUR SAVINGS, OR DID
YOU JUST BREAK EVEN?

Saved	52
Broke even	36
Decreased savings	10
Not ascertained	0
Don't know	2
Total	100

A67. WHAT KINDS OF SAVINGS OR INVESTMENTS - FOR
EXAMPLE, STOCKS AND BONDS, REAL ESTATE, OR BUSINESS
INVESTMENTS - HAVE YOU ACCUMULATED UP TILL NOW?

Percent of
nonretired
respondents

Mentions savings accounts, government bonds, deposits in savings and loan associations and credit unions	79
Mentions corporate stocks and/or bonds	12
Mentions non-corporate business investments	1
Mentions farms or other real estate, not counting respondents home	17
Mentions some savings or investments not covered above	2
Total	*

A68. HOW MUCH DO YOU HAVE RIGHT NOW ALTOGETHER IN
SAVINGS AND INVESTMENTS - NOT COUNTING YOUR HOME?

Less than $100	8
$100-499	7
$500-1999	13
$2000-4999	21
$5000-9999	17
$10,000-24,999	17
$25,000-49,999	6
$50,000-99,999	1
$100,000 or more	0
Not ascertained, don't know	10
Total	100

A69. CAN YOU THINK OF ANY SOURCES OF RETIREMENT INCOME
YOU'LL HAVE OTHER THAN THE ONES WE'VE TALKED ABOUT, SUCH
AS VETERANS' BENEFITS, PENSIONS FROM ANOTHER COMPANY, ETC.?

Yes	5
No	94
Don't know	0
Not ascertained	1
Total	100

A70. WHAT WILL THEY BE?

Government pensions or pensions, not ascertained whether government (include local, state, and Federal governments)	2.0
Non-government pensions	2.0
Dividends, rent, interest, trust funds, or royalties	0.8
Combinations of the above	0.0
Other sources	0.0
Don't know	0.0
Not ascertained	0.5
Not asked this question	94.7
Total	100.0

---

*
Adds to more than 100 percent because some respondents had more than
one kind of savings or investments.

A71. HOW MUCH WILL YOU GET FROM THIS SOURCE?	Percent of nonretired respondents
$1-49 per month	1.9
$50-99	0.3
$100-149	0.4
$150-199	0.3
$200-249	0.1
$250-299	0.1
$300 and over	0.0
Don't know	1.6
Not ascertained	0.6
Not asked this question	94.7
Total	100.0

A72.   DO YOU PLAN TO MAKE ANY MAJOR PURCHASES - OF, FOR
EXAMPLE, A CAR, A REFRIGERATOR, OR A TV SET - BEFORE
RETIRING?

Yes	50
No	39
Don't know	10
Not ascertained	1
Total	100

A73.   WHAT WILL YOU BUY?

House or farm trailer	0.9
Car	35.9
Major household durables (TV set, refrigerator or freezer, washing machine, clothes dryer, cook stove or range, furniture, dishwasher, air conditioner)	11.7
Additions and/or repairs to house	0.3
Major hobby or other recreational items (except TV)	0.2
Other	0.4
Don't know	0.1
Not ascertained	0.5
Not asked this question	50.0
Total	100.0

(QUESTION B1 WAS NOT CODED).

B2. WHAT IS THE HOURLY WAGE RATE FOR THIS JOB?

Less than $2.75	3
$2.75-2.99	8
$3.00-3.24	30
$3.25-3.49	23
$3.50-3.74	9
$3.75-3.99	8
$4.00 and over	18
Don't know	0
Not ascertained	1
Total	100

B3. IS YOUR WORK FLEXIBLE, OR DO YOU HAVE TO DO MUCH
THE SAME THINGS OVER AND OVER?

Work is flexible	43
Work is repetitious	56
Work is flexible and work is repetitious	1
Don't know	0
Not ascertained	0
Total	100

B4. DO YOU ORGANIZE YOUR OWN WORK OR VARY ITS PACE?

Yes	61
No	38
Don't know	0
Not ascertained	1
Total	100

B5. HOW MANY YEARS HAVE YOU WORKED FOR THE COMPANY YOU'RE
WITH NOW?

Less than 10 years	5
10-14	16
15-19	18
20-24	20
25-29	9
30-39	26
40 and over	6
Don't know	-
Not ascertained	-
Total	100

B6. DO YOU FEEL THAT YOUR WORK IS DRUDGERY, OR IS IT ALL RIGHT, OR DO YOU ENJOY THE WORK?	Percent of nonretired respondents
Enjoy very much	7
Enjoy; enjoy with qualifications	56
Pro-con; netural; all right	24
Dislike; dislike with qualifications	6
Dislike very much; drudgery	6
Don't know	-
Not ascertained	1
Total	100

B7. IS IT HARD FOR YOU TO KEEP UP WITH YOUR WORK?	
Yes	8
Yes and no; mixed response	10
No	82
Don't know	0
Not ascertained	0
Total	100

B8. IS THE PLACE YOU WORK IN PLEASANT OR NOT?	
Pleasant	60
Neither pleasant nor unpleasant; pro-con; neutral	19
Unpleasant	18
Don't know	0
Not ascertained	3
Total	100

B9. HAS YOUR DECISION ABOUT WHEN TO RETIRE BEEN INFLUENCED BY ANY CHANGES MADE ON YOUR JOB IN THE LAST FEW YEARS - FOR EXAMPLE, BY AUTOMATION OR BY A SHIFT TO ANOTHER JOB?	
Yes	11
No	88
Don't know	0
Not ascertained	1
Total	100

B10. HOW HAVE THESE CHANGES AFFECTED THE DECISION?	
Changes have influenced respondent to retire earlier than he would have otherwise	5.8
Changes have influenced respondent to retire later than he would have otherwise	0.8
Other	0.3
Don't know	-
Not ascertained	3.6
Not asked this question	89.5
Total	100.0

B11. IF YOU WERE TO CONTINUE WORKING WHERE YOU ARE,
WOULD YOU MOVE INTO A BETTER JOB FAIRLY SOON, WOULD
YOU KEEP ON DOING ABOUT THE SAME THING, OR WOULD YOU
BE MOVED TO A LESS SATISFACTORY JOB?

Percent of
nonretired
respondents

Respondent would move to <u>better</u> job	2
Respondent would remain on <u>same</u> or similar job	88
Respondent would be moved to <u>worse</u> job	2
Don't know	4
Not ascertained	4
Total	100

B12. WHAT ABOUT THE PEOPLE YOU WORK WITH - ARE THEY
ABOUT YOUR AGE, OR ARE THEY YOUNGER?

About same age	10
Some same, some younger	42
Mostly younger	48
Don't know	0
Not ascertained	0
Total	100

B13. WOULD YOU MISS SEEING THE PEOPLE YOU WORK WITH IF
YOU CHANGED JOBS, OR WOULDN'T YOU REALLY CARE?

Would miss them; would miss some	52
Would miss some but not others	6
Would not miss them (work alone); would not miss some	37
Don't know	1
Not ascertained	4
Total	100

B14. IS YOUR FOREMAN DIFFICULT TO GET ALONG WITH,
OR EASY?

Very easy	15
Easy	50
Neither easy nor difficult; neutral	25
Difficult	6
Very difficult	1
Don't know	0
Not ascertained	3
Total	100

B15. HOW ABOUT YOUR WORK LAST YEAR: HOW MANY WEEKS
PAID VACATION DID YOU TAKE OFF?

1 week	7
2 weeks	17
3 weeks	24
4 weeks	27
5-7 weeks	1
8 weeks	-
9 weeks and over	-
Don't know	-
Not ascertained	1
No weeks vacation	23
Total	100

	Percent of nonretired respondents

B16.   HOW MANY WEEKS WERE YOU UNEMPLOYED OR LAID OFF?

1 week	6.8
2 weeks	6.2
3	6.2
4	3.2
5-7	1.9
8	0.8
9 or more	0.6
Don't know	-
Not ascertained	0.5
No weeks unemployed	73.8
Total	100.0

B17.   HOW MANY WEEKS WERE YOU ILL OR NOT WORKING FOR ANY OTHER REASON?

1 week	10.0
2 weeks	4.2
3	2.7
4	3.7
5-7	4.1
8	3.6
9 and over	4.9
Don't know	-
Not ascertained	0.4
No weeks ill	66.4
Total	100.0

B18.   THEN, HOW MANY WEEKS DID YOU ACTUALLY WORK AT YOUR JOB IN 1966?

1-13 weeks	0
14-26	1
27-39	3
40-47	28
48-49	44
50-51	18
52	6
Don't know	-
Not ascertained	0
Total	100

B19.   DID YOU ALSO HAVE A SECOND JOB ANYTIME IN 1966?

Yes	4
No	96
Total	100

B20. ABOUT HOW MANY HOURS IN TOTAL DID YOU WORK
IN 1966 ON AN EXTRA JOB?

Less than 200 hours	0.5
200-399	0.7
400-599	1.0
600-799	0.3
800-999	0.3
1000-1499	0.1
1500-2000	-
Don't know	0.5
Not ascertained	1.1
Did not have extra job	95.5
Total	100.0

B21. IF IT WERE POSSIBLE FOR YOU TO WORK MORE HOURS
A WEEK AND RECEIVE A CORRESPONDINGLY HIGHER PAYCHECK,
WOULD YOU WANT TO DO IT?

Would like to; would like to very much	18
Would like to, with qualifications	9
Would and would not; pro-con	2
Would not like to, with qualifications	3
Would not like to (at all); can't work more than I am now	67
Don't know	0
Not ascertained	1
Total	100

B22. WHAT ABOUT FEWER HOURS WITH A CORRESPONDING CUT IN
WEEKLY PAY - WOULD YOU LIKE THIS?

Would like to; would like to very much	11
Would like to, with qualifications	5
Would and would not; pro-con	1
Would not like to, with qualifications	3
Would not like to (at all); can't work less than I am now	79
Don't know	0
Not ascertained	1
Total	100

B23. SOME PEOPLE FEEL AS HEALTHY AND ACTIVE AS THEY DID
SEVERAL YEARS AGO, WHILE OTHERS FEEL THAT THEIR HEALTH IS
NOT QUITE AS GOOD AS IT WAS THEN. HOW DO YOU FEEL?

Feel much better now	-
Feel better now	6
Feel same, as good	36
Feel worse	45
Feel much worse	1
Don't know	0
No comparison given	12
Total	100

	Percent of nonretired respondents

B24. WHY IS THAT?

Respondent gives a work-related reason for declining health	2.9
Respondent mentions a specific, but nonwork-related (or not ascertained whether work-related), illness or injury	20.8
Respondent refers generally to a gradual decline of health associated with advancing age	18.5
Other reasons	1.1
Don't know	0.3
Not ascertained	2.1
Not asked this question	54.3
Total	100.0

B25. ABOUT HOW MANY WORKDAYS HAVE YOU LOST BECAUSE OF ILLNESS DURING THE LAST FIVE YEARS?

Less than 10 workdays lost	43
10-50	30
More than 50	27
Don't know	0
Total	100

B26, B27. HAVE YOU HAD AN ILLNESS, PHYSICAL CONDITION OR NERVOUS CONDITION WHICH LIMITS THE TYPE OF WORK OR THE AMOUNT OF WORK YOU CAN DO?   HOW MUCH DOES IT LIMIT YOUR WORK?

Yes, complete limitation, "can't work at all"	1
Yes, severe limitation on work	2
Yes, some limitation on work (must rest, mentions "part-time work"; occasional limit on work; can't lift heavy objects, reports periods of pain, sickness, etc.)	15
Yes, but no limitation on work	1
No, illness, physical or nervous condition	80
Yes, limitation on work not ascertained	1
Don't know	0
Not ascertained whether has disability	0
Total	100

B28. HOW DO YOU GET FROM YOUR HOME TO YOUR WORK - BY CAR, BY BUS, BY CAR POOL, OR WHAT?

Car	75
Car pool	14
Bus, train, subway, other mass transportation	7
Other	4
Don't know	0
Not ascertained	0
Total	100

B29. HOW LONG DOES THE TRIP TO WORK TAKE?

Less than 15 minutes	22
15 to 30 minutes	49
More than 30 minutes	27
Depends; varying times; more than one checked	1
Don't know	0
Not ascertained	1
Total	100

B30. IS THE TRIP VERY ANNOYING, OR IS IT JUST A
MINOR INCONVENIENCE, OR DO YOU ENJOY IT?

Very annoying	2
Annoying	16
O.K.; all right; neutral response; depends	31
Enjoyable	48
Very enjoyable	1
Don't know	0
Not ascertained	2
Total	100

PART III: QUESTIONS ASKED OF RETIRED AUTO WORKERS

SECTION A: RETIREMENT ATTITUDES

A1. HAVE YOU BEEN TO ANY MEETINGS OR CLASSES ABOUT
THE NEGOTIATED EARLY RETIREMENT PROVISIONS?

Percent of retired respondents

Yes	28
No	72
Total	100

A2. DID YOU GO TO MORE THAN ONE MEETING?

Yes	19.2
No	8.1
Not ascertained, don't know	0.7
Not asked this question	72.0
Total	100.0

A3.   DID YOUR WIFE GO ALONG WITH YOU?

Yes	5.9
No	12.1
Not ascertained, don't know	0.2
Not asked this question	81.8
Total	100.0

A4.   DO YOU THINK THAT THE WRITTEN MATERIAL FROM THE UNION
AND THE COMPANY HAS DESCRIBED THE PROGRAM CLEARLY ENOUGH?

Yes	83
No	12
Don't know	3
Not ascertained	2
Total	100

A5.   WHAT PARTS NEED MORE EXPLANATION?

Parts covering eligibility	0.2
Parts covering benefits	3.9
Both eligibility and benefits	2.0
Other	3.2
Don't know (nothing specific mentioned)	3.9
Not ascertained	3.3
Not asked this question	83.5
Total	100.0

A6.   WHAT DO YOU THINK ABOUT THE EARLY RETIREMENT PLAN
IN GENERAL - IS IT A GOOD THING FOR UAW MEMBERS, OR NOT
SO GOOD?

Plan is very good	29
Plan is good, not bad	55
Neutral response or mixed feelings ("plan is fair," etc.)	5
Plan is not so good, is bad	3
Plan is very bad	-
Depends (if can afford it, if wants to, etc.)	5
Don't know	1
Not ascertained	2
Total	100

SECTION C: INFORMATION FROM RETIRED

C1.   WHEN DID YOU RETIRE?

AGE WHEN RETIRED:

Age 57 or earlier	2
Age 58	4
Age 59	21
Age 60	29
Age 61	21
Age 62	20
Age 63 or later	3
Total	100

TIME WHEN RETIRED:

December 1965 or before	26
January-June 1966	28
July-December 1966	22
1967	24
Don't know	-
Not ascertained	0
Total	100

C2.   ARE YOU RECEIVING REGULAR, SPECIAL, OR DISABILITY EARLY
RETIREMENT BENEFITS?

Regular	90
Special	3
Disability*	7
Don't know	0
Not ascertained	-
Not asked this question	0
Total	100

C3.   HAD YOU PLANNED TO RETIRE WHEN YOU DID, OR DID YOU
RETIRE UNEXPECTEDLY?

Retired as planned	68
Retired unexpectedly (include here if made plans but had to change them)	25
Other	0
Don't know	0
Not ascertained	0
Not asked this question	7
Total	100

---

*Disabled retirees were not asked questions C3-C41.

Percent of
retired
C4a-b. WHY DID YOU (MAKE THE DECISION TO) RETIRE THEN?   respondents

Health reasons	27
Financial reasons	16
Job reasons	9
Family reasons	3
Recreational reasons, "to enjoy life"	7
Reason referring specifically to retirement age or eligibility	10
Other	3
Respondent refers to having worked long enough, to being tired of working, etc.	15
Not ascertained, don't know	3
Not asked this question	7
Total	100

C5. HOW IMPORTANT WERE THE SUPPLEMENTAL EARLY RETIREMENT
BENEFITS IN YOUR DECISION TO RETIRE?

Very important	55
Important	25
Neither important nor unimportant; "had a little effect," etc.	5
Unimportant	5
Don't know	-
Not ascertained	3
Not asked this question	7
Total	100

C6. WOULD YOU HAVE RETIRED WHEN YOU DID IF THE EARLY
RETIREMENT PROVISION HAD NOT BEEN IN EFFECT?

Yes	12
No	79
Don't know	2
Not ascertained	0
Not asked this question	7
Total	100

C7. HOW DID YOU FEEL ABOUT RETIRING WHEN YOU DID?

Very good; very satisfied, very glad to retire	29
Good, satisfied	45
Good and bad, neutral	9
Bad, dissatisfied	3
Very bad, very dissatisfied, very unhappy about retiring	1
Don't know	1
Not ascertained	6
Not asked this question	6
Total	100

Question C8. was not coded.

C9. WHAT WAS YOUR HOURLY WAGE RATE?

Less than $2.75	8
$2.75-2.99	13
$3.00-3.24	30
$3.25-3.49	18
$3.50-3.74	9
$3.75-3.99	7
$4.00 or more	8
Don't know	0
Not ascertained	0
Not asked this question	7
Total	100

C10. WERE YOU ABLE TO KEEP UP WITH THE WORK EASILY,
OR WAS IT GETTING TO BE A PHYSICAL STRAIN BEFORE YOU RETIRED?

Respondent was able to keep up easily	33
Keeping up was neither easy nor difficult	15
Work was getting to be a physical strain	42
Don't know	-
Not ascertained	4
Not asked this question	6
Total	100

C11. WHAT ABOUT THE PEOPLE YOU WORKED WITH - WERE THEY
ABOUT YOUR AGE, OR WERE THEY YOUNGER?

Same age	11
Some same, some younger	47
Mostly younger	36
Don't know	-
Not ascertained	-
Not asked this question	6
Total	100

C12. WAS YOUR WORK DRUDGERY, OR WAS IT ALL RIGHT,
OR DID YOU ENJOY IT?

Enjoyed very much	7
Enjoyed	48
Pro-con; neutral; all right	23
Disliked	6
Disliked very much; drudgery	8
Don't know	0
Not ascertained	1
Not asked this question	7
Total	100

Percent of
retired
respondents

C13. WAS THE PLACE YOU WORKED IN PLEASANT OR NOT?

Pleasant	54
Neither pleasant nor unpleasant; pro-con; neutral; OK	17
Unpleasant	18
Don't know	-
Not ascertained	4
Not asked this question	7
Total	100

C14. WAS YOUR WORK FLEXIBLE, OR DID YOU HAVE TO DO MUCH
THE SAME THINGS OVER AND OVER?

Work was flexible	42
Both	1
Work was repetitious	51
Don't know	-
Not ascertained	-
Not asked this question	6
Total	100

C15. DID YOU ORGANIZE YOUR OWN WORK OR VARY ITS PACE?

Yes	54
No	40
Don't know	-
Not ascertained	-
Not asked this question	6
Total	100

C16. HOW DID YOU GET FROM YOUR HOME TO YOUR WORK - BY CAR,
BY BUS, BY CAR POOL, OR WHAT?

Car	72
Car pool	10
Bus, train, subway, other mass transportation	7
Other (walk, "it varies," etc.)	5
Don't know	-
Not ascertained	-
Not asked this question	6
Total	100

C17. HOW LONG DID THE TRIP TO WORK TAKE?

Less than 15 minutes	16
15 to 30 minutes	53
More than 30 minutes	24
Depends: varying times	0
Don't know	-
Not ascertained	-
Not asked this question	7
Total	100

Percent of
retired
respondents

C18. WAS THE TRIP RATHER ANNOYING, OR WAS IT JUST
A MINOR INCONVENIENCE, OR DID YOU ENJOY IT?

Very annoying	2
Annoying	20
OK; all right; other neutral response; depends	34
Enjoyable	35
Very enjoyable	1
Don't know	0
Not ascertained	1
Not asked this question	7
Total	100

C19. WAS YOUR FOREMAN DIFFICULT TO GET ALONG WITH,
OR EASY?

Very easy	16
Easy	48
Neither (or both) easy nor difficult; neutral response	19
Difficult	7
Very difficult	2
Don't know	-
Not ascertained	1
Not asked this question	7
Total	100

C20. DID HE URGE YOU TO RETIRE WHEN YOU DID?

Yes	4
No	90
Don't know	-
Not ascertained	-
Not asked this question	6
Total	100

C21. DID THE UNION (ALSO) URGE RETIREMENT?

Yes	9
No	84
Don't know	-
Not ascertained	1
Not asked this question	6
Total	100

C22. WHAT ABOUT YOUR FELLOW WORKERS (- DID THEY URGE
YOU TO RETIRE)?

Yes	19
No	74
Don't know	-
Not ascertained	0
Not asked this question	7
Total	100

C23. WAS YOUR RETIREMENT DECISION INFLUENCED BY ANY CHANGES   Percent of
MADE ON YOUR JOB IN THE LAST FEW YEARS BEFORE YOU RETIRED -   retired
<u>FOR EXAMPLE, BY AUTOMATION OR BY A SHIFT TO ANOTHER JOB?</u>   respondents

Yes	16
No	78
Don't know	-
Not ascertained	-
Not asked this question	6
Total	100

C24. <u>HOW DID THESE CHANGES AFFECT THE DECISION?</u>

Changes influenced respondent to retire earlier than he would have otherwise	13.7
Changes influenced respondent to retire later than he would have otherwise	-
Other	0.2
Don't know	-
Not ascertained	1.8
Not asked this question	84.3
Total	100.0

C25, C26. THINKING BACK TO THE LAST FEW YEARS BEFORE YOU
RETIRED, WERE YOU BOTHERED BY ILLNESS OR HEALTH PROBLEMS THAT
AFFECTED YOUR WORK? ABOUT HOW MANY WEEKS OF WORK DID YOU LOSE
<u>BECAUSE OF YOUR HEALTH DURING THE TWO YEARS BEFORE YOU RETIRED?</u>

None lost	68
1-2 weeks	3
3-4 weeks	3
5-8 weeks	7
9-12 weeks	6
More than 12 weeks	10
Don't know	0
Not ascertained	3
Total	100

C27, C28. HOW ABOUT UNEMPLOYMENT OR LACK OF WORK - WERE
YOU ABLE TO WORK AS MUCH AS YOU WANTED BEFORE RETIREMENT?
ABOUT HOW MANY WEEKS OF WORK DID YOU LOSE BECAUSE OF UN-
<u>EMPLOYMENT DURING THE TWO YEARS BEFORE YOU RETIRED?</u>

None lost	96
1-2 weeks	1
3-4 weeks	1
5-8 weeks	1
9-12 weeks	0
More than 12 weeks	0
Don't know	1
Not ascertained	0
Total	100

		Percent of retired respondents
C29. DID YOU DISCUSS RETIREMENT WITH YOUR (WIFE/HUSBAND) BEFORE YOU RETIRED?		
Yes		74
No		6
Don't know		-
Not ascertained		0
Not asked this question, not married		20
Total		100

C30. HOW DID YOUR (WIFE/HUSBAND) FEEL ABOUT YOUR RETIRING WHEN YOU DID?

Highly pleased, very satisfied	10
Pleased, satisfied, O.K.	48
Pro-con; neutral	14
Displeased, dissatisfied	4
Highly displeased, very dissatisfied	0
Don't know	1
Not ascertained	3
Not asked this question, not married	20
Total	100

C31. HAVE YOU HAD A CHANCE TO WORK FOR MONEY SINCE YOUR RETIREMENT?

Yes	27
No	66
Don't know	-
Not ascertained	0
Not asked this question	7
Total	100

C32. HAVE YOU WORKED AT ALL SINCE YOU RETIRED?

Yes	11.7
No	15.1
Don't know	-
Not ascertained	0.2
Not asked this question	73.0
Total	100.0

C33. WHEN DID YOU LAST WORK FOR MONEY?

1965	0.2
1966	1.8
1967; currently working	9.4
Don't know	-
Not ascertained	0.3
Not asked this question	88.3
Total	100.0

C34. DID YOU WORK FOR SOMEONE ELSE, OR YOURSELF,
OR WHAT?

Percent of
retired
respondents

Someone else	10.4
Self	1.2
Both someone else and self	0.2
Other	-
Don't know	-
Not ascertained	-
Not asked this question	88.2
	100.0

C35. DID YOU WORK FULL-TIME OR PART-TIME?

Full-time	0.5
Part-time	11.2
Other	-
Don't know	-
Not ascertained	-
Not asked this question	88.3
Total	100.0

C36. HAVE YOU WORKED BECAUSE YOU NEEDED THE MONEY,
OR MAINLY BECAUSE YOU WANTED TO DO IT, OR WHAT?

Needed income	2.1
Wanted to work	2.5
Needed income and wanted to work	1.3
Wanted to keep busy	3.5
Needed income and wanted to keep busy	0.5
Wanted to work and wanted to keep busy	0.2
Needed income, wanted to work, and wanted to keep busy	-
Other, with or without any of above	1.2
Not ascertained, don't know	0.5
Not asked this question	88.2
Total	100.0

C37. DID YOU DO ANY WORK LIKE THIS BEFORE YOU RETIRED?

Yes	5.6
No	5.9
Don't know	-
Not ascertained	0.2
Not asked this question	88.3
Total	100.0

C38. HAVE YOU ENJOYED THIS WORK MORE THAN YOUR UAW JOB?

Yes	5.8
No	5.4
Don't know	-
Not ascertained	0.5
Not asked this question	88.3
Total	100.0

	Percent of retired respondents

C39. WHAT ABOUT YOUR WORK HAVE YOU ESPECIALLY LIKED?

Flexibility of time: being able to work when respondent feels like it; being able to work part-time	0.5
Being one's own boss	0.2
Less taxing, less strenous nature of work	0.8
Specific reference to non-repetitive nature of the work (as opposed to repetitious assembly-line work) and/or ability to control the pace of the work	0.7
The people respondent now works with	2.1
Lack of necessity to travel to work	-
Other	1.5
Don't know	-
Not ascertained	-
Not asked this question	94.2
Total	100.0

C40. WOULD YOU LIKE TO HAVE SOME KIND OF JOB OR WAY TO EARN SOME MONEY?

Yes	17
No	47
Don't know	1
Not ascertained	1
Not asked this question	34
Total	100

C41. (IF YES) DO YOU WANT TO WORK BECAUSE YOU NEED THE MONEY, OR MAINLY BECAUSE YOU WANT TO DO IT, OR WHAT?

Need income	4.0
Want to work	2.5
Need income and want to work	2.0
Want to keep busy	6.8
Need income and want to keep busy	1.8
Want to work and want to keep busy	-
Need income, want to work, and want to keep busy	-
Other, with or without any of above	0.2
Not ascertained, don't know	0.2
Not asked this question	82.5
Total	100.0

C42. HAD YOU ACCUMULATED ANY SAVINGS OR INVESTMENTS - FOR EXAMPLE, STOCKS AND BONDS, REAL ESTATE, OR BUSINESS INVESTMENTS - WHEN YOU RETIRED?

Yes	81
No	18
Don't know	-
Not ascertained	1
Total	100

	Percent of retired respondents

C43. NOT COUNTING YOUR HOME, HOW MUCH DID THESE
SAVINGS AND INVESTMENTS AMOUNT TO?

Less than $100	1
$100-499	4
$500-1999	12
$2000-4999	16
$5000-9999	19
$10,000-24,999	19
$25,000-49,999	5
$50,000-99,999	2
$100,000 or more	-
Not ascertained, don't know	22
Total	100

C44. WHAT ABOUT NOW, WOULD YOU HAVE MORE OR
LESS IN SAVINGS THAN WHEN YOU RETIRED?

More	18
Same (or none either time)	55
Less	26
Don't know	-
Not ascertained	1
Total	100

C45. WAS THIS AN UNEXPECTED DECREASE?

Yes	12.3
No	13.5
Don't know	0.2
Not ascertained	0.3
Not asked this question	73.7
Total	100.0

C46. HOW MUCH INCOME PER MONTH ARE YOU GETTING FROM
YOUR NEGOTIATED PENSION?

$1-99 per month	1
$100-199	5
$200-249	6
$250-299	10
$300-349	18
$350-399	39
$400 or more	19
Don't know	0
Not ascertained	2
Total	100

C47. WILL YOU CONTINUE TO RECEIVE THE SAME AMOUNT AS
LONG AS YOU LIVE?

Yes	9
No	88
Don't know	2
Not ascertained	1
Total	100

C48. ARE YOU (AND YOUR SPOUSE) RECEIVING SOCIAL SECURITY BENEFITS NOW?	Percent of retired respondents
Yes	47.9
No	52.1
Total	100.0

C49. HOW MUCH PER MONTH DID YOU GET?

$1-99 per month	3.8
$100-149	32.7
$150-199	4.9
$200-249	2.6
$250 or more	1.6
"The maximum"	0.0
Don't know	0.2
Not ascertained	2.0
None	52.2
Total	100.0

C50. WHEN WILL YOU START TO DRAW THEM?

Age 62 (or before)	32
63	1
64	0
65	13
After age 65	0
Don't know	4
Not ascertained	2
Not asked this question	48
Total	100

C51. HAVE YOU KEPT SOME LIFE INSURANCE SINCE YOU RETIRED?

Yes	84
Yes, but amount will change in future	12
No	4
Don't know	0
Total	100

C52. HOW MUCH DOES IT AMOUNT TO?

$1-1500	10
$1501-3500	11
$3501-5500	3
$5501-7500	29
$7501-9500	23
$9501-14,499	12
$14,500 or more	3
Don't know	3
Not ascertained	1
None	5
Total	100

C53. IS YOUR (WIFE/HUSBAND) ELIGIBLE FOR SURVIVOR'S BENEFITS FROM THE NEGOTIATED PENSION PLAN?	Percent of retired respondents
Yes	31
No	48
Don't know	6
Not ascertained	1
Not married	14
Total	100

C54. DOES YOUR (WIFE/HUSBAND) GET ANY OTHER RETIREMENT PENSION?	
Yes	8
No	75
Don't know	1
Not ascertained	2
Not married	14
Total	100

C55. HOW MUCH DOES (SHE/HE) GET?	
$1-49 per month	1.2
$50-99	0.7
$100-149	1.2
$150-199	0.7
$200-249	0.0
$250-299	1.0
$300 or more	2.0
Don't know	1.2
Not ascertained	0.3
None, not married	91.7
Total	100.0

C56. DO YOU (OR YOUR SPOUSE) (OR ANYONE ELSE IN THE FAMILY) RECEIVE ANY WAGES OR SALARIES NOW?	
Yes	34
No	63
Don't know	0
Not ascertained	3
Total	100

C57. WHO RECEIVES THE MONEY?	
Respondent alone	2.5
Respondent and others	3.0
Spouse only	15.9
Other combinations	12.6
Not asked this question	66.0
Total	100.0

	Percent of retired respondents
C58. HOW MUCH IS IT BEFORE DEDUCTIONS FOR TAXES OR ANYTHING ELSE?	

$1-99 per month	3.0
$100-199	3.6
$200-299	3.5
$300-399	3.5
$400-499	3.5
$500-749	5.9
$750 or more	1.5
Don't know	5.2
Not ascertained	4.3
Not asked this question	66.0
Total	100.0

C59. TYPES OF INCOME RECEIVED BY RESPONDENT AND HIS FAMILY

A professional practice or a trade	2.3
A business in which your family has a financial interest	0.7
Farming or market gardening	2.3
Dividents, rent, interest, trust funds, annuities or royalties	50.8
Any pensions other than those we've already talked about	3.8
Unemployment compensation, supplementary unemployment benefits, or sick or accident benefits	3.3
Anything else, such as alimony, welfare, or help from relatives	1.5
Total	*

Question C60. was not coded.

C61. HOW ABOUT YOUR CURRENT LIVING EXPENSES - ARE YOU SPENDING LESS THAN BEFORE YOU RETIRED, OR MORE, OR THE SAME? (IF LESS) IS IT A LOT LESS?

Spending less	18
Spending a lot less	6
Spending more	20
Same	56
Don't know	0
Total	100

---

*
Does not add to 100 since all workers did not receive non-wage (or non-pension) income.

C62. WHAT ARE THE TINGS THAT MAKE A DIFFERENCE IN YOUR EXPENSES? (ANYTHING ELSE?)	Percent of retired respondents
Medical and dental expenses	2.5
Change in debt position: paid off mortgage, paid off car, incurred debts, made necessary purchases	3.7
Change in financial responsibility for family or change in number of members of family unit	1.2
Change in specific ordinary living expenses: rent, light, heat, food, clothes, taxes, routine transportation, etc.	22.8
Changes associated with expenses for recreation, travel for pleasure, etc.	3.9
General reference to "prices" or cost of living	4.9
Have to spend less, economize, less to spend; wanted to spend more, wanted a higher living standard	4.1
Other references	1.3
Don't know, not ascertained	-
Not asked this question	55.6
Total	100.0

C63. ARE YOU GIVING ANY FINANCIAL HELP TO (YOUR CHILDREN OR OTHER) RELATIVES?	
Yes	21
No, none	78
Don't know whether giving aid	-
Not ascertained	1
Total	100

C64. ARE YOU RECEIVING FINANCIAL SUPPORT (FROM YOUR CHILDREN) FROM RELATIVES, OR FROM ANYONE LIKE THAT?	
Yes	0.2
No, none	99.5
Don't know whether receiving aid	0.0
Not ascertained	0.3
Total	100.0

C65. HOW DOES YOUR INCOME NOW COMPARE WITH YOUR INCOME THE YEAR BEFORE YOU RETIRED - IS IT CLOSER TO ¼ AS LARGE, ½ AS LARGE, OR ALMOST AS LARGE AS BEFORE YOU RETIRED?	
Less than ¼; 0-19%	0
¼, about a quarter; 20-29%	9
Smaller, but not ascertained, don't know how much; 30-39%	6
½, about a half; 40-59%	41
60-79%	23
Almost as large or the same; 80-100%	18
Larger (than pre-retirement income)	0
Don't know whether larger or smaller	1
Not ascertained	2
Total	100

	Percent of retired respondents
C66. CONSIDERING INCOME AND EXPENSES, ARE YOU LIVING ABOUT AS WELL AS BEFORE YOU RETIRED, NOT QUITE AS WELL, OR WHAT?	
Much better living standard	0
Better, somewhat better	6
About the same	72
Lower, somewhat lower, not as good	17
Much lower, much worse	1
Don't know	2
Not ascertained	2
Total	100

C67. DO YOU FEEL THAT YOU HAVE ENOUGH TO LIVE COMFORTABLY?

Yes	7.6
No	10.5
Not asked this question	81.9
Total	100.0

C68. DO YOU DO ANY WORK WITHOUT PAY FOR CHURCH, OR CHARITY (OR YOUR CHILDREN)?

Yes	35
No	65
Total	100

C69. ARE YOU DOING MORE OR LESS OF THIS THAN BEFORE YOU RETIRED?

More	16.5
Same	15.4
Less	2.6
Don't know	-
Not ascertained	-
Not asked this question	65.5
Total	100.0

C70. DO YOU HAVE ANY HOBBIES YOU HAVE SPENT TIME ON SINCE YOU RETIRED?

Yes	59
No	41
Total	100

	Percent of retired respondents
C71. WHAT ARE THEY?	
Active hobbies: gardening, carpentry, woodworking, "working around the house", "handywork", etc.	23
Inactive hobbies: collecting, writing, photography, etc.	8
Sports, games, other recreational activities	24
Travel, vacationing, etc.	3
Relaxing, loafing, sitting around, "playing with grandchildren", etc.	0
Other	1
Don't know, not ascertained	0
Not asked this question	41
Total	100

C72. ARE YOU DEVOTING MORE OR LESS TIME TO THEM THAN BEFORE YOU RETIRED?

More	46
Same	8
Less	3
Don't know	0
Not ascertained	2
Not asked this question	41
Total	100

C73. WHAT ABOUT YOUR HEALTH? SOME PEOPLE FEEL AS HEALTHY AND ACTIVE AS THEY DID SEVERAL YEARS AGO, WHILE OTHERS FEEL THAT THEIR HEALTH IS NOT QUITE AS GOOD AS IT WAS THEN. HOW DO YOU FEEL?

Much better	1
Better	20
Feel same, as healthy as several years ago	34
Worse, health not quite as good	31
Much worse	3
Don't know	0
Not ascertained	11
Not asked this question	-
Total	100

C74. HAS THIS CHANGE HAPPENED MAINLY SINCE YOU RETIRED?

Yes	25
No	27
Don't know	0
Not ascertained	3
Not asked this question	45
Total	100

Percent of
retired
respondents

C75. HAVE YOU MOVED SINCE YOU RETIRED?

Yes	9
No	91
Don't know	-
Not ascertained	0
Total	100

C76. WHY DID YOU MOVE?

To go to a better climate	0.7
To get a smaller, easier-to-keep, and/or less expensive house or apartment	1.8
To be nearer relatives	0.7
To go to a community with certain desirable features, such as a retirement community	0.0
Other reasons	4.6
Don't know	0.0
Not ascertained	1.6
Not asked this question	90.6
Total	100.0

C77. GENERALLY SPEAKING, HOW DO YOU FEEL ABOUT YOUR LIFE SINCE RETIREMENT?

Very good, very favorable, enthusiastic	24
Good, favorable	50
Pro-con, neutral	12
Bad, not good, unfavorable	7
Very bad, very unfavorable	2
Don't know	3
Not ascertained	2
Total	100

C78. HAVE THINGS TURNED OUT ABOUT AS YOU HAD EXPECTED?

Yes	78
"Some things have, others haven't"	5
No	10
Don't know	4
Not ascertained	3
Total	100

C79. HOW ABOUT OTHER PEOPLE YOU KNOW WHO ARE RETIRED: HOW ARE THEY GETTING ALONG?

Very well	14
Well; some are doing well	45
Neither well nor badly; just OK; some well, some not	20
Badly; some are doing badly	4
Very badly	0
Don't know	14
Not ascertained	3
Total	100

BIBLIOGRAPHY

Listed below are books and articles published or prepared in 1968 by the staff of the Economic Behavior Program of the Survey Research Center.

Dunkelberg, William C. and Frank P. Stafford. The cost of financing automobile purchases. *Review of Economics and Statistics,* 1969.

Katona, George, James N. Morgan, and Richard E. Barfield. Retirement in prospect and retrospect. *Trends in Early Retirement* (Occasional Papers in Gerontology No. 4). Ann Arbor: The University of Michigan Institute of Gerontology, March 1969, 27-49.

Katona, George and Eva Mueller. *Consumer Response to Income Increases* (An Investigation Conducted in the Year of the Tax Cut). Washington, D.C.: Brookings Institution, 1968.

Katona, George. On the Function of Behavioral Theory and Behavioral Research in Economics. *American Economic Review,* LVIII, March 1968, 146-150.

Katona, George. Consumer Behavior: Theory and Findings on Expectations and Aspirations. Proceedings, *American Economic Review,* LVIII, 2, May 1968, 19-30.

Katona, George. Consumer Behavior and Monetary Policy. In *Geldtheorie und Geldpolitik* (Festschrift for Guenter Schmoelders). Berlin, Germany: Duncker and Humbolt, 1968, 117-132.

Lansing, John B., Charles Wade Clifton, and James N. Morgan. *New Homes and Poor People.* Ann Arbor: Institute for Social Research, 1969.

Morgan, James N. Family Use of Credit. *Journal of Home Economics, 60,* January 1968.

Morgan, James N. Some pilot studies of communication and consensus in the family. *Public Opinion Quarterly, 32,* 1, Spring 1968, 113-121.

Morgan, James N. The supply of effort, the measurement of well-being, and the dynamics of improvement. *American Economic Review, 58,* May 1968.

Morgan, James N. Survey analysis: applications in economics. In *International Encyclopedia of the Social Sciences, 15,* New York: Macmillan, 1968, 429-436.

Mueller, Eva. *Technological Advance in an Expanding Economy: Its Impact on a Cross-section of the Labor Force.* In press, to be released in September 1969.

Sonquist, John A. Problems of getting sociological data in and out of a computer. Paper read at the American Sociological Association, Boston, August 1968, 22 p.

Stafford, Frank P. Concentration and labor earnings: comment. *American Economic Review, 58,* 1, March 1968, 174-181.

Stafford, Frank P. Student family size in relation to current and expected income. *Journal of Political Economy,* 1969.

> Data collected by the Economic Behavior Program are available on either punched cards or computer tapes, together with a detailed code describing the content of the cards or tapes. Thus, interested scholars or other parties may obtain or prepare further analysis beyond that presented in this volume.

SURVEY RESEARCH CENTER PUBLICATIONS

Survey Research Center publications should be ordered by author and title from the Publications Division, Department B, Institute for Social Research, The University of Michigan, P.O. Box 1248, Ann Arbor, Michigan 48106.

1960 Survey of Consumer Finances. 1961. $4 (paperbound), 310 pp.

1961 Survey of Consumer Finances. G. Katona, C. A. Lininger, J. N. Morgan, and E. Mueller. 1962. $4 (paperbound), $5 (cloth), 150 pp.

1962 Survey of Consumer Finances. G. Katona, C. A. Lininger, and R. F. Kosobud. 1963. $4 (paperbound), 310 pp.

1963 Survey of Consumer Finances. G. Katona, C. A. Lininger, and E. Mueller. 1964. $4 (paperbound), 262 pp.

1964 Survey of Consumer Finances. G. Katona, C. A. Lininger, and E. Mueller. 1965. $4 (paperbound), 245 pp.

1965 Survey of Consumer Finances. G. Katona, E. Mueller, J. Schmiedeskamp, and J. A. Sonquist. 1966. $4 (paperbound), $6 (cloth).

1966 Survey of Consumer Finances. G. Katona, E. Mueller, J. Schmiedeskamp, and J. A. Sonquist. 1967. $4 (paperbound), 303 pp.

1967 Survey of Consumer Finances. G. Katona, J. N. Morgan, J. Schmiedeskamp, and J. A. Sonquist. 1968. $5 (paperbound), $7 (cloth), 343 pp.

1968 Survey of Consumer Finances. G. Katona, W. C. Dunkelberg, J. Schmiedeskamp, and F. P. Stafford. 1969. $5 (paperbound), $7 (cloth), 287 pp.

Automobile Ownership and Residential Density. John B. Lansing and Gary Hendricks. 1967. $3, 230 pp.

The Geographical Mobility of Labor. John B. Lansing and Eva L. Mueller. 1967. $6.50, 421 pp.

Multiple Classification Analysis. James N. Morgan, John A. Sonquist and Frank M. Andrews. 1967. $3.

Productive Americans: A Study of How Individuals Contribute to Economic Progress. James N. Morgan, Ismail Sirageldin, and Nancy Baerwaldt. 1966. $5, 546 pp.

Residential Location and Urban Mobility: The Second Wave of Interviews. John B. Lansing. 1966. $2.50 (paperbound), 115 pp.

Private Pensions and Individual Saving. George Katona. 1965. $1.50 (paperbound), $2.50 (cloth), 114 pp.

Consumer Behavior of Individual Families Over Two and Three Years. Richard F. Kosobud and James N. Morgan (Editors). 1964. $5 (paperbound), $6 (cloth), 208 pp.

Residential Location and Urban Mobility. John B. Lansing and Eva Mueller. 1964. $2 (paperbound), 142 pp.

Residential Location and Urban Mobility: A Multivariate Analysis. John B. Lansing and Nancy Barth. 1964. $2 (paperbound), 98 pp.

The Travel Market, 1964-1965. John B. Lansing. 1965 $4 (cloth), 112 pp.

The Changing Travel Market. John B. Lansing and Dwight M. Blood. 1964. $10 (cloth), 374 pp.

The Detection of Interaction Effects. John A. Sonquist and James N. Morgan. 1964. $3 (paperbound), 292 pp.

The Geographic Mobility of Labor, a First Report. John B. Lansing, Eva Mueller, William Ladd, and Nancy Barth. 1963. $3.95 (paperbound), 328 pp.

The Travel Market 1958, 1959-1960, 1961-1962. John B. Lansing, Eva Mueller, and others. Reprinted 1963 (originally issued as three separate reports). $10, 388 pp.

The Travel Market 1955, 1956, 1957. John B. Lansing and Ernest Lillienstein. Reprinted 1963 (originally issued as three separate reports). $10, 524 pp.

*Package of three available for $25.00.

Location Decisions and Industrial Mobility in Michigan, 1961. Eva Mueller, Arnold Wilken, and Margaret Wood. 1962. $2.50 (paperbound), $3 (cloth), 115 pp.

OTHER BOOKS BY MEMBERS OF
THE ECONOMIC BEHAVIOR PROGRAM

Transportation and Economic Policy. John B. Lansing. Free Press, 1966.

The Mass Consumption Society. George Katona. McGraw-Hill, 1964.

Income and Welfare in the United States. J. N. Morgan, M. H. David, W. J. Cohen, and H. E. Brazer. McGraw-Hill, 1962.

An Investigation of Response Error. J. B. Lansing, G. P. Ginsburg, and K. Braaten. Bureau of Economic and Business Research, University of Illinois, 1961.

The Powerful Consumer. George Katona. McGraw-Hill, 1960.

Business Looks at Banks: A Study of Business Behavior. G. Katona, S. Steinkamp, and A. Lauterbach. University of Michigan Press, 1957.

Consumer Economics. James N. Morgan. Prentice-Hall, 1955.

Contributions of Survey Methods to Economics. G. Katona, L. R. Klein, J. B. Lansing, and J. N. Morgan. Columbia University Press, 1957.

Psychological Analysis of Economic Behavior. George Katona. McGraw-Hill, 1951. (Paperback edition published in 1963.)

Economic Behavior of the Affluent. Robin Barlow, H. E. Brazer, and J. N. Morgan. Washington, D. C.: Brookings Institution, 1966.

Living Patterns and Attitudes in the Detroit Region. John B. Lansing and Gary Hendricks. A report for TALUS (Detroit Regional Transportation and Land Use Study), 1967, 241 pp. (Available only from TALUS, 1248 Washington Blvd., Detroit, Mich. 48226—$5 to nongovernmental agencies.)